The Platformisation of Consumer Culture

A Digital Methods Guide

Alessandro Caliandro,
Alessandro Gandini,
Lucia Bainotti,
Guido Anselmi

Amsterdam University Press

This book project was financially supported by:

Fondazione Cariplo (Bando 2020, Ricerca Sociale: Scienza Tecnologia e Società. Project name: "The value of digital data: Enhancing citizens' awareness and voice about surveillance capitalism (V-DATA)."

The University of Milan under the project SPOTIGEM — Music genres in the age of Spotify (Project No. 1072), funded by the SEED 2019 call.

We are very grateful to Dr Angeles Briones for curating the data visualisations in the book.

Cover illustration: Unsplash

Cover design: Coördesign, Leiden
Lay-out: Crius Group, Hulshout

ISBN   978 94 6372 956 7
e-ISBN   978 90 4855 510 9
DOI   10.5117/9789463729567
NUR   811 9789048555109

Table of Contents

I.   Introduction

Digital Methods, Consumer Culture, and the Question of Platformisation

This book aims at providing the reader with a set of research strategies and techniques for using digital methods to explore the processes of *platformisation of consumer culture* unfolding within digital environments (Caliandro et al., 2024). In the new century, most consumer activities migrated onto digital platforms: as a result, consumer culture gradually went through a process of platformisation (Duffy et al., 2019). The systems of meanings and practices consumers articulate around products, brands, or services are increasingly shaped by the socio-technical architecture of digital environments themselves (Carah and Angus, 2018) – besides and beyond traditional social institutions, such as class (Bourdieu, 1984), subcultures (Schouten and McAlexander, 1995), or communities (Muñiz and O'Guinn, 2001). Although social classes as well as consumer subcultures and communities still exist, and, indeed, exert a strong influence on consumer activities, such social formations have been profoundly reconfigured by the advent of digital media (Marres, 2017). Given these conditions, we argue that digital methods provide useful conceptual and practical tools to understand the emerging phenomenon of platformisation of consumer culture.

In the last decade, digital methods affirmed itself as the main methodological paradigm for studying the internet from a sociological perspective. Over the years, thanks to digital methods, scholars have cast a light upon several key and emerging socio-cultural phenomena: among them, the so-called like economy (Gerlitz and Helmond, 2013), echo chambers (Colleoni et al., 2014), social bots (Bessi and Ferrara, 2016), and fake news (Gray et al., 2020), to name a few. From the outset, digital methods privileged *politics* as their main field of research – intended as both the *politics of the medium* (e.g., algorithms) and *politics within the medium* (e.g., climate change) (Rogers, 2010). Curiously, consumption and consumer culture received scant attention within digital methods studies. This represents a notable gap, since consumption is not simply one topic among many others that might

Caliandro, A., A. Gandini, L. Bainotti, G. Anselmi, *The Platformisation of Consumer Culture: A Digital Methods Guide*. Amsterdam: Amsterdam University Press, 2024
DOI 10.5117/9789463729567_INTRO

be interesting to explore on the internet; rather, it is a key phenomenon that underpins the logic of the functioning of the contemporary digital landscape. Consider that, for example, among the applications that dominate the contemporary 2.0 Web (as well as governing its functioning), there are commercial platforms like Google, Twitter, TikTok, Amazon, Uber, or Airbnb, whose business models consist in extracting data from consumers in order to deliver them products, experiences, and advertising (Srnicek, 2017). Moreover, several interesting and current consumer phenomena are *natively digital*, such as virality, influencer marketing, or brand publics. Yet, few consumer culture and marketing scholars have addressed these phenomena using digital methods (Humphreys and Wang, 2018; Berger et al., 2020; Schöps et al., 2020; Airoldi, 2021a; 2021b; Schöps et al., 2022).

Consumer culture is not an easy concept to define. A pivotal definition of the term was provided by Arnould and Thompson in their seminal 2005 article "Consumer Culture Theory (CCT)," in which they conceptualise consumer culture as an "interconnected system of commercially produced images, texts, objects that groups use – through the construction of overlapping and even conflicting practices, identities, and meanings – to make collective sense of their environments and to orient their members' experiences and lives" (Arnould and Thompson, 2005, p. 869). More than fifteen years later, we can safely argue that this complex system of meanings has been deeply re-mediated, re-shaped, and re-configured by the likewise complex system of digital devices (such as search engines, algorithms, or reputational metrics) populating the internet, and especially by digital platforms, considered as commercial environments where consumers spend most of their time (WeAreSocial, 2023). Consider, for example, that social media platforms are the first source of information people refer to if they want to find out about a product or brand (Mangold and Faulds, 2009; Tuten and Solomon, 2017) or interact with other like-minded consumers (Brodie et al., 2013).

While CCT does not draw specifically on the concepts of "platform" and "platformisation," it has a long tradition of studies on "digitisation" (Hagberg and Kjellber, 2020), intended as a process of reconfiguration of markets brought about by digital technologies, whereby cultural production is no longer centralised within traditional market and media institutions (e.g., brands, marketing and advertising companies, mass media, etc.), but rather it is dispersed within an heterogeneous network of stakeholders (e.g., regular consumers, influencers, brand communities, brand managers, software developers, etc.) (Dolbec and Fisher, 2015), which coalesce and act in innovative (Von Hippel, 2005; Füller et al., 2007) and unexpected ways (Jankins, 2006; Parmentier and Fischer, 2015). Specifically, and drawing primarily on assemblage theory[1] (DeLanda, 2006; Canniford and Bajde, 2015; Hoffman and Novak, 2018), CCT scholars have argued that it is not only (human) consumers who *engage* in symbolic activities through objects of consumption, and it is not only objects of consumption (i.e., brands, products, services) that *mediate* processes of cultural production. Indeed, increasingly, it is mechanical agents themselves (such as digital networks, environments, devices, apps, etc.) that play a key role in shaping the construction of identity, social relations, ideologies, and worldviews (Denegri-Knott and Molesworth, 2010; Belk, 2013; Arvidsson and Caliandro, 2016; Sörum and Fuentes, 2023). Consider, for example, how digital networks favour collaboration and value creation among geographically dispersed consumers (Schau et al. 2009; Figueiredo and Scaraboto, 2016); assemblages of food images and posts trigger consumers' desire (Kozinets et al., 2017); selfies destabilise brand images (Rokka and Canniford, 2016); car-sharing apps deteriorate communitarian bonds among consumers and affective connections with brands (Bardhi and Eckhardt, 2012); recommendation algorithms shape music taste (Airoldi, 2021b); and micro-targeted ads stimulate consumers' self-reflection, pushing them to resist automation and surveillance (Leung et al. 2018; Ruckenstein and Granroth; 2020).

As valuable and insightful as all these contributions are, they draw on small-scale empirical research based on qualitative online and offline methods. Instead, we argue that addressing these kinds of topics with a Digital Methods approach could significantly contribute to consumer culture and marketing literature, shedding light on the mechanisms through which digital consumer culture is produced, articulated, and circulated on a large scale, as well as on the complex interplay between digital infrastructures and participatory cultures in shaping consumers' identities, practices, and discourses. In addition to the methodological limitations in the literature on digitisation, Airoldi and Rokka (2022) highlight a theoretical one. Research in this area, they contend, seems to be caught in an unsolvable tension between *liquification* (Bardhi and Eckhardt, 2017) and *datafication* (Van Dijck, 2014). In fact, on the one hand, digitisation is framed as an empowering force that favours "liquid" forms of consumption (i.e., access-based, ephemeral, de-materialised, individualised), which "potentially emancipate

---

1   Assemblage theory conceptualises society as a complex entity continuously formed and re-formed by "assemblages," that is, "heterogeneous groupings of entities, consisting of emergent properties and capacities" (Schöps, 2022, p. 13). Assemblages are networks made of people as well as material (e.g., products) and expressive components (e.g., communicative acts), which are in constant interplay and exchange. Such ontological "instability" constantly "territorialise or deterritorialise the identity of an assemblage" (Schöps, 2022, p. 14).

consumers from social and geographical boundaries while creating value" (Airoldi and Rokka, 2022, p. 412). On the other hand, digitisation is seen as an oppressing force of surveillance (Darmody and Zwick, 2020) that, by converting every aspect of social life into data, disempowers consumers (Zwick et al., 2008; Cova, and Dalli, 2009; Thompson, 2019) by transforming their "volition into reinforcement and action into conditioned response" (Zuboff, 2019, p. 378). Airoldi and Rokka (2022) try to recompose such a contradiction by introducing the concept of "algorithmic articulation." Reflecting on the power exerted by algorithms on consumer behaviour (Beer, 2017), the authors exhort researchers to always put algorithmic and consumer agency within a dialectic relation: algorithms endow technical features and logics that constrain consumers' activities but, at the same time, consumers manipulate those very features and logics to achieve their own goals. Consider, for example, how the Twitter algorithm pushes mainstream or polarised hashtags to the trending topics (Gruzd and Roy, 2014; Valensise et al. 2023), but also how, at the same time, fandoms (like those of One Direction or BTS) hijack the Twitter algorithm (e.g., through massive and coordinated retweeting) in order to position their "own personal agendas" within the trending topics (e.g., news of concerts or anti-racist messages) (Arvidsson et al., 2016; Treré and Bonini, 2022).

In this book, following the exhortation of Airoldi and Rokka, we propose a methodological guide to help researchers explore processes of platformisation of consumer culture by keeping together the mutual influence of platforms' technical infrastructures and digital participatory cultures populating (and using) them (Caliandro and Anselmi, 2021; Rogers and Giorgi, 2023).

Platforms, Platformisation, and Platformisation of Consumer Culture

When talking about platforms, we commonly refer to big-tech companies such as Google, Apple, Facebook/Meta, Amazon, and Microsoft (GAFAM). According to Srnicek, platforms are "digital infrastructures that enable two or more groups to interact; they position themselves as intermediaries that bring together different users: advertisers, service providers, producers, suppliers and physical objects" (2017, p. 48). This "position" is not neutral (Gillespie, 2010), since platforms are explicitly designed and meant to extract data from the very same users they host. These massive and systematic processes of data extraction are pivotal for the business models of digital platforms, which employ user data for: a) internal marketing purposes (i.e., increasing the platform's traffic); b) selling them to third parties (for their own advertising and marketing scopes); c) developing new products and/or markets (vocal assistants, self-driving cars, etc.) (Arvidsson, 2019). In order to meet their business purposes, platforms not only need an enclosed space in which to monitor, track, and predict user behaviour, but they also need to design spaces in which to corral users' activities into standardised patterns of action in order to make their behaviours predictable (Zuboff, 2019). For example, social media (e.g., Instagram) or sharing platforms (e.g., Airbnb) are especially suited for these purposes, since they provide users with free tools to produce creative content, create communities, and express their identities (Marwick, 2015). All these tools, however, are purposely designed to capture such social-cultural processes, transform them into data points, and convert them into marketing and business products (Van Dijk and Poell, 2013). The result is an emerging global socio-economic model that Shoshana Zuboff calls *surveillance capitalism* (Zuboff, 2015).

A key concept for understanding platform logics and impact is "platformisation," which Poell et al. (2019, p. 1) define as "the penetration of infrastructures, economic processes and governmental frameworks of digital platforms in different economic sectors and spheres of life, as well as the reorganisation of cultural practices and imaginations around these platforms." Studies on platformisation have been gaining traction in recent years and cover different key sociological topics. Regarding the more technical aspects of the phenomenon, Helmond (2015, p. 1) points out that the open web has been progressively "colonised" by social media infrastructures, describing the process as the *platformisation of the web*, which she defines as "the extension of social media platforms into the rest of the web and their drive to make external web data platform-ready." The tendency of digital platforms to extend themselves beyond the domain of their digital boundaries in order to "datafy" the "surrounding reality" has a precise economic goal, which is strictly connected to how capitalism works today (Van Dijck, 2014). Srnicek describes this using the concept of *platform capitalism*, intended as an emerging mode of production based on the massive accumulation of digital data and the control of the technologies through which data are collected, stored, managed, and analysed. Such a mode of production has been initiated by few multinational tech companies (such as Google, Facebook, or Apple), which have not only monopolised the market in which they operate (e.g., Facebook for social networking sites, or Amazon for e-commerce), but also hegemonised their business logics across the whole digital economy. Drawing on the concept of platform capitalism (and considering its growing importance in the economy of

Western countries), Van Dijk et al. (2018) elaborated the notion of a *platform society*. According to Van Dijk et al., both the business logic and functioning of digital platforms are re-configuring the structure of many key social institutions, impacting upon the ways in which we experience the city, use public transportation, get cured, or access knowledge. More recently, reflecting on the relations between digital platforms and cultural industries, Duffy et al. (2019, p. 276) have posited the impending *platformisation of culture*, referring to a process of culture production that involves the "penetration of economic, governmental, and infrastructural extensions of digital platforms into the web and app ecosystems, fundamentally affecting the operations of the cultural industries." In two special issues of the journal *Social Media + Society* dedicated to the platformisation of cultural production, Duffy et al. (2019) and Nieborg et al. (2020) explore this phenomenon across many example. For instance, looking at how Instagram and Vine offer ad hoc technical and symbolic means of cultural production and self-promotion to marginalised communities (i.e., queer influencers) (Duguay, 2019), how communities of influencers collaborate to manipulate the Instagram algorithm to gain visibility for their posts (O'Meara, 2019), or how Spotify's algorithmic and human curators are supplanting traditional cultural intermediaries to become new music gatekeepers (Bonini and Gandini, 2019). Finally, drawing on the tradition of cultural studies (Hall, 1980), Van Es and Poell (2020) have introduced the concept of *platform imaginary*, intended as a process of penetration of platforms' logics into users' mentalities. By interviewing members of the Dutch public service media (who increasingly use social media to disseminate public broadcasting content), Van Es and Poell underline how a mentality is growing in which people are apparently more preoccupied with delivering content able to engage, reach, or create community with their audience than they are with producing content capable of promoting key public values within their audience (such as independence, trustworthiness, pluriformity, etc.).

Marketing and consumer culture literature has also investigated the platformisation phenomenon, focusing on the role of platforms as *intermediaries* between different market actors (Boudreau, 2017; Täuscher and Laudien, 2018) as well as on the kind of value that platforms offer to companies and customers (Gielens and Steenkamp, 2019). For example, Perren and Kozinets (2018) studied how platforms reconfigure economic and social exchanges among peer-to-peer networks of providers and recipients (of product, services, and content). Based on an ethnographic study of 193 cases, the authors identified four ideal types of platforms, which differ according to the kind of value they provide: "Forums connect actors, Enablers equip actors, Matchmakers pair actors, and Hubs centralise exchange" (Perren and Kozinets, 2018, p. 20). Employing a more consumer-centred perspective and drawing on the case of the Reclame Aqui (the largest Latin American consumer feedback platform), Kozinets et al. (2021) reflect instead on how platform affordances empower consumers. In particular, they conclude that the socio-technical architecture of Reclame Aqui empowers consumers, insofar as it offers them a "discovery affordance that informs choice, a narration affordance that provides them with an opportunity to voice complaints, a contact affordance through which they can seek justice, and a meta-voice affordance that includes their evaluation in an important reputation rating" (Kozinets et al., 2021, p. 447). Finally, Wichmann et al. explored the phenomenon of *platformisation of brands*, which consists in a process of brands transforming themselves into "commercial hubs" that "transcend the specific product brand by including third-party complementary products, services, and content to occupy the broader category space and address consumer needs more holistically" (2022, p. 110; see also Zhu and Furr, 2016). According to the authors, the emergence and hegemony of digital "aggregator platforms" (like Amazon or Zalando) poses a serious threat to brands, since such aggregators "diminish brand differentiation and foster price competition by featuring many similar or even identical offerings at different prices from competing suppliers" (Wichmann et al,. 2022, pp. 109–110). By contrast, Wichmann et al. provide a step-by-step guide to transforming brands into "brand flagship platforms," that is, assemblages of different "building blocks" (transaction, community, benchmarking, guidance, inspiration) that allow companies to provide ad hoc kinds of values to different market segments. For example, Nike is a "brand platform" insofar as it offers, among other things, an online shop for selling shoes and a run club (Nike Run Club) aggregating a community of running enthusiasts; in this way, Nike increases both its *economic* and *linking* value (Cova, 1997) with customers. However, this interesting and innovative strand of research is more concerned with the processes of value creation that emerge within the relations among platforms' users, rather than the processes of cultural production embedded within the technical infrastructure of platforms (Caliandro et al., 2024).

With this book, we are contributing to this emergent strand of studies on platformisation with a specific focus on consumer culture, zooming in on culture in an *anthropological* sense, i.e., intended as the complex set of values, symbols, identities, discourses, and narratives that emerge from the interactions between platforms' technicalities and the everyday digital practices of platform users, rather than the relationship between cultural industries (or markets) and platforms (Caliandro et al., 2024). To do so, we take advantage of computational and digital methods, rather than solely ethnographic and qualitative ones (Pink et al., 2015; Salmons, 2016). Employing an interpretative approach to digital methods (Caliandro and Gandini, 2017; Airoldi, 2021a; Vicari and Kirby, 2023), we offer methodological guidance to go beyond the "classical" dichotomy between the *shallow volume* of big data and the *localised richness* of small data (Adler-Nissen et al., 2021; Cambrosio et al., 2020).

Finally, taking inspiration from Beer (2019), we focus on those "quirks of digital culture" – that is, those small online cultural phenomena that usually pass unnoticed and/or are considered frivolous – that, if made visible and studied systematically through the appropriate methods, are nonetheless capable of enlightening the structure and functioning of the global system of digital consumer culture (Latour et al., 2012; Geertz, 1979). In so doing, we present a set of case studies that underline the methodological relevance of these "quirks," and demonstrate how they can be turned to our advantage for the purpose of researching emergent digital consumer cultures and the role that platforms (and their affordances) play within them.

Using Digital Methods for Addressing the Platformisation of Consumer Culture

In order to study the process of platformisation of consumer culture within digital environments, we employ a *qualitative approach to digital methods* (Caliandro and Gandini, 2017). This exhorts the researcher to both *follow the medium* and *the users* when exploring digital environments (Audy Martínek et al. 2023), especially if s/he wants to understand cultural processes unfolding within them (Caliandro, 2018). On the one hand, the researcher has to "follow the medium" in order to observe how digital devices (e.g., algorithms, links, likes, etc.) structure online communication and interaction within internet spaces – (to do so, s/he can also take advantage of "traditional" digital methods techniques, such as API calling or co-hashtag analysis) (Rogers, 2019). On the other hand, the researcher must also "follow the users," in order to understand how internet users *use* digital devices to fulfil specific scopes and, ultimately, influence processes of online communication and interaction – (to do so, s/he can "repurpose" traditional qualitative techniques, such as content analysis or non-participant observation) (Bainotti et al., 2021).

We contend that this approach is particularly suitable for studying digital platform affordances, which are crucial elements for understanding sociocultural dynamics emerging in digital social environments. Affordances consist in a set of contextual constraints and props that shape the usage of technology, and which emerge at the intersection between the devices' properties and the users' perception of their utility. In turn, these perceptions are shaped by the cultural meanings and practices of use shared by the social groups that users belong to (Bucher and Helmond, 2017). This complex array of constraints and props "determines the socially mediated possibilities that the devices offer for action" (Fernández-Ardèvol et al., 2020, p. 3). When it comes to digital platforms such as social media, affordances can be seen at the intersection between *platform politics* (Gillespie, 2010) and *cultures of use* (Rieder et al. 2018), that is, between the technical architecture of a platform, which shapes patterns of communication (e.g., algorithms) and the collective practices of those social groups that use the platform and its technicalities for specific communicative purposes (e.g., participatory cultures) (Rieder et al. 2020).

From an empirical point of view, we focus on two intertwined dimensions that are useful when studying social media affordances: *grammars* (Gerlitz and Rieder, 2018) and *vernaculars* (Burgess, 2006). The concept of grammar refers to the fact that every digital environment corrals activities into specific "units of actions" and, in addition, provides the means to perform such actions (Agre, 1994). For example, Twitter drives users towards reactive interactions rather than conversational ones; at the same time, it provides them with retweets, that is, the very means that allow them to pursue reactive interactions. The term vernacular derives from Burgess's notion of *vernacular creativity* (2006), which is intended as a particular form of cultural production initiated by "ordinary" internet users (Atton, 2001), who, with no professional means and business purposes, create aesthetic artefacts through which they capture, represent, and reflect on mundane aspects of their everyday life (Negus and Pickering, 2004). In relation to digital media, vernaculars refer to those linguistic conventions characterising a specific digital environment (Manovich, 2017). Consider, for example, Instagram Stories. Instagram Stories are digital devices that permit users to simulate intimate interactions. In order to convey a sense of intimacy to their audiences, storymakers tend to articulate visual narrations in which they open their backstage to the public. This linguistic convention comes from Instagram influencers, who carefully craft and promote it through their public performances (Audrezet et al., 2020; Abidin, 2021). From the intersection between digital media grammars and vernaculars stem *platform vernaculars* (Gibbs et al., 2015). The term platform vernacular "refers to the different narrative patterns that shape content and the flow of information" (Niederer and Colombo, 2019, p. 55) across a given platform, which are not solely driven by the creativity of individual users, but rather are shaped by the "specificities of the platform, its material architecture, and the collective cultural practices that operate on and through it" (Gibbs et al., 2015, pp. 257–258). Throughout the book, we will show the reader how to *follow the medium* in order to study digital media's grammars, and how to *follow the users* in order to explore digital media's vernaculars – and, ultimately, how to take advantage of the intersection of these two perspectives.

Along this line, the ultimate scope of the book is therefore not to focus (specifically) on platform vernaculars – which are generic artefacts that can be found in the whole spectrum of cultural production on the internet – but rather to take advantage of platforms' grammars and vernaculars to cast a light upon a key and yet understudied aspect of consumer culture research: *digital consumer imaginaries*. Although it recalls supposedly childish concepts like "fantasy" or "daydreaming," imagination plays a pivotal role in consumer culture (Schau, 2000; Bajde, 2012). As clearly pointed out by Arnould and Thompson (2018, p. 22), imagination is by no means trivial; instead, it is something researchers need to pay significant attention when studying consumption, since imagination: "(1) links corporeality (the body and the physical sensations) and abstract reasoning (thought) to yield knowledge (intelligence), and (2) is central to the construction and expression of identities and realities." Put differently, imagination is the "virtual" space where consumers construct their ideas of the world, society, and self, while objects of consumption (brands, ads, commercial products, etc.) are the instruments they use to trigger or manifest their own imagination (Lury, 1996; Anderson, 1997). This last point is crucial: while imagination can be spurred by an individual's drive, it is nonetheless intrinsically structured and, in some sense, constrained, scaffolded, and channelled by the market (along with its heterogeneous array of commercial products and symbols) (Wallendorf and Arnould, 1988). Yet, despite how important real and concrete consumer imagination is, it remains something ephemeral (as it exists, forms, and develops inside the minds of consumers) and thus difficult to grasp from an empirical point of view (as can be inferred from consumers' accounts or behaviours, and nothing else). Nevertheless, this state of things changed with the advent of digital media and "digitisation" (Hagberg and Kjellber, 2020). Consequently, classical manifestations of consumer imaginaries, such as self-presentation strategies (Schau and Gilly, 2003), consumer narratives (Van Laer et al. 2017), or practices of community building (Caliandro, 2014) are not only clearly visible now, but they are somehow captured and made tangible by digital infrastructures (boyd, 2011). Moreover, many of the elements of such infrastructures can be considered as objects of consumption per se, as digital apps or algorithms (Denegri-Knott et. al. 2020; Airoldi and Rokka, 2022). Therefore, in the contemporary digital age, we can argue that consumer imagination is shaped by another important external force beyond that of the market, that is, *platformisation.*

Based on this understanding, we introduce the new concept of *digital consumer imaginary*, which we define as the cultural construction of identity, society, and reality elaborated and enacted by consumers through consumption objects. This digital consumer imaginary is not only re-shaped, re-constructed, and re-configured by digital platforms, but also made visible, traceable, and measurable by them. It is not intended as a set of narratives elaborated by a specific consumer about, for example, the properties of a digital object of consumption (Mardon et al., 2022), or how an algorithm feeds her/him with specific ads or brand promotions (Schellewald, 2022), or even a consumer narrative enabled by a digital device (Sörum and Fuentes, 2023). Rather, it is the result of an assemblage of dispersed pieces of consumer expression and symbolic productions that are collated by both the technicalities of the platform and the technical means of data collection and analysis through which researchers explore the platform. Therefore, insofar as we consider digital platforms to be privileged places in which to observe digital consumer imaginaries, we also deem digital methods to be a privileged means of tracing, measuring, and analysing them. By taking advantage of digital methods as well as ad hoc case studies, we will show that digital consumer imaginaries consist of a complex set of contents, discourses, narrations, and visual repertoires (co-created by human and non-human actors) emerging at the intersection of digital platforms grammars and vernaculars. Through them, users represent the process of consumer culture production itself – by, for example, reflecting (implicitly or explicitly) on what is meaningful, appropriate, authentic, or desirable about the consumption of products, brands, and services (Caliandro and Anselmi, 2021). Obviously, this does not cover all the multiple manifestations of consumer cultural processes on digital platforms (Chochoy et al., 2020; Rokka, 2021); nevertheless, it is one of the most visible and most suitable methods as it gives us an immediate cognition of the ongoing processes of platformisation of consumer culture.

Scope and Structure of the Book

In the different chapters that compose this book, we present a systematic set of digital research techniques to study the processes of platformisation of consumer culture, and thus explore the different kinds of digital consumer imaginaries emerging around products and brands on digital media. To do so, we will elaborate, describe, and provide a set of methodological guidelines to map out the processes of ordering, circulation, and curation of consumer culture enacted by digital media affordances (Beer, 2019) – with the ultimate aim of understanding the kind of consumer culture users, create, encounter, and interact with when using digital platforms. To achieve this goal, we do not provide the reader with a canonical set of chapters in which different research techniques and their possible methodological implications for both digital methods and consumer culture theory are discussed. On the contrary, taking explicit inspiration from Bounegru et al.'s (2018) *Field guide to fake news and other information disorders*, we develop ad hoc case studies through which we offer a "collection of research recipes" for using digital methods to explore the platformisation of consumer culture within digital environments. Specifically, we present eight case studies:

1. Consuming Nostalgia on Facebook
2. YouTube and the Radicalisation (?) of Consumption
3. The Platformisation of Music Genres on Spotify
4. Exploring the Role of Fake News and Bots in Brand Communication on Twitter and Their Impact on Brand Value and Consumer Culture
5. Instagram Influencers at the Crossroads between Publics and Communities
6. Assessing the Impact of *Kitchen Nightmares* through TripAdvisor
7. Thinking of the Same Place: the Trivialisation of the Sharing Economy on Airbnb
8. Ephemeral Content and Ephemeral Consumption on TikTok

In addition to the chapters featuring ad hoc case studies, the book comprises a *Methodological Framework*, in which we clarify, justify, and contextualise our methodological strategies and choices, and a *Conclusion*, in which we outline a systematic definition of the platformisation of consumer culture from a theoretical perspective.

We expect this book to be relevant for readers already acquainted with digital methods, since a basic understanding of these techniques is necessary to address the complex phenomenon of platformisation of consumer culture. In other words, this is not a handbook for learning digital methods (for this, we refer the reader to specific textbooks already available on the market, such as Richard Rogers' *Doing digital methods* (2019) or Alessandro Caliandro and Alessandro Gandini's *Qualitative research in digital environments* (2017)). Nevertheless, all the techniques of data collection, analysis, and visualisation employed in the chapters are carefully described, and links to ad hoc tutorials for digital methods tools will be provided throughout the text.

Before delving into the contents of the book, a final clarification is due. Since this is not a methodological handbook, we dared to take some "intellectual liberties," of the kind that one is usually not willing to take when writing a paper for a scientific journal. While obviously maintaining scientific rigour, we also used the book as an occasion to: 1) explore topics and research questions that resonate with our personal and intellectual curiosity, rather than focusing on pressing research issues in the academic debate; and 2) elaborate some new (and sometimes "quirky") theoretical concepts that can be useful for framing the novelty of consumer culture processes as they play out on digital platforms, such as "radicalisation of consumption," "subversive fake news," or the *Kitchen Nightmares* effect." Naturally, the elaboration of such new theoretical concepts did not stem solely from the creative drive of the authors, but from our systematic data analysis. Moreover, it fulfils a scientific necessity: studies on the platformisation of consumer culture are still in their infancy. Therefore, on the one hand, we need new conceptual categories to orient and guide the analysis of our datasets: considering that a research field focused on the study of platformisation of consumer culture through digital methods does not exist yet, sometimes we had to create our own categories, heuristics, and concepts. On the other hand, we developed some "quirky" new concepts to stimulate the imagination of the readers, and, hopefully, to encourage them to undertake the journey of the study of platformisation of consumer culture (either theoretically or empirically) by further developing or even discarding our theoretical intuitions. This way, we hope that a new strand of research will emerge from the case studies, methodological recipes, conceptual elaborations, and theoretical intuitions presented in this book.

References

Abidin, C. (2021). Singaporean influencers and Covid-19 on Instagram stories. *Celebrity Studies*, 12(4), 693–698. https://doi.org/10.1080/19392397.2021.1967604.

Adler-Nissen, R., Eggeling, K. A. and Wangen, P. (2021). Machine anthropology: A view from international relations. *Big Data & Society*, 8(2). https://doi.org/10.1177/20539517211063690.

Agre, P. E. (1994). Surveillance and capture: Two models of privacy. *The Information Society*, 10(2), 101–127. https://doi.org/10.1080/01972243.1994.9960162.

Airoldi, M. (2021a). Digital traces of taste: Methodological pathways for consumer research. *Consumption Markets and Culture*, *24*(1), 97–117. https://doi.org/10.108 0/10253866.2019.1690998.

Airoldi, M. (2021b). The techno-social reproduction of taste boundaries on digital platforms: The case of music on YouTube. *Poetics*, 89. https://doi.org/10.1016/j. poetic.2021.101563.

Airoldi, M. and Rokka, J. (2022). Algorithmic consumer culture. *Consumption Markets and Culture*, *25*(5), 411–428. https://doi.org/10.1080/10253866.2022.2084726.

Anderson, W. (1997). T*he future of the self: Inventing the postmodern person*. Penguin Putnam Inc.

Arnould, E. J. and Thompson, C. J. (2005). Consumer culture theory (CCT): Twenty years of research. *Journal of Consumer Research*, *31*(4), 868–882. https://doi. org/10.1086/426626.

Arnould, E. J., and Thompson, C. J (2018). *Consumer culture theory*. Sage.

Arvidsson, A (2019). *Changemakers: The industrious future of the digital economy*. Polity Press.

Arvidsson, A. and Caliandro, A. (2016). Brand public. *Journal of Consumer Research*, *42*(5), 727–748. https://doi.org/10.1093/jcr/ucv053.

Arvidsson, A., Caliandro, A., Airoldi, M., and Barina, S. (2016). Crowds and value: Italian directioners on Twitter. *Information, Communication and Society*, *19*(7), 921–939. https://doi.org/10.1080/1369118X.2015.1064462.

Atton, C. (2001). The mundane and its reproduction in alternative media. *Journal of Mundane Behavior*, *2*(1), 122–137. http://researchrepository.napier.ac.uk/id/ eprint/3620.

Audrezet, A., De Kerviler, G., and Moulard, J. G. (2020). Authenticity under threat: When social media influencers need to go beyond self-presentation. *Journal of Business Research*, *117*. 557–569.https://doi.org/10.1016/j.jbusres.2018.07.008.

Audy Martínek, P., Caliandro, A., and Denegri-Knott, J. (2023). Digital practices tracing: Studying consumer lurking in digital environments. *Journal of Marketing Management*, 39(3/4), 244–274. https://doi.org/10.1080/0267257X.2022.2105385.

Bainotti, L., Caliandro, A., and Gandini, A. (2021). From archive cultures to ephemeral content, and back: Studying Instagram Stories with digital methods. *New Media and Society*, 23(12), 3656–3676. https://doi.org/10.1177/1461444820960071.

Bardhi, F. and Eckhardt, G. M. (2012). Access-based consumption: The case of car sharing. *Journal of Consumer Research*, *39*(4), 881–898. https://doi. org/10.1086/666376.

Bardhi, F. and Eckhardt, G. M. (2017). Liquid consumption. *Journal of Consumer Research*, *44*(3), 582–597. https://doi.org/10.1093/jcr/ucx050.

Bajde, D. (2012). Mapping the imaginary of charitable giving. *Consumption Markets and Culture*, *15*(4), 358–373. https://doi.org/10.1080/10253866.2012.659433.

Beer, D. (2017). The social power of algorithms. *Information, Communication and Society, 20*(1), 1–13. https://doi.org/10.1080/1369118X.2016.1216147.

Beer, D. (2019). *The quirks of digital culture.* Emerald Group Publishing.

Belk, R. W. (2013). Extended self in a digital world. *Journal of Consumer Research, 40*(3), 477–500. https://doi.org/10.1086/671052.

Berger, J., Humphreys, A., Ludwig, S., Moe, W. W., Netzer, O., and Schweidel, D. A. (2020). Uniting the tribes: Using text for marketing insight. *Journal of Marketing, 84*(1), 1–25. https://doi.org/10.1177/0022242919873106.

Bessi, A. and Ferrara, E. (2016). Social bots distort the 2016 US Presidential election online discussion. *First Monday, 21*(11/7). https://doi.org/10.5210/fm.v21i11.7090.

Bonini, T., and Gandini, A. (2019). First week is editorial, second week is algorithmic: Platform gatekeepers and the platformisation of music curation. *Social Media+ Society, 5*(4). https://doi.org/10.1177/2056305119880006.

Boudreau, K. J. (2017). Platform boundary choices and governance: Opening-up while still coordinating and orchestrating. In J. Furman, A. Gawer, B. S. Silverman, and S. Stern (Eds.), *Entrepreneurship, innovation, and platforms* (pp. 227–297). Emerald Publishing Limited.

Bounegru L., Gray J., Venturini T., and Mauri, M. (2018). *A field guide to "fake news" and other information disorders.* Public Data Lab.

Bourdieu, P. (1984). *Distinction: A social critique of the judgement of taste.* Harvard University Press.

boyd, d. (2011). Social networking sites as networked publics: Affordances, dynamics and implication. In Z. Papacharissi (Ed.), *A networked self: Identity community and culture on social network sites* (pp. 39–58). Routledge.

Brodie, R. J., Ilic, A., Juric, B., and Hollebeek, L. (2013). Consumer engagement in a virtual brand community: An exploratory analysis. *Journal of Business Research, 66*(1), 105–114. https://doi.org/10.1016/j.jbusres.2011.07.029.

Bucher, T. and Helmond, A. (2017). The affordances of social media platforms. In J. Burgess, T. Poell, and A. Marwick (Eds.), *The SAGE handbook of social media* (pp. 233–253). Sage.

Burgess, J. (2006). Hearing ordinary voices: Cultural studies, vernacular creativity and digital storytelling. *Continuum: Journal of Media and Cultural Studies, 20*(2), 201–214. https://doi.org/10.1080/10304310600641737.

Caliandro, A. (2014). Ethnography in digital spaces: Ethnography of virtual worlds, netnography, and digital ethnography. In R. Denny and P. Sunderland (Eds.), *Handbook of anthropology in business* (pp. 658–680). Left Coast Press.

Caliandro, A. (2018). Digital methods for ethnography: Analytical concepts for ethnographers exploring social media environments, *Journal of Contemporary Ethnography, 47*(5), 551–578. https://doi.org/10.1177/0891241617702.

Caliandro A. and Gandini A. (2017). *Qualitative research in digital environments: A research toolkit.* Routledge.

Caliandro, A. and Anselmi, G. (2021). Affordances-based brand relations: An inquiry on memetic brands on Instagram. *Social Media+ Society, 7*(2). https://doi.org/10.1177/20563051211021367.

Caliandro, A., Gandini, A., Bainotti, L., and Anselmi, G. (2024). The platformization of consumer culture: A theoretical framework. *Marketing Theory.* https://journals.sagepub.com/doi/10.1177/14705931231225537

Cambrosio, A., Cointet, J. P., and Abdo, A. H. (2020). Beyond networks: Aligning qualitative and computational science studies. *Quantitative Science Studies, 1*(3), 1017–1024. https://doi.org/10.1162/qss_a_00055.

Canniford, R. and Bajde, D. (2015). *Assembling consumption: Researching actors, networks and markets.* Routledge.

Carah, N. and Angus, D. (2018). Algorithmic brand culture: Participatory labour, machine learning and branding on social media. *Media, Culture and Society, 40*(2), 178–194. https://doi.org/10.1177/016344371875464.

Cochoy, F., Licoppe, C., McIntyre, M. P., and Sörum, N. (2020). Digitalizing consumer society: Equipment and devices of digital consumption. *Journal of Cultural Economy, 13*(1), 1–11. https://doi.org/10.1080/17530350.2019.1702576.

Colleoni, E., Rozza, A., and Arvidsson, A. (2014). Echo chamber or public sphere? Predicting political orientation and measuring political homophily in Twitter using big data. *Journal of communication, 64*(2), 317–332. https://doi.org/10.1111/jcom.12084.

Cova, B. (1997). Community and consumption: Towards a definition of the "linking value" of product or services. *European Journal of Marketing, 31*(3/4), 297–316. https://doi.org/10.1108/03090569710162380.

Cova, B. and Dalli, D. (2009). Working consumers: The next step in marketing theory? *Marketing Theory, 9*(3), 315–339. https://doi.org/10.1177/147059310933814.

Darmody, A. and Zwick, D. (2020). Manipulate to empower: Hyper-relevance and the contradictions of marketing in the age of surveillance capitalism. *Big Data and Society, 7*(1). https://doi.org/10.1177/205395172090411.

DeLanda, M. (2006). *A new philosophy of society: Assemblage theory and social complexity.* Continuum.

Denegri-Knott, J. and Molesworth, M. (2010). Concepts and practices of digital virtual consumption. *Consumption, Markets and Culture, 13*(2), 109–132. https://doi.org/10.1080/10253860903562130.

Denegri-Knott, J., Jenkins, R. and Lindley, S. (2020). What is digital possession and how to study it: A conversation with Russell Belk, Rebecca Mardon, Giana M. Eckhardt, Varala Maraj, Will Odom, Massimo Airoldi, Alessandro Caliandro, Mike Molesworth, and Alessandro Gandini. *Journal of Marketing Management, 36*(9/10), 942–971. https://doi.org/10.1080/0267257X.2020.1761864.

Dolbec, P. Y. and Fischer, E. (2015). Refashioning a field? Connected consumers and institutional dynamics in markets. *Journal of Consumer Research*, *41*(6), 1447–1468. https://doi.org/10.1086/680671.

Duffy, B. E., Poell, T., and Nieborg, D. B. (2019). Platform practices in the cultural industries: Creativity, labor, and citizenship. *Social Media+ Society*, 5(4). https://doi.org/10.1177/2056305119879672.

Duguay, S. (2019). Running the numbers: Modes of microcelebrity labor in queer women's self-representation on Instagram and Vine. *Social Media+ Society*, *5*(4). https://doi.org/10.1177/2056305119894002.

Fernández-Ardèvol, M., Belotti, F., Ieracitano, F., Mulargia, S., Rosales, A., and Comunello, F. (2020). "I do it my way": Idioms of practice and digital media ideologies of adolescents and older adults. *New Media and Society*, *24*(1), 31–49. https://doi.org/10.1177/1461444820959298.

Figueiredo, B. and Scaraboto, D. (2016). The systemic creation of value through circulation in collaborative consumer networks. *Journal of Consumer Research*, *43*(4), 509–533. https://doi.org/10.1093/jcr/ucw038.

Füller, J., Jawecki, G., and Mühlbacher, H. (2007). Innovation creation by online basketball communities. *Journal of Business Research*, *60*(1), 60–71. https://doi.org/10.1016/j.jbusres.2006.09.019.

Geertz, C. (1973). *The interpretation of cultures*. New York: Basic books.

Gerlitz, C. and Helmond, A. (2013). The like economy: Social buttons and the data-intensive web. *New Media and Society*, *15*(8), 1348–1365. https://doi.org/10.1177/1461444812472322.

Gerlitz, C. and Rieder, B. (2018). Tweets are not created equal: Investigating Twitter's client ecosystem. *International Journal of Communication*, *12*, 528–547. 1932–8036/20180005.

Gibbs, M., Meese, J., Arnold, M., Nansen, B., and Carter, M. (2015). #Funeral and Instagram: Death, social media, and platform vernacular. *Information, Communication and Society*, *18*(3), 255–268. https://doi.org/10.1080/1369118X.2014.987152.

Gielens, K. and Steenkamp, J. B. E. (2019). Branding in the era of digital (dis) intermediation. *International Journal of Research in Marketing*, *36*(3), 367–384. https://doi.org/10.1016/j.ijresmar.2019.01.005.

Gillespie, T. (2010). The politics of "platforms". *New Media and Society*, *12*(3), 347–364. https://doi.org/10.1177/1461444809342733.

Gray, J., Bounegru, L., and Venturini, T. (2020). "Fake news" as infrastructural uncanny. *New Media and Society*, *22*(2), 317–341. https://doi.org/10.1177/1461444819856912.

Gruzd, A. and Roy, J. (2014). Investigating political polarization on Twitter: A Canadian perspective. *Policy and Internet*, *6*(1), 28–45. https://doi.org/10.1002/1944-2866.POI354.

Hall, S. (1980). Encoding/decoding. In S. Hall, D. Hobson, A. Lowe, and P. Willis (Eds). *Culture, Media, Language* (pp. 128–38). Hutchinson.

Hagberg, J. and Kjellberg, H. (2020). Digitalized markets. *Consumption Markets and Culture*, *23*(2), 97–109. https://doi.org/10.1080/10253866.2020.1694209.

Helmond, A. (2015). The platformisation of the web: Making web data platform ready. *Social Media+ Society*, *1*(2). https://doi.org/10.1177/2056305115603080.

Hoffman, D. L. and Novak, T. P. (2018). Consumer and object experience in the internet of things: An assemblage theory approach. *Journal of Consumer Research*, *44*(6), 1178–1204. https://doi.org/10.1093/jcr/ucx105.

Humphreys, A. and Wang, R. J. H. (2018). Automated text analysis for consumer research. *Journal of Consumer Research*, *44*(6), 1274–1306. https://doi.org/10.1093/jcr/ucx104.

Jenkins, H. (2006). *Convergence culture: Where old and new media collide*. New York University Press.

Kozinets, R., Patterson, A., and Ashman, R. (2017). Networks of desire: How technology increases our passion to consume. *Journal of Consumer Research*, *43*(5), 659–682. https://doi.org/10.1093/jcr/ucw061.

Kozinets, R. V., Ferreira, D. A., and Chimenti, P. (2021). How do platforms empower consumers? Insights from the affordances and constraints of Reclame Aqui. *Journal of Consumer Research*, 48(3), 428–455. https://doi.org/10.1093/jcr/ucab014.

Latour, B., Jensen, P., Venturini, T., Grauwin, S., and Boullier, D. (2012). The whole is always smaller than its parts: A digital test of Gabriel Tardes' monads. *The British journal of sociology*, *63*(4), 590–615. https://doi.org/10.1111/j.1468-4446.2012.01428.x.

Leung, E., Paolacci, G., and Puntoni, S. (2018). Man versus machine: Resisting automation in identity-based consumer behavior. *Journal of Marketing Research*, *55*(6), 818–831. https://doi.org/10.1177/0022243718818423.

Lury, C. (1996). *Consumer culture*. Rutgers University Press.

Mangold, W. G. and Faulds, D. J. (2009). Social media: The new hybrid element of the promotion mix. *Business horizons*, *52*(4), 357–365. https://doi.org/10.1016/j.bushor.2009.03.002.

Manovich, L. (2017). Instagram and contemporary image. Manovich.net. http://manovich.net/index.php/projects/instagram-and-contemporary-image.

Mardon, R., Denegri-Knott, J., and Molesworth, M. (2022). "Kind of mine, kind of not": Digital possessions and affordance misalignment. *Journal of Consumer Research*, *50*(2), 255–281. https://doi.org/10.1093/jcr/ucac057.

Marres, N. (2017). *Digital sociology: The reinvention of social research*. John Wiley and Sons.

Marwick, A. E. (2015). Instafame: Luxury selfies in the attention economy. *Public culture*, *27*(1/75), 137–160. https://doi.org/10.1215/08992363-2798379.

Muniz, A. M. and O'Guinn, T. C. (2001). Brand community. *Journal of Consumer Research*, *27*(4), 412–432. https://doi.org/10.1086/319618.

Negus, K. and Pickering, M. (2004). *Creativity, communication and cultural value.* Sage.

Nieborg, D. B., Duffy, B. E., and Poell, T. (2020). Studying platforms and cultural production: Methods, institutions, and practices. *Social Media+ Society, 6*(3), https://doi.org/10.1177/2056305120943273.

Niedeer, S. and Colombo, G. (2019). Visual methodologies for networked images: Designing visualizations for collaborative research, cross platform analysis, and public participation. *Diseña, 14,* 40–67. https://doi.org/10.7764/disena.14.40-67.

O'Meara, V. (2019). Weapons of the chic: Instagram influencer engagement pods as practices of resistance to Instagram platform labor. *Social Media+ Society, 5*(4), https://doi.org/10.1177/2056305119879671.

Parmentier, M. A., and Fischer, E. (2015). Things fall apart: The dynamics of brand audience dissipation. *Journal of Consumer Research, 41*(5), 1228–1251. https://doi.org/10.1177/2056305119879671.

Perren, R. and Kozinets, R. V. (2018). Lateral exchange markets: How social platforms operate in a networked economy. *Journal of Marketing, 82*(1), 20–36. https://doi.org/10.1509/jm.14.0250.

Pink, S., Horst, H., Postill, J., Hjorth, L., Lewis, T., and Tacchi, J. (2015). *Digital ethnography: Principles and practice.* Sage.

Poell, T., Nieborg, D., and Van Dijck, J. (2019). Platformisation. *Internet Policy Review, 8*(4), 1–13. doi:10.14763/2019.4.1425.

Rieder, B., Matamoros-Fernández, A., and Coromina, O. (2018). From ranking algorithms to "ranking cultures": Investigating the modulation of visibility in YouTube search results. *Convergence, 24*(1), 50–68. https://doi.org/10.1177/1354856517736982.

Rieder, B., Coromina, O., and Matamoros-Fernandez, A. (2020). Mapping YouTube: A quantitative exploration of a platformed media system. *First Monday, 25*(8). 0.5210/fm.v25i8.10667.

Rogers, R. (2010). Internet research: The question of method. A keynote address from the YouTube and the 2008 election cycle in the United States conference. *Journal of Information Technology and Politics, 7,* 241–260. https://doi.org/10.1080/19331681003753438.

Rogers, R. (2019). *Doing Digital Methods.* Sage.

Rogers, R. and Giorgi, G. (2023). What is a meme, technically speaking?. *Information, Communication and Society,* 1–19, https://doi.org/10.1080/1369118X.2023.2174790.

Rokka, J. (2021). Consumer culture theory's future in marketing. *Journal of Marketing Theory and Practice, 29*(1), 114–124. https://doi.org/10.1080/10696679.2020.1860685.

Rokka, J. and Canniford, R. (2016). Heterotopian selfies: How social media destabilizes brand assemblages. *European Journal of Marketing, 50*(9/10), 1789–1813. https://doi.org/10.1108/EJM-08-2015-0517.

Ruckenstein, M. and Granroth, J. (2020). Algorithms, advertising and the intimacy of surveillance. *Journal of Cultural Economy*, *13*(1), 12–24. https://doi.org/10.108 0/17530350.2019.1574866.

Salmons, J. (2016). *Doing qualitative research online*. Sage.

Schau, H. J. (2000). Consumer imagination, identity and self-expression. In S. J. Hoch and R. J. Mayer (Eds.), *NA – Advances in Consumer Research*, 27 (pp. 50–56). Association for Consumer Research.

Schau, H. J. and Gilly, M. C. (2003). We are what we post? Self-presentation in personal web space. *Journal of Consumer Research*, *30*(3), 385–404. https://doi. org/10.1086/378616.

Schau, H. J., Muñiz Jr, A. M., and Arnould, E. J. (2009). How brand community practices create value. *Journal of Marketing*, *73*(5), 30–51. https://doi.org/10.1509/ jmkg.73.5.30.

Schellewald, A. (2022). Theorizing "stories about algorithms" as a mechanism in the formation and maintenance of algorithmic imaginaries. *Social Media+ Society*, *8*(1), https://doi.org/10.1177/20563051221077025.

Schöps, J. D.(2022). *Digital Markets as Performative Assemblages* (PhD dissertation), Leopold-Franzens-Universität Innsbruck.

Schöps, J. D., Kogler, S., and Hemetsberger, A. (2020). (De-)stabilizing the digitized fashion market on Instagram-dynamics of visual performative assemblages. *Consumption Markets and Culture*, *23*(2), 195–213. https://doi.org/10.1080/1025 3866.2019.1657099.

Schöps, J. D., Reinhardt, C., and Hemetsberger, A. (2022). Sticky market webs of con-nection–human and nonhuman market co-codification dynamics across social media. *European Journal of Marketing*, *56*(13), 78–104. https://doi.org/10.1108/ EJM-10-2020-0750.

Schouten, J. W. and McAlexander, J. H. (1995). Subcultures of consumption: An ethnography of the new bikers. *Journal of Consumer Research*, *22*(1), 43–61. https://doi.org/10.1086/209434.

Sörum, N. and Fuentes, C. (2023). How sociotechnical imaginaries shape consum-ers' experiences of and responses to commercial data collection practices. *Consumption Markets and Culture*, 26(1), 24–46. https://doi.org/10.1080/10253 866.2022.2124977.

Srnicek, N. (2017). *Platform capitalism*. Polity Press.

Täuscher, K. and Laudien, S.V. (2018). Understanding platform business models: A mixed methods study of marketplaces. *European Management Journal*, *36*(3), 319–329. https://doi.org/10.1016/j.emj.2017.06.005.

Thompson, C. J. (2019). The "big data" myth and the pitfalls of 'thick data' op-portunism: On the need for a different ontology of markets and consumption.

Journal of Marketing Management, 35(3–4), 207–230. https://doi.org/10.1080/02 67257X.2019.1579751.

Treré, E. and Bonini, T. (2022). Amplification, evasion, hijacking: Algorithms as repertoire for social movements and the struggle for visibility. *Social Movement Studies*, 1–17. https://doi.org/10.1080/14742837.2022.2143345.

Tuten, T. L. and Solomon, M. R. (2017). *Social media marketing*. Sage.

Valensise, C. M., Cinelli, M., and Quattrociocchi, W. (2023). The drivers of online polarization: Fitting models to data. *Information Sciences, 642*. https://doi. org/10.1016/j.ins.2023.119152.

Van Dijck, J. (2014). Datafication, dataism and dataveillance: Big Data between scientific paradigm and ideology. *Surveillance and Society, 12*(2), 197–208. https:// doi.org/10.24908/ss.v12i2.4776.

Van Dijck, J. and Poell, T. (2013). Understanding social media logic. *Media and Communication, 1*(1), 2–14. https://ssrn.com/abstract=2309065.

Van Dijck, J., Poell, T., and De Waal, M. (2018). *The platform society: Public values in a connective world*. Oxford University Press.

Van Es, K. and Poell, T. (2020). Platform imaginaries and Dutch public service media. *Social Media+ Society, 6*(2), https://doi.org/10.1177/2056305120933289.

Van Laer, T., Edson Escalas, J., Ludwig, S., and Van Den Hende, E. A. (2019). What happens in Vegas stays on TripAdvisor? A theory and technique to understand narrativity in consumer reviews. *Journal of Consumer Research, 46*(2), 267–285. https://doi.org/10.1093/jcr/ucy067.

Vicari, S. and Kirby, D. (2023). Digital platforms as socio-cultural artifacts: Developing digital methods for cultural research. *Information, Communication and Society, 26*(9), 1733–1755. https://doi.org/10.1080/1369118X.2022.2027498.

Von Hippel, E. (2005). *Democratizing innovation*. MIT Press.

Wallendorf, M. and Arnould, E. J. (1988). "My favorite things": A cross-cultural inquiry into object attachment, possessiveness, and social linkage. *Journal of Consumer Research, 14*(4), 531–547. https://doi.org/10.1086/209134.

WeAreSocial (2023). Digital 2023: Your ultimate guide to the evolving digital world. WeAreSocial.com. https://wearesocial.com/uk/blog/2023/01/digital-2023/.

Wichmann, J. R., Wiegand, N., and Reinartz, W. J. (2022). The platformization of brands. *Journal of Marketing, 86*(1), 109–131. https://doi.org/10.1177/00222429211054073.

Zhu, F. and Furr, N. (April 2016). Products to platforms: Making the leap. *Harvard Business Review, 94*(4), 72–78. https://hbr.org/2016/04/products-to-platforms-making-the-leap.

Zuboff, S. (2015). Big other: Surveillance capitalism and the prospects of an information civilization. *Journal of Information Technology, 30*(1), 75–89. https://doi. org/10.1057/jit.2015.5.

Zuboff, S. (2019). *The age of surveillance capitalism: The fight for a human future at the new frontier of power.* Profile Books.

Zwick, D., Bonsu, S. K., and Darmody, A. (2008). Putting consumers to work: Co-creation and new marketing govern-mentality. *Journal of Consumer Culture,* *8*(2), 163–196. https://doi.org/10.1177/1469540508090089.

II. Methodological Framework

A Qualitative Approach to Digital Methods

As illustrated in the Introduction, this book is grounded upon a qualitative approach to digital methods. But what are digital methods? Digital methods employ "online tools and data for the purposes of social and medium research" (Rogers, 2017, p. 75), with the broader scope of studying socio-cultural conditions and changes (Rogers, 2013). More than a set of digital techniques, digital methods are, first and foremost, an epistemological paradigm. In fact, digital methods rest on the premise that digital environments (such as blogs, search engines, and, of course, platforms) can be considered as *sources of methods*, rather than just *objects of study* (Rogers, 2009). To fully take advantage of such a new and invaluable repository of methods, researchers must learn how to *follow the medium*, meaning, to make use of and take inspiration from those *natively digital methods* that digital environments apply to themselves to gather, order, organise, rank and, rate digital data – as with APIs, algorithms, tags, retweets, likes, hashtags, etc. (Caliandro, 2014) – (for instance, retweets are devices through which users establish new social relations as well as, at the same time, the very natively digital metrics through which one can measure such relations) (Ruppert et al., 2013). Specifically, by following the medium, digital methods aim at understanding how digital infrastructures structure communication and interaction playing out on digital media; in so doing, they are primarily concerned with mapping online discourses and social formations (Marres, 2017).

More recently, digital methods scholars have argued that it is not enough to simply *follow the medium* in order to fully grasp the socio-cultural processes manifesting in online environments (Hutchinson, 2016; Caliandro, 2018) – it is necessary to *follow the actors*, too (Latour, 2005). In fact, to exclusively follow the medium carries the risk of producing merely "descriptive" accounts, thus lacking theoretical depth (Severson, 2019). In order to follow the actors, beyond observing how digital devices structure online communication and interaction, a researcher must also pay attention to how users *use* digital devices as well as how such use impacts the structure of online communication and interaction. For example, Bruns et al. (2016)

Caliandro, A., A. Gandini, L. Bainotti, G. Anselmi, *The Platformisation of Consumer Culture: A Digital Methods Guide*. Amsterdam: Amsterdam University Press, 2024
DOI 10.5117/9789463729567_II

stress that different practices of use of the same digital device (the Twitter hashtag, #) can be conducive to the generation of quite different communicative spaces. These range from *acute events* (communicative spaces emerging around hashtags like #breakingnews or #charliehebdo, whereby users "engage in gatewatching activities") to *media events* (communicative spaces emerging around hashtags like #masterchef or #electionday, whereby users "use Twitter as a second-screen channel") (2016, pp. 27–29).

Following this same line of thought, and in order to take better advantage of digital methods for understanding cultural processes unfolding on digital media (especially related to brands, products, and consumers), in the book *Qualitative research in digital environments* Caliandro and Gandini (2017) propose a qualitative approach to digital methods. Simply put, this approach consists in systematically integrating qualitative research techniques (e.g., ethnographic content analysis, non-participant observation, narrations analysis, etc.) into "traditional" digital methods inquiries (e.g., mapping the natural clustering of hashtags emerging around a brand on Twitter). This qualitative approach to digital methods has been fruitfully applied to investigate several key consumer culture topics, such as the transformation of brand communities into publics within social media platforms (Arvidsson and Caliandro, 2016); the micro-celebrity practices of teenage music fans on Twitter (Arvidsson et al., 2016); the processes through which the socio-technical architecture of YouTube shapes music tastes (Airoldi et al., 2016) as well as authenticity-related boundary works of music listeners (Airoldi, 2021); the co-creation of brand image between customers and brands on Instagram (Schöps et al., 2020); the memefication of brands relations on Instagram (Caliandro and Anselmi; 2021). This approach is based on the combination of three main research strategies that Caliandro and Gandini call: *follow the thing, follow the medium, follow the natives* (see also Caliandro, 2018). As Caliandro and Gandini (2017, p. 63) put it:

> [To follow the thing, the medium, the natives] is an exhortation to researchers to start their digital enquiries by following the circulation of an empirical object (such as a topic of discussion, a political issue or a brand) within a given online environment or across different online environments, with the aim to observe the:
> 1) the social formations naturally emerging from the processes of online communication structuring enacted by digital devices; and
> 2) the cultural formations naturally emerging from the practices of use of digital devices enacted by users, as well as from the interactions among users and digital devices.

In the present book, we draw on the same logic, but with two epistemological updates: 1) we do not talk of "things" to follow but rather of "traces," since we recognise that any digital object (e.g., a branded hashtags) is, fundamentally, a digital trace left behind by some kind of online actor acting on a given digital environment (Corchia, 2022); consequently, 2) we do not speak of "natives" anymore but of "users," implying that a user can be (indifferently) a human or a non-human actor (Latour, 2005).

In the following paragraphs, we will unpack the three aforementioned research strategies (*follow the traces, follow the medium, follow the users*) by: a) providing more methodological context and justification; b) describing how we applied them to the specific case studies featured in the different chapters of the book; and c) reflecting on how they helped us to explore and understand the platformisation of consumer culture. Before continuing, a last premise is due: to comprehensively study the platformisation of consumer culture, one has to simultaneously follow the traces, the medium, and the actors. In fact, in each chapter we employ a combination of those three strategies – even though, sometimes, some were more dominant than others. Nonetheless, to enable their full understanding, we present them here below separately and as stand-alone ones.

Follow the Traces

Generally, all digital data can be considered as *digital traces*. As Salganik argues, digital traces are akin to what sociologists call "observational data," that is, "data that results from observing a social system without intervening in some ways" (2019, p. 13). In fact, all digital data is the by-product of some kind of activity performed by users on and/or through digital media. Venturini et al. (2018, p.6) put it more formally, describing a digital trace as:

> Any inscription produced by a digital medium in its mediation of collective actions – for instance, a post published on a blog and a hyperlink connecting two websites or the log of an e-commerce transaction. We call this particular type of inscriptions "traces" as a reminder that they are (most often) generated by purposes other than academic research.

As a result of global processes of datafication and platformisation, consumers leave behind a countless number of traces during their daily whereabouts within digital environments, for example by searching, browsing, liking, linking, saving content on a wishlist, buying, posting comments or reviews, etc. (Deighton, 2019; Audy Martínek et al., 2023). Such traces materialise in two main kinds of digital data: *user-generated content* (data that are deliberately produced by users during their interactions with digital devices, e.g., posting a selfie on Instagram) and *transactional data* (data that are generated as a by-product of users' online activities, e.g., visiting a website) (Caliandro and Gandini, 2017).

According to Airoldi (2021), digital traces can be used as both *research objects* and *methodological tools* for research purposes. For example, one can analyse co-hashtag networks emerging around a given brand on Twitter (e.g., #cocacola) to map the macro discourse users articulate around it; alternatively, one can take advantage of a hashtag to sample and/or detect specific consumers' conversations (e.g., #boycottcocacola) within a broader stream of tweets referring to a certain brand (e.g., #cocacola). Therefore, by "simply" following the digital traces that users leave behind, it is possible to investigate complex cultural phenomena and observe how they are re-configured by digital platforms' affordances (Airoldi, 2021). This is, for instance, what Airoldi et al. (2016) did in their socio-technical exploration of music taste on YouTube. By following (and re-aggregating) the patterns of co-viewing related to music videos, the authors observed how YouTube's users collaborate (among themselves and the platform's algorithm) to co-create crowd-based categorisation of music genres. In the process, the authors noted the emergence of new "crowd-generated" music categories (such as Relaxing Music or Music for Babies), which are "characterised by what may be seen as *situational* culture of music reception by digital audiences" (Airoldi et al., 2016, p. 3).

The chapters of the book in which the *follow the traces* strategy is at the core of the empirical work are Chapter 4 ("Exploring the Role of Fake News and Bots in Brand Communication on Twitter and Their Impact on Brand Value and Consumer Culture"), Chapter 6 ("Assessing the Impact of *Kitchen Nightmares* through TripAdvisor"), and Chapter 7 ("Thinking of the Same Place: The Trivialisation of the Sharing Economy on Airbnb"). Here, we mostly employ computational techniques – that is, automated procedures of meta-data and keywords extraction and counting – to achieve this goal.

Exploring the Role of Fake News and Bots in Brand Communication on Twitter and Their Impact on Brand Value and Consumer Culture

Fake news has a notoriously nefarious impact on online brand reputation, which can be further magnified by the activity of social bots (Di Domenico and Visentin, 2020). In this chapter, we investigate the relationship between fake news and bots as well as its impact on brand value and consumer culture. To do so, we analysed a dataset of 461,303 tweets related to Pepsi, New Balance, and Twitter Inc. itself. Specifically, we followed the traces left by brand-related fake news and bots (i.e., the number of posts generated over time) in order to verify if, and to what extent, there is a relation between fake news outlets and bots. Our analysis permitted us to discover that the activities of fake news and bots seem to be quite disconnected, as if fake news' creators and bots had separate "businesses on their own." Fake news creators are mostly human actors that create or exploit brand-related fake news to push their political agendas (e.g., make America great again!), rather than to tank brands' reputation or value; while bots simply piggyback existing controversies triggered by fake news to boost their visibility and, thus, sell commercial products to Twitter audiences. This insight is the basis of further qualitative analysis that allowed us to shed light on a peculiar aspect of platformisation of culture on Twitter. Similarly to bots, human users follow a platformised logic of cultural production: this does not necessarily mean that, when creating and posting fake news, users adhere to a general social media logic of content production (Van Dijck and Poell, 2013), but rather that they *use* fake news as a platform to convey their (very) own *political imaginary* (Caliandro et al., 2021) – and not so much to talk about brands per se. We speak of "political imaginary" because we found no traces of coherent and organised political debates among users (e.g., pushing specific political programmes or manifestos), but rather individualised narrations envisioning a generic (better) future. In this sense, we deem fake news related to brands as having a "subversive" function rather than a "toxic" one – if compared to traditional political fake news.

Assessing the Impact of Kitchen Nightmares through TripAdvisor

Watching the Italian episodes of *Kitchen Nightmares*, one has the impression that chef Antonino Cannavacciuolo (Gordon Ramsay's counterpart) has the power to positively change the destiny of hopeless food businesses. However, it is legitimate to ask about the extent to which Cannavacciuolo's operations actually have an impact on a large pool of restaurants. Therefore, we articulated the following research question: *How are the restaurants doing after the ending of the show? Are they still in business? Did they improve their services and practices? Did they go back to their old bad habits?* To answer these questions, we followed the traces left by customers visiting restaurants appearing on *Kitchen Nightmares Italy* on Tripadvisor (i.e., 5,608 reviews). We did not focus so much on the review content (for example, in order to study consumers' display of food expertise or taste), but rather on reviews as proxies to assess the impact of the TV show on real food business. In so doing, we employed the number of reviews and rating scores to measure the level of success (or unsuccessfulness) of each restaurant. Then, we took advantage of the storytelling techniques users articulate within the texts of the reviews to explain why a restaurant was successful or not – that is why, after the airing of the show, the restaurant improved or not its business. We discovered that, in most of the cases, the restaurants worsen their conditions or return to their previous status quo (i.e., business troubles). We think this happens because of a peculiar interaction between *Kitchen Nightmares* and the affordances of the Tripadvisor platform: although the TV show increases restaurants' fame, it sets too high expectations in the minds of customers, who are inevitably frustrated when they visit the restaurants after the TV programme has finished; then, to voice their discontent, customers go on TripAdvisor, which registers and amplifies it. Of course, all this reflects negatively on the restaurants' reputation (and business in general), but it also enhances the reputation of the TV show.

Thinking of the Same Place: The Trivialisation of the Sharing Economy on Airbnb

The popularisation of the sharing economy, and in particular of the platform Airbnb, has revolutionised the hospitality sector. Many consumers today opt for the experiential value of renting an apartment or a room when they travel, as opposed to the service that a hotel accommodation would offer. However, we do have empirical evidence of Airbnb acting as something radically different than a sharing facilitator: research has underlined how the short term rental platform feeds the dynamics of income concentration and gentrification. Simultaneously, we observe that people still refer to Airbnb as something that has a definite "convivial" aura, something "less cold and standardised" than a hotel room. In this chapter, we try to solve this apparent conundrum by questioning the consumer cultures underpinning Airbnb. Using consumer reviews and ratings to explore the ways in which Airbnb users produce and perform this aura of conviviality, we also assess how much of this performance is built upon a "standard repertoire" of affection that the platform is able to mobilise. Similar to Chapter 6, in this chapter we follow the reviews posted by customers on Airbnb not so much to explore their experiences as guests or their cultural tastes in terms of hospitality, but rather as proxies to intercept a broader platformised cultural phenomenon: the transformation of the sharing experience into a mere consumption practice. Drawing on automated analysis of rating scores and keyword extractions, we observe that the majority of reviews aim at conveying some sort of emotional warmth, and address Airbnb as a venue for convivial sharing; however, in practice, most of the time the content is rote and stereotypical. Hosts are "wonderful" or "excellent" because they provide basic services (i.e., directions to places or a welcome drink), and most of the time, these descriptions feel part of an emotional "contract" binding the guests to testify to the value of the host towards the platform. It seems like the platform, notwithstanding its role in concentrating rental income, was able to mobilise (and consume, to some extent) the imaginary of the sharing economy, making it part of the consumer experience and building commercial value upon it.

Follow the Medium

As illustrated earlier, the principle of *following the medium* lays at the very foundation of the digital methods paradigm. By following the medium, digital methods take the nature and affordances of the digital environments seriously by studying how these structure communications and interactions among social actors (Caliandro and Gandini, 2017). In the domain of empirical research on platformisation of consumer culture, to follow the medium means to observe how specific digital devices operating on platforms (such as, technical features, interfaces, algorithms, APIs, etc.) shape the flows of online consumers' conversations as well as patterns of content production. Consider, for example, how, customarily, the Instagram algorithm favours, pushes, and makes more visible highly engaging content usually posted by prominent content creators. This, in turn, influences users' purchases, the way in which they perceive brands and products, but also how they assess authenticity in consumption, and how consumption practices should be properly performed and consumer goods publicly displayed (Audrezet et al., 2018; Mardon et al., 2023). Arvidsson and Caliandro's work on brand publics (2016) is a classical example of the development of the *follow the medium* strategy in consumer culture research. The authors collected 9,000 tweets featuring the hashtag #louisvuitton, and analysed how users' conversations around the brand were structured by Twitter infrastructure (e.g., #s, RTs, (at the time) 180 characters, etc.), paying particular attention to the kind of social formations emerging from the intersection between the platform infrastructure and users' practices of posting around the brand. Thanks to this kind of analysis, the authors were able to theorise the shift from brand communities to brand publics in the age of "social media-fueled consumer culture" (2016, p. 728).

In the present book, ad hoc applications of the *follow the medium* strategy can be found in Chapter 1 (*Consuming Nostalgia on Facebook*), Chapter 2 (*YouTube and the Radicalisation (?) of Consumption*), Chapter 3 (*The Platformisation of Music Genres on Spotify*), and Chapter 5 (*Instagram Influencers at the Crossroad between Publics and Communities*).

Consuming Nostalgia on Facebook

Nostalgia is a very powerful marketing tool. Building on the notion of "consumer nostalgia" (Cross, 2015), we investigated how social media users express nostalgia in relation to (material and cultural) consumer goods and what the role played by consumption is in the development of a nostalgic imaginary and discourse. Specifically, in this chapter, we follow the medium in the sense that we study how Facebook Pages dedicated to the '80s structure generic sentiments of nostalgia and channel them towards specific consumption experiences and practices. By observing the high occurrence and circulation of certain types of posts, created by Pages' administrators to trigger interactions and cohesion among followers, we show that, on the Facebook platform, nostalgia does not emerge as an undistinguished magma but finds expression around particular consumption objects from the '80s (e.g., ads, cartoons, TV shows, etc.). This insight tells us something interesting about the platformisation of nostalgic consumer culture; in fact, despite the increasing importance of experience (Pine and Gilmore, 2011) and access-based consumption (Bardhi and Eckhardt, 2012) in digital environments, a peculiar feature of the imaginary of nostalgia on Facebook is the persistence of references to material consumer goods.

YouTube and the Radicalisation (?) of Consumption

In this chapter, we investigate a typical phenomenon related to the platformisation of culture, which nonetheless has never been explored in relation to consumption: that is, "radicalisation." In a famous *New York Times* article, Zeynep Tufekci (2018) calls YouTube "The Great Radicaliser," referring to the tendency of the platform's algorithm to push far-right content to users. Building on this insight, in this chapter we question whether the YouTube platform applies the same logic to consumption as well. Specifically, we ask: *Does the YouTube algorithm contribute to radicalising processes of consumption? And if so, how and to what extent? Is YouTube pushing users to view homogeneous content that encourages them to stick with a specific consumer niche as well as funnelling them towards more extreme and controversial versions of the same niche?* Here we follow the medium in the sense that we study how the YouTube platform structures flows of information to understand if, and to what extent, YouTube is able to "radicalise" consumers' taste. Specifically, by observing how the YouTube algorithm positions (7,429) vegetarian videos over time (15 years) on the homepage, we found that, first, although it is not possible to maintain that YouTube concurs to radicalise consumers per se, it nonetheless pushes them towards some forms of "indoctrination" about vegetarianism. Second, for those users who are willing to do so, YouTube suggests some paths of video consumption that encourage them to explore more complex and narrower versions of vegetarianism, such as veganism, keto vegetarianism, vegetarian Tex-Mex cuisine, and Indian cuisine. This insight is extremely important, since it shows that the phenomenon of radicalisation of consumption on YouTube may not necessarily be a negative one, and can sometimes be framed as a neutral one – just like there is nothing wrong for a vegetarian to mix her dietary regime with elements of veganism. Furthermore, it also allows us to reflect on the fact that although platforms aim at standardising the cultural experience of consumers, standardisation of consumption is not a necessary and mandatory outcome.

The Platformisation of Music Genres on Spotify

Chapter 3 is similar to Chapter 2, in the sense that we follow processes of structuration of music consumption on Spotify. Existing research on music consumption suggests that the preferences of music listeners in recent years have shifted from a genre-based kind of consumption, where listening habits are shaped around typical music styles (e.g., rock, pop, metal, folk, etc.), to "situational" forms of music consumption, where moods and the social context wherein music is listened to play a more important role than the adherence to a particular genre (Airoldi et al., 2016). In this chapter, we employ the newly-created SpotiGem tool to query the Spotify API and thus analyse a set of genre-based playlists vis-à-vis mood-based ones, to observe the extent to which playlist composition has shifted away from genre-specific subcultural boundaries. We show that genre consistency still maintains significant relevance in playlist construction, for both users and the Spotify platform, and that even in "mood-based" or "situation-based" playlists there tends to be a certain convergence towards a small number of genres, as opposed to an increase in heterogeneity.

Instagram Influencers at the Crossroads between Publics and Communities

In this chapter, we map social formations emerging around influencers' accounts on Instagram. Influencers are key social actors shaping how consumption is organised in the digital society. To fully unpack their role, it is relevant to consider their practices at the crossroads between brand publics and communities. On the one hand, Instagram content creators are urged to nurture their audience and create "communities" based on long lasting, consistent, and intimate relationships. On the other hand, they can be considered branded personae who attract more ephemeral interactions, similar to what happens in a brand public (Arvidsson and Caliandro, 2016). In light of this complexity, we ask: *In which ways do brand publics and influencer communities coexist on Instagram? What is the relationship between these hybrid social formations and the platformisation of consumer culture?* To answer this question, our analysis focuses on the flow of communication, the structure of interaction, and the type of communication that characterises influencers' social formations on Instagram by blending metric analysis and comment analysis. Based on this analysis, we show that the coexistence of features typical of both brand publics and communities around the influencer persona leads to the formation of *hybrid influencer publics* – social formations characterised by the coexistence of mediation and interaction, the emphasis on affective forms of communication, and the presence of a mediated form of identity. The hybrid nature of influencers' social formations is fuelled by, and contributes to promoting, the platformisation of consumer culture.

Follow the Users

The third strategy consists in *following the users*, that is, focusing on practices of content production enacted by consumers within digital platforms, rather than only on their digital traces or on the technicality of platforms per se. Users are not only subject to digital devices, but also actively use and reappropriate them to accomplish specific communicative and interactional goals (Bruns et al., 2016). Of course, the users' strategies of media manipulation do not happen in a social void; indeed, they are profoundly shaped by the affordances of digital platforms (Bucher and Helmond, 2017). In this regard, we draw on the idea that consumers' digital practices of content production increasingly tend to follow, adhere to, and reproduce the logics and aesthetics of platforms themselves (Leaver et al., 2020; Zulli and Zulli,

2020; Caliandro and Anselmi, 2021). In recent years, consumption and media scholars pointed out that, in the increasingly platformised web ecosystem (Helmond, 2015), online consumers tend, very often, to use brands (and products in general) not so much as key symbolic resources for identity work (Thompson, 2014) or community building (Muñiz and O'Guinn, 2001), but rather as *platforms* to stage private identities and emotions (Arvidsson and Caliandro, 2016; Eckhardt and Bardhi, 2020). Interestingly, such personal drives of self-expression do not take random and idiosyncratic forms; instead, they tend to coalesce into a few typical and standardised patterns (Wiggins and Bowers, 2015; Schöps et al., 2020) – notwithstanding that they are enacted by dispersed users that do not necessarily interact among each other or are not necessarily aware of their reciprocal existence (Georgakopoulou, 2021). This is due to an *affordance effect*; that is, this happens because the affordances of digital platforms, with their complex intertwining of *grammars* and *vernaculars*, bear the constitutive power to shape users' patterns of content production (Hallinan et al., 2023). This phenomenon has been, for example, empirically explored by Caliandro and Anselmi (2021) in their study on *memetic brands* on Instagram. Drawing on the analysis of 757,776 Instagram branded-posts generated by "regular" users, the authors show how the practices of production of such pieces of content tend to follow a *memetic logic*. That is, the technical structure and the visual repertoires circulating on Instagram "push" users to create branded posts displaying a very repetitive and standardised visual aesthetic, which repeats itself from user to user with only minimal tweaks at every iteration – much like a classic meme does (Shifman, 2014).

A very direct and systematic application of the *follow the users* strategy is featured in Chapter 8: *Ephemeral Content and Ephemeral Consumption on TikTok*. In this chapter, we follow the users, in the sense that we pay particular attention to how TikTok's templates and algorithmic logics are incorporated into users' everyday practices of content production as well as of interaction within the platform itself. TikTok is characterised by a stream of video content, the ephemerality of which is due to the large number of short video clips, their limited permanence on the For You page, and their volatile visibility connected to the algorithmic curation of content. A substantial number of TikTok clips are related to the display of consumer goods and access-based consumption (Bardhi and Eckhardt, 2012), two elements that highlight the increasing ephemerality of consumer practices. Such elements are amplified by the memetic behaviours encouraged by the platform in the form of "challenges," which increase the circulation of ephemeral content and, at the same time, feed the ephemeral dimension of consumption. The purpose of this chapter is, therefore, to analyse how TikTok's architecture prompts practices of ephemeral consumption, here intended as forms of ephemeral digital consumption (rather than other forms of fast-paced and temporary consumption, such as fast fashion). More specifically, we answer the following research questions: *What is the role of TikTok affordances in prompting practices of ephemeral consumption? What are the main practices and templates through which ephemeral consumption unfolds on TikTok?* By mixing hashtag analysis, sound analysis, and the visual analysis of TikTok videos, this chapter provides further understanding of how platform affordances can stimulate the emergence of ephemeral consumption practices. By focusing on one TikTok challenge, the #shoechallenge, results show that ephemeral consumption on TikTok is characterised by: a) the ubiquitous display of consumption; b) the limited temporality of video clips; c) the situational nature of users' performances; and d) the attempts at attention-seeking in an algorithmically mediated and memetic platform (Zulli and Zulli, 2020).

A Brief Overview of Research Techniques

In order to follow digital traces, the medium, and the users, we employed and combined a variety of data collection, computational, quantitative, and qualitative techniques. Each of these techniques is clearly introduced and described in ad hoc sections within each chapter of the book. Below, we provide an introductory list (along with useful references).

Data collection techniques: APIs calling (Gerlitz and Rieder, 2013), scraping (Landers et al., 2016), corporate dashboards (i.e., CrowdTangle) (Punziano et al., 2022), online free tools (Bainotti et al., 2021), online databases (i.e., Inside Airbnb) (Anselmi et al., 2021).

Computational techniques: automated keyword extraction, topic modeling (Nelson, 2020), tf-idf (Qaiser and Ali 2018), bot detection (Bessi and Ferrara, 2016).

Quantitative techniques: network analysis (Venturini et al. 2021), co-hashtag analysis (Marres and Gerlitz, 2016), social media metrics analysis (Rogers, 2018).

Qualitative methods: online observation (Abidin and De Seta, 2020), ethnographic content analysis (Altheide, 1987), qualitative visual analysis (Rose, 2016), qualitative sentiment analysis, narrations analysis (Caliandro and Gandini, 2017).

A Brief Appendix on Digital Social Research in the Post-Api Era

A last insight we want to address is the monumental change that is transforming the field of research as we are writing this book: in July 2023, an update to the APIs used by Twitter made them useless for academic (or commercial) research (Porter, 2023). This is definitely part of a larger trend that has seen major platforms close down their data capture APIs, or neutralise services (e.g., Netvizz), which the academic community commonly utilised to acquire data (Bruns, 2019). First, Facebook and Instagram have stopped providing access to data (to then make them accessible, under certain conditions, through the Meta-owned platform CrowdTangle) (Lawler, 2022); now, Twitter and Reddit have become unavailable too (Peters, 2023; Mehta and Singh, 2023). While this kind of evolution is consistent with monopolistic behaviour from platforms, pointed at maximising control over data while reducing public scrutiny from independent researchers at a minimum, this state of things also begs the question of what kind of study researchers should undertake if they are unable to rely on platform-provided data, in a "post-API" era (Freelon 2018; Perriam et al., 2020).

From a purely technical standpoint, the answer to this question is relatively simple: *scraping.* As long as data gets visualised on a screen, it may be captured by a screen scraper; however this course of action comes with practical, legal, ethical, and methodological complexities.

First of all, writing a screen scraper is significantly more complex than accessing APIs: the latter often leverages pre-compiled tools or, at the very least, pieces of software (typically, if there is an API, there is a Python package that can be employed to access that API). Writing a scraper instead relies on carefully analysing the webpage to be scraped, getting familiar with its DOM[1] structure and then writing a piece of software, which is: a) far more complex than the few lines of code typically needed to make an API call; and b) subject to a relentless "cat and mouse" game with the page owner changing the layout of the page, precisely to avoid being scraped.

Contributions on the legal and ethical side of screen scraping are many and well established (Mancosu and Vegetti, 2020; Bainotti et al., 2021; Landers et al., 2016). From an ethical standpoint, the main issue is data privacy: the general consensus on this seems to have settled on allowing scraping as long as the researchers make a sensible effort to protect users'

---

1   DOM stands for Document Object Model, which is a "programming interface for web documents. It represents the page so that programs can change the document structure, style, and content" (Developer Mozilla, 2023).

privacy, meaning that data should not be published without anonymisation, should be used for research purposes only, and should be stored in a format and style that prevents data thefts or leakages. Legal issues also depend upon the jurisdiction of the researchers; if we were to look at the terms and conditions of platforms, scraping should be considered as illegal – however, luckily different jurisdictions allow data capture for "public good" endeavours such as research – in general, EU states are far more lenient than US states (Mancosu and Vegetti, 2020). The complexities of scraping from a methodological standpoint are also multifaceted, however, the most important one is related to research replication: firstly, different scrapers written at different points in time may return different results due to changes in the architecture of a page (it should be noted that this also happens with API, albeit less frequently). Secondly, being less standardised, scraping depends upon the individual researchers' skill as a programmer, which further complicates the replicability of research while simultaneously excluding less technically competent researchers, again depriving the field of valuable contributions because of a technical barrier.

The collapse of open APIs, however, also has positive implications for the digital methods/computational field: the abundance of data has made social researchers dependent upon platforms and has, in general, dulled critical thinking (Tromble, 2021). For example, digital research has become Twitter-centric, essentially confirming (due to the very generous data policy) Twitter's role as a global agora, meaning that research has played along with a commercial strategy developed by a (would-be) monopolistic platform. Less generous data APIs also means the freedom to experiment with other platforms and other approaches, like tracing user level behaviour and the effect of algorithmic recommendations (cf. Rama et al., 2022) or pivoting to "small screens" and tracing user behaviour at a far more basic level (Audy Martínek et al., 2023) – for example, understanding how people use their smartphones throughout the day (Caliandro et al., 2021b, Caliandro, 2021).

Notwithstanding this daunting scenario, which Axel Bruns (2019) dubbed the "APIcalypse," we believe that the present volume maintains a methodological validity and utility. First, we provide alternative methods of data collection (namely, online scrapers, custom-made scrapers, free online databases); second, APIs will not cease to exist, although, unfortunately, they will be available, primarily, in a private version and for a fee. It may also be the case that the closure of the APIs is a blessing in disguise, pushing the field to explore other pathways, both from a methodological and empirical point of view. Almost certainly, it will push digital research outside the

"Twitter orbit," leading researchers to explore different platforms, and so different forms of platformisation of consumer culture – as we have done in this book.

References

Abidin, C. and de Seta, G. (2020). Doing digital ethnography: Private messages from the field. *Journal of Digital Social Research*, 2(1), 1–19. http://doi.org/10.33621/jdsr.

Airoldi, M. (2021). Digital traces of taste: Methodological pathways for consumer research. *Consumption Markets and Culture*, 24(1), 97–117. https://doi.org/10.1080/10253866.2019.1690998.

Airoldi, M., Beraldo, D., and Gandini, A. (2016). Follow the algorithm: An exploratory investigation of music on YouTube. *Poetics*, 57, 1–13. https://doi.org/10.1016/j.poetic.2016.05.001.

Altheide, D. (1987). Reflections: Ethnographic content analysis. *Qualitative Sociology*, 10, 65–77. https://doi.org/10.1007/BF00988269.

Anselmi, G., Chiappini, L., and Prestileo, F. (2021). The greedy unicorn: Airbnb and capital concentration in 12 European cities. *City, Culture and Society*, 27. https://doi.org/10.1016/j.ccs.2021.100412.

Arvidsson, A. and Caliandro, A. (2016). Brand public. *Journal of Consumer Research*, 42(5), 727–748. https://doi.org/10.1093/jcr/ucv053.

Audrezet, A., De Kerviler, G., and Moulard, J. G. (2020). Authenticity under threat: When social media influencers need to go beyond self-presentation. *Journal of Business Research*, 117, 557–569. https://doi.org/10.1016/j.jbusres.2018.07.008.

Audy Martínek, P., Caliandro, A., and Denegri-Knott, J. (2023). Digital practices tracing: Studying consumer lurking in digital environments. *Journal of Marketing Management*, 39(3/4), 244–274. https://doi.org/10.1080/0267257X.2022.2105385.

Bainotti, L., Caliandro, A., and Gandini, A. (2021). From archive cultures to ephemeral content, and back: Studying Instagram Stories with digital methods. *New Media and Society*, 23(12), 3656–3676. https://doi.org/10.1177/1461444820960071.

Bardhi, F. and Eckhardt, G. M. (2012). Access-based consumption: The case of car sharing. *Journal of Consumer Research*, 39(4), 881–898. https://doi.org/10.1086/666376.

Bessi, A. and Ferrara, E. (2016). Social bots distort the 2016 US Presidential election online discussion. *First Monday*, 21(11/7), https://doi.org/10.5210/fm.v21i11.7090.

Bruns, A. (2019). After the "APIcalypse": Social media platforms and their fight against critical scholarly research. *Information, Communication and Society*, 22(11), 1544–1566. https://doi.org/10.1080/1369118X.2019.1637447.

Bruns, A., Moon, B., Paul, A., and Münch, F. (2016). Towards a typology of hashtag publics: A large-scale comparative study of user engagement across trending topics. *Communication Research and Practice*, 2(1), 20–46.

Bucher, T. and Helmond, A. (2017). The affordances of social media platforms. In J. Burgess, T. Poell, and A. Marwick (Eds.), *The SAGE handbook of social media* (pp. 233–253). Sage.

Caliandro, A. (2014). Ethnography in digital spaces: Ethnography of virtual worlds, netnography, and digital ethnography. In R. Denny and P. Sunderland (Eds.), *Handbook of anthropology in business* (pp. 658–680). Left Coast Press.

Caliandro, A. (2018). Digital methods for ethnography: Analytical concepts for ethnographers exploring social media environments, *Journal of Contemporary Ethnography*, 47(5), 551–578. https://doi.org/10.1177/0891241617702.

Caliandro, A. (2021). Repurposing digital methods in a post-API research environment: Methodological and ethical implications. *Italian Sociological Review*, 11(4S), 225–225. https://doi.org/10.13136/isr.v11i4S.433.

Caliandro A. and Gandini A. (2017), *Qualitative research in digital environments: A research toolkit*. Routledge.

Caliandro, A. and Anselmi, G. (2021). Affordances-based brand relations: An inquiry on memetic brands on Instagram. *Social Media+ Society*, 7(2). https://doi.org/10.1177/20563051211021367.

Caliandro, A., Garavaglia, E. and Anselmi, G. (2021a). Studying ageism on social media: An exploration of ageing discourses related to Covid-19 in the Italian Twittersphere. *Rassegna Italiana di Sociologia*, 62(2), 343–375. 10.1423/101848.

Caliandro, A., Garavaglia, E., Sturiale, V., and Di Leva, A. (2021b). Older people and smartphone practices in everyday life: An inquiry on digital sociality of Italian older users. *The Communication Review*, 24(1), 47–78. https://doi.org/10.1080/10714421.2021.1904771.

Corchia, L. (2022). Digital trace data analysis. In A. Ceron (Ed.), *Elgar encyclopedia of technology and politics* (pp. 72–77). Edward Elgar Publishing.

Cross, G. (2015). *Consumed nostalgia: Memory in the age of fast capitalism*. Columbia University Press.

Deighton, J. (2019). Big data. *Consumption Markets and Culture*, 22(1), 68–73. https://doi.org/10.1080/10253866.2017.1422902.

Developer Mozilla (2023). Introduction to the DOM. Developer.mozilla.org. https://developer.mozilla.org/en-US/docs/Web/API/Document_Object_Model/Introduction.

Di Domenico, G. and Visentin, M. (2020). Fake news or true lies? Reflections about problematic contents in marketing. *International Journal of Market Research*, 62(4), 409–417. https://doi.org/10.1177/147078532093471.

Eckhardt, G. M. and Bardhi, F. (2020). New dynamics of social status and distinction. *Marketing Theory*, *20*(1), 85–102. https://doi.org/10.1177/1470593119856650.

Freelon, D. (2018). Computational research in the post-API age. *Political Communication*, *35*(4), 665–668. https://doi.org/10.1080/10584609.2018.1477506.

Georgakopoulou, A. (2021). Small stories as curated formats on social media: The intersection of affordances, values and practices. *System*, *102*. https://doi.org/10.1016/j.system.2021.102620.

Gerlitz, C. and Rieder, B. (2013). Mining one percent of Twitter: Collections, baselines, sampling. *M/C Journal*, *16*(2). https://doi.org/10.5204/mcj.620.

Hallinan, B., Kim, B., Scharlach, R., Trillò, T., Mizoroki, S., and Shifman, L. (2023). Mapping the transnational imaginary of social media genres. *New Media and Society*, *25*(3), 559–583. https://doi.org/10.1177/14614448211012372.

Helmond, A. (2015). The platformisation of the web: Making web data platform ready. *Social Media+ Society*, *1*(2), https://doi.org/10.1177/2056305115603080.

Hutchinson, J. (2016). An introduction to digital media research methods: How to research and the implications of new media data. *Communication Research and Practice*, *2*(1), 1–6. https://doi.org/10.1080/22041451.2016.1155307.

Landers, R. N., Brusso, R. C., Cavanaugh, K. J., and Collmus, A. B. (2016). A primer on theory-driven web scraping: Automatic extraction of big data from the internet for use in psychological research. *Psychological methods*, *21*(4), 475–492. https://doi.org/10.1037/met0000081.

Latour, B. (2005). *Reassembling the social: An introduction to actor-network theory.* Oxford University Press.

Lawler, R. (2022, June 23). Meta reportedly plans to shut down CrowdTangle. *The Verge*. https://www.theverge.com/2022/6/23/23180357/meta-crowdtangle-shut-down-facebook-misinformation-viral-news-tracker.

Leaver, T., Highfield, T., and Abidin, C. (2020). *Instagram: Visual social media cultures.* John Wiley and Sons.

Mancosu, M. and Vegetti, F. (2020). What you can scrape and what is right to scrape: A proposal for a tool to collect public Facebook data. *Social Media+ Society*, *6*(3). https://doi.org/10.1177/20563051209407.

Mardon, R., Cocker, H., and Daunt, K. (2023). When parasocial relationships turn sour: Social media influencers, eroded and exploitative intimacies, and anti-fan communities. *Journal of Marketing Management*, 1–31. https://doi.org/10.1080/0267257X.2022.2149609.

Marres, N. (2017). *Digital sociology: The reinvention of social research.* John Wiley and Sons.

Marres, N. and Gerlitz, C. (2016). Interface methods: Renegotiating relations between digital social research, STS and sociology. *The Sociological Review*, *64*(1), 21–46. https://doi.org/10.1111/1467-954X.12314.

Mehta, I and Singh, M. (2023, February 2). Twitter to end free access to its API in Elon Musk's latest monetization push. TechCrunch+. https://techcrunch.com/2023/02/01/twitter-to-end-free-access-to-its-api/?guce_referrer=aHR0cHM6Ly93d3cuZ29vZ2xlLmNvbS8andguce_referrer_sig=AQAAALa-1teLuMQH-mTRzKDMQSh67Oxqjx4GMhdj7lQMQbzcn-nQBoTZn-VMj7m5eeGvwz1Vik-osOKYGl3nHn_t18WaEbakGDMDwodwrKcpN3OpocXdVf-xhJxuE1SyQnXe-CouLDoUWA7zpd1M5R3VYoLM-5r1Lg23A4D4qblugWgcVC8andguccounter=2.

Muñiz, A. M., and O'Guinn, T. C. (2001). Brand community. *Journal of Consumer Research*, 27(4), 412–432. https://doi.org/10.1086/319618.

Nelson, L. K. (2020). Computational grounded theory: A methodological framework. *Sociological Methods and Research*, 49(1), 3–42. ttps://doi.org/10.1177/0049124117729703.

Perriam, J., Birkbak, A., and Freeman, A. (2020). Digital methods in a post-API environment. *International Journal of Social Research Methodology*, 23(3), 277–290.

Peters, J. (2023, June 6). It's not just Apollo: Other Reddit apps are shutting down, too. *The Verge*. https://www.theverge.com/2023/6/8/23754616/reddit-third-party-apps-api-shutdown-rif-reddplanet-sync.

Pine, J. and Gilmore, J.H. (2011). *The experience economy: Work is theater and every business a Stage*. Harvard Business Review Press.

Porter, J. (2023, March 30). Twitter announces new API pricing, posing a challenge for small developers. *The Verge*. https://www.theverge.com/2023/3/30/23662832/twitter-api-tiers-free-bot-novelty-accounts-basic-enterprice-monthly-price.

Punziano, G., Trezza, D., and Acampa, S. (2022). Russian-Ukraine war and institutional use of memetic communication: methodological opportunities and challenges. *Mediascapes Journal*, 20(2), 70–90. https://rosa.uniroma1.it/rosa03/mediascapes/article/view/18036.

Qaiser, S. and Ali, R. (2018). Text mining: Use of TF-IDF to examine the relevance of words to documents. *International Journal of Computer Applications*, 181(1), 25–29. 10.5120/ijca2018917395.

Rama, I., Bainotti, L., Gandini, A., Giorgi, G., Semenzin, S., Agosti, C., Corona, G., and Romano, S. (2022). The platformization of gender and sexual identities: An algorithmic analysis of Pornhub. *Porn Studies*, 10(2), 154–173. https://doi.org/10.1080/23268743.2022.2066566.

Rogers, R. (2009). *The end of the virtual: Digital methods*. Amsterdam University Press.

Rogers, R. (2013). *Digital methods*. MIT press.

Rogers, R. (2017). Foundations of Digital Methods: Query Design. In M. T. Schäfer and K. van Es (Eds.), *The datafied society: Studying culture through data* (pp. 75–94). Amsterdam University Press.

Rogers, R. (2018). Otherwise engaged: Social media from vanity metrics to critical analytics. *International Journal of Communication, 12*, 23. 1932–8036/20180005.

Rose, G. (2016). *Visual methodologies: An introduction to researching with visual materials*. Sage.

Ruppert, E., Law, J., and Savage, M. (2013). Reassembling social science methods: The challenge of digital devices. *Theory, Culture and Society, 30*(4), 22–46. https://doi.org/10.1177/0263276413484941.

Salganik, M. J. (2019). *Bit by bit: Social research in the digital age*. Princeton University Press.

Schöps, J. D., Kogler, S., and Hemetsberger, A. (2020). (De-)stabilizing the digitized fashion market on Instagram-dynamics of visual performative assemblages. *Consumption Markets and Culture, 23*(2), 195–213. https://doi.org/10.1080/1025 3866.2019.1657099.

Severson, P. (2019). How critical digital method development can strengthen studies of media and terrorism. In R. de La Brosse and K. Holt (Eds.), *Media and Journalism in an Age of Terrorism* (pp. 168–184). Cambridge Scholars Publishing.

Shifman, L. (2014). The cultural logic of photo-based meme genres. *Journal of Visual Culture*, 13(3), 340–358. https://doi.org/10.1177/1470412914546577.

Thompson, C. J. (2014). The politics of consumer identity work. *Journal of Consumer Research, 40*(5), iii–vii. ttps://doi.org/10.1086/673381.

Tromble, R. (2021). Where have all the data gone? A critical reflection on academic digital research in the post-API age. *Social Media+ Society, 7*(1), https://doi.org/10.1177/2056305121988929.

Tufekci, Z. (2018, March 10). YouTube, the great radicalizer. *New York Times*. https://www.nytimes.com/2018/03/10/opinion/sunday/youtube-politics-radical.html.

Van Dijck, J. and Poell, T. (2013). Understanding social media logic. *Media and Communication, 1*(1), 2–14. https://ssrn.com/abstract=2309065.

Venturini, T., Bounegru, L., Gray, J., and Rogers, R. (2018). A reality check (list) for digital methods. *New Media and Society, 20*(11), 4195–4217. https://doi.org/10.1177/1461444818769236.

Venturini, T., Jacomy, M., and Jensen, P. (2021). What do we see when we look at networks: Visual network analysis, relational ambiguity, and force-directed layouts. *Big Data and Society, 8*(1), https://doi.org/10.1177/20539517211018488.

Wiggins, B. E. and Bowers, G. B. (2015). Memes as genre: A structurational analysis of the memescape. *New Media and Society, 17*(11), 1886–1906. https://doi.org/10.1177/1461444814535194.

Zulli, D. and Zulli, D. J. (2020). Extending the Internet meme: Conceptualizing technological mimesis and imitation publics on the TikTok platform. *New Media and Society, 24*(8), 1872–1890. https://doi.org/10.1177/1461444820983603.

1.   Consuming Nostalgia on Facebook

Abstract

Building on the notion of "consumer nostalgia," in this chapter we explore how nostalgia is represented on Facebook through consumer goods, and how Facebook structures and fosters the circulation of a nostalgic imaginary. Based on the analysis of 63 Facebook Pages dedicated to the 1980s, we show that nostalgia on the Facebook platform does not emerge as an undistinguished magma, but rather finds expression around particular consumption objects from the '80s (e.g. ads, cartoons, TV shows, etc.), which allow users to deploy (and position themselves around) specific grammars and vernaculars. Despite the increasing importance of experience and access-based consumption in digital environments, a peculiar feature of the imaginary of nostalgia on Facebook turns out to be the persistence of references to material consumer goods.

Keywords: Pages, '80s, CrowdTangle, visual analysis, materiality.

In the 21st century, nostalgia has confirmed itself as a powerful cultural force (Bauman, 2019; Gandini, 2020; Tanner, 2020) and the domain of consumption is among those where nostalgia has been most impactful. As argued by cultural critic Simon Reynolds (2011), pop culture has been experiencing a phase of "retromania," characterised by the reprise of past trends, especially in fashion and music, and by the fetishisation and idealisation of the past as a source of authenticity. Beginning in the early 2000s, this "retromania" is apparently set to endure; not coincidentally, this trend is taking place in parallel with the mainstream affirmation of hipster culture, which glorifies authenticity and uses the past to "resignify" old production practices and products as cool (Scott, 2017; Michael, 2015; Scheirmer, 2014).

In marketing, nostalgia has long been recognised as having a significant impact on consumption choices, driving people's preferences and behaviours (Holbrook, 1993; Goulding, 2002; Lasaleta et al., 2021). Holbrook and Schindler (1991, p. 330) define nostalgia in marketing as "(a) preference

Caliandro, A., A. Gandini, L. Bainotti, G. Anselmi, *The Platformisation of Consumer Culture: A Digital Methods Guide*. Amsterdam: Amsterdam University Press, 2024
DOI 10.5117/9789463729567_CH01

(general liking, positive attitude or favourable effect) towards experiences associated with objects (people, places or things) that were more common (popular, fashionable or widely circulated) when one was younger (in early adulthood, in adolescence, in childhood or even before birth)." This runs alongside generational sociology, which posits the relevance of the sharing of common experiences by people who became adults in the same time frame and socio-cultural context (Wilson, 2014; Bristow, 2016) and thus experienced the same "zeitgeist" (Krause, 2019). This translates into an interest in consumption items of the past. Suggesting a connection between age and the development of taste, Holbrook and Schindler (2003) theorised the concept of "nostalgic bonding," claiming that interaction with a certain product during a critical period of preference formation (stretching through adolescence and early adulthood) can create a lifelong preference for that object. More recently, Cross (2015) has highlighted the growth of what he calls "consumer nostalgia": attuned to fast capitalist logics of commodification of products and aligned with increasingly ephemeral forms of consumption of both cultural and material goods, an market of consumers who share "common consumer memories" is emerging. Hartmann and Brunk (2019) further underline that nostalgia in marketing and branding has the key function of producing "enchantment" around products, building on different "modes" of nostalgia –in their account: reluctant, progressive, or playful – to serve the purpose of creating an emotional bond with the consumer.

Unsurprisingly, social media such as Facebook and Instagram are important spaces for the observation of how nostalgia can be a "cultural glue" that brings together different kinds of consumers, with varying economic and cultural capital, in the sharing of and engagement with (material and cultural) consumer goods of the past. This is well represented by the emergence of numerous groups and pages with evocative titles such as *nostalgia*, *vintage*, or *retronaut* (Niemeyer, 2014), or that explicitly refer to decades and generational groups (Giorgi, 2022). However, the modalities through which social media users express a nostalgic sentiment towards products have been only sporadically addressed. Experiment-based research on Pinterest (Youn and Jin, 2017) suggests that nostalgia has a strong influence on consumer attitudes towards a certain brand, and that it might play a significant role in purchase intentions as a process of social influence by users of this platform. Yet, the relationship between nostalgia and consumer goods on mainstream social media, and the role their affordances play in fostering the propagation of consumer nostalgia, deserve greater attention.

In this chapter, we explore how social media users express nostalgia in relation to (material and cultural) consumer goods, and what the role of consumption is in the development of a nostalgic imaginary and discourse. In particular, we ask: *is nostalgia for consumer goods on social media accompanied by the production of specific grammars and vernaculars? If so, what types of consumer goods or practices feature within the nostalgic social media imaginary, and which role do they play?*

To answer these questions, we turn to Facebook. As said, this platform is peculiarly characterised by the presence of a plethora of "generational" pages, whose titles explicitly mention a certain decade and whereby a variety of content is produced within a broad nostalgic discourse (Giorgi, 2022). For our study, we focused in particular on the numerous Facebook Pages dedicated to the 1980s. This decade represents a useful proxy to operationalise consumer nostalgia on social media, as conceived by Cross (2015), given that consumption items of the 1980s are made objects of idealisation by consumers of various demographics. Different from Facebook Groups, Pages are usually "vertical" social spaces managed by one or more administrators who get to decide what content to publish and when. Generally, Pages followers tend to be passive users who react to content rather than actively participate in its co-creation and interact with it (and with each other) using reaction buttons and the comments section. For these reasons, Pages may be considered a privileged space in which to observe how the Facebook platform and its affordances contribute to structuring and organising the production of a nostalgic imaginary and discourse around consumption and the engagement of users around consumer objects from the past.

Data Collection and Methods

To collect data from Facebook's Pages we used CrowdTangle. This is a public insights tool owned and operated by Meta, Facebook's mother company. It allows users to track, monitor, and collect data from Meta's social media platforms – Facebook and Instagram – as well as from Reddit and Twitter[1] (Fan, 2022). Following an approval procedure, academics can freely access and use the CrowdTangle dashboard; this provides access to data from Facebook and the other, aforementioned platforms, albeit with some important limitations. Focusing only on Facebook, CrowdTangle's dashboard currently hosts 7M+ pages, groups, and verified profiles (Miles, 2022a). These do not cover the entire Facebook population but undoubtedly represent a generous

---

[1] It is worth mentioning that, as we were finalising the editing of this book, rumours abound that Meta is planning to shut down CrowdTangle (Lawler, 2022).

sample – consider also that one can also upload manually those pages/ groups/profiles currently not tracked by CrowdTangle. From this pool of data, the researcher can access contents (e.g., posts of a given page), interactions (e.g., likes, shares, reactions, etc.), Page likes, and various statistics related to a specific Page or Group, such as likes, followers, followers growth, video views, etc. Instead, it is not possible to access comments, demographic data, page reach, traffic and clicks, private posts and profiles, paid or boosted posts[2] (Miles, 2022a).

   In our case, we used CrowdTangle as follows. First, via the dashboard, we searched for all the Pages containing the Italian phrase "anni 80" (*the '80s*). We decided to analyse only Italian Pages in order to better navigate the various cultural references contained in them – all the authors of this book are Italian. In doing so, we obtained a long list of Pages (200+) from which we retained only those with at least 100 followers. In addition, we kept in our sample those Pages associating the '80s with another decade, such as the '70–'80s or the '80–'90s. We excluded those Pages referencing more than two decades (for example *All from the '70s, '80s, and '90s*). This allowed us to obtain a final database composed of 63 Pages. Subsequently, using the "Historical Data" function, we collected all the posts from these Pages and stored them in a unique .csv file. Theoretically, this function allows researchers to go back in time using a custom time range – the CrowdTangle team assures that "you can export the history of any account going back to the very first post they made on Facebook" (Miles, 2022b) – and get up to 300,000 posts. However, in our case, the tool retrieved only 119,754 posts, ranging from January 19, 2017 to January 18, 2022 (the day we launched the search). This is because, as the CrowdTangle team further clarifies, "followers data goes back to August 2017"; consequently, other data and metadata related to Pages might be incomplete (Miles, 2022c). Nonetheless, we deemed the dataset to be large enough to conduct an exploratory research about consumer nostalgia on Facebook. Along with posts, CrowdTangle also retrieved a lot of other useful metadata, such as: *Page Name, Followers* (per page), *Page Created at, Post Created at, Type, Total Interactions, Likes, Comments, Shares, Reactions* (i.e., Love, Wow, Haha, Sad, Angry, and Care), *Post URL, Message, Overperforming Score.*[3]

2   Anyone interested in monitoring paid or boosted posts can take advantage of another free tool, that is, Facebook Ad Library: https://www.facebook.com/ads/library/?active_status=allandad_ type=allandcountry=ITandsort_data[direction]=descandsort_data[mode]=relevancy_month-ly_groupedandmedia_type=all.
3   The Overperforming Score indicates whether a post did better than expected, compared to the average rate of interactions of a given page. As the definition provided by the CrowdTangle

Once collected, we undertook quantitative and qualitative analyses on the data. From a quantitative perspective, we first developed a general description of Pages drawing on the statistics provided by CrowdTangle (Rogers, 2018; Geboers et al., 2022); then, we analysed the content of posts taking advantage of automated text analysis techniques (Krippendorff, 2012). As far as the qualitative analysis is concerned, we first performed a manual categorisation of the Pages, focusing on two main categories: *Topic* and *Page Use* (Caliandro and Gandini, 2017). "Topic" refers to the main theme of discussion around which conversations across these pages unfold. This resulted in the identification of 12 topics: *Generic* (where a generic reference to the '80s was present, e.g., solo anni 80/*only 8os*); *Ads*; *Cartoons*; *Music*; *Toys*; *Movies*; *Soccer*; *Food*; *Place* (e.g., anni 80 italiani/*The 8os in Italy*); *Cars*; *TV*; *Entertainment* (Pages generically dealing with movies, songs, and cartoons). "Page Use" refers to the attitude towards – and the "cultural use" of – the '80s expressed by Page titles. As a result, we identified four sub-categories: *Nostalgia* (titles that express an explicit sentiment of nostalgia towards the '80s, e.g., Nostalgie degli anni 80-90/*'8o–'gos Nostalgia*); *Community* (titles that express a sense of belonging around the '80s, e.g. Noi degli anni 80 e 90/We, people from the '80–'90s); *Self-Expression* (i.e., titles that use the '80s as a "platform" for self-expression, e.g. Anni 80. Io c'ero/*The '8os: I was there*); *Neutral* (i.e., titles not expressing a particular attitude, e.g. Anni 80/*The '8os*). Such a coding scheme proved to be particularly fruitful, insofar as – after an initial exploration of the dataset – we soon realised that it was suitable to categorise all posts in the dataset. In fact, as we will see later with respect to the topic, it is not uncommon to find, for example, posts about movies and cartoons within pages dedicated to music. The same goes for attitude, as all the posts we analysed tended to have the same attitude towards the '80s described above. In other words, from the categorisation of Page titles, we derived a coding scheme that was also used for the qualitative analysis of posts.

Subsequently, we zoomed in on the visual dimension of a sub-sample of 260 randomly extracted posts, with the goal of highlighting the different visual grammars of nostalgia on Facebook. To do so, we performed a qualitative visual analysis (Rose, 2016) aimed at providing an ethnographic account of the visual elements that characterise these posts (Altheide, 1987). Rather

team states: "Every post is compared to a benchmark, which is the expected value of that post. The equation is: score = actual / expected. So if a post has 100 interactions and its benchmark was 50, that's 100/50 = 2.0x. To generate the benchmarks, we take the last 100 posts from a given account and of a given post type (link post, image post, etc.). We drop the top and bottom 25% of those 100 posts, and calculate the mean number of interactions that the middle 50% of the posts have at each age (15 minutes old, 60 minutes old, 5 hours old, etc.)" (Integrity Transparency, 2022).

than operating a structured and systematic visual content analysis (e.g., Krippendorf, 2012), we paid particular attention to the different ways in which a nostalgic sentiment has been expressed by Page owners, as these directly emerged from the visual data, and accounted for them in an ethnographic way, without counting how many times these appear in the dataset. Such an approach allowed us to grasp the organising principles underpinning the visual representations of nostalgic imaginaries on Facebook. More specifically, we first looked at the compositional nature of images, paying attention to how the construction of the image contributes to the creation of certain narrations and representations (Rose, 2016). Then, we developed an interpretative analysis of the images by taking into consideration both their visual and textual dimensions (in the form of captions) – an analysis that was conducive to the identification of the main grammars underpinning them (see also Thurlow et al., 2020). The interpretative categories we identified (*grammar of celebration, grammar of memorialisation, and grammar of techno-longing*) emerged directly from the analysis of the visual data, following a grounded theory approach (Charmaz, 2000).

Lastly, since the comment section is the only place where ordinary users are allowed to create content on Pages, we decided to conduct a narration analysis (Caliandro and Gandini, 2017) on a sample of comments, so as to further investigate the ways in which users position themselves and their identities in relation to nostalgic content. To this end, we identified the most commented ten posts in the dataset and analysed the related comments in an ethnographic way. This analysis was very useful for spotting users' vernacular narrations about consumer nostalgia, and investigating their internal structure (Georgakopoulou, 2021). Three main narrations were identified, which we named: *reminiscent, playful,* and *experiential.* These are discussed in the final section of this chapter.

Descriptive Overview: Quantitative Analysis

As said, our dataset comprises 119,754 posts, created between January 19, 2017 and January 18, 2022 and posted within 63 Pages. Looking at Fig. 1.1, from 2017, a constant growth of posts is visible; this stabilises in 2020, with a little deflection in 2021.

In total, these posts generated 312,918,411 views, 79,077,379 interactions, 49,507,640 likes, 17,581,524 shares, and 4,059,734 comments. It is interesting to note the high number of shares and comments, which, as usual, do not exceed "classical" passive forms of engagement (i.e., views and likes), but

Post per year

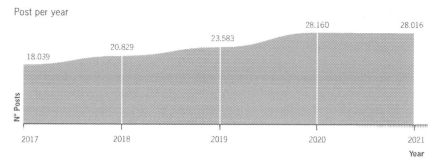

Fig. 1.1. The timeline shows the growth of posts (produced by all of the 63 Pages analysed) per year (2017–2021; data for 2022 is not shown because we can only retrieve posts for 18 days).

	Page Name	Total Interactions	Interaction Rate	Avg Posts Per Day	Views on Owned Videos	Page Followers	Growth % and #
	Average Total	4,803.69	0.270%	1.12	7,959.72	59,150.24	+0.44%
1	Solo anni 80	74,791	0.178%	9.14	---	656,694	+0.00% +27
2	Anni 80/90 Io C'Ero	58,415	1.557%	5.14	10,163	104,266	+0.22% +232
3	soloanni80 il calcio piu' bello del mondo	50,376	1.783%	7.71	---	52,507	+0.92% +478
4	Remember 80/90	31,663	0.298%	5.57	---	272,708	+0.08% +218
5	Anni 80 le Girls dei cartoni animati the original	28,545	0.258%	9.14	---	172,975	+0.05% +88
6	TUTTO SPOT 80	20,772	0.759%	1.29	301,918	304,591	+0.25% +745
7	Vecchi tempi. Giocattoli e Ricordi anni 80-90	18,380	1.459%	1.14	71,158	157,785	+0.33% +519
8	80 Voglia di trash	9,514	0.482%	1.43	81,788	197,461	+0.12% +243
9	Altro Calcio Anni '80-'90	8,305	0.452%	2.43	---	107,930	+0.10% +108
10	Musica degli Anni 70 & 80	5,629	1.158%	0.14	75,731	486,015	+0.05% +252
11	Noi degli 80-90	5,383	0.029%	12.86	---	203,819	-0.02% -32
12	Gli Anni 80	3,986	0.271%	4.29	---	48,778	+0.15% +72
13	Ridateci gli anni 80/90	3,045	0.104%	4	---	103,677	-0.01% -8
14	Giocattoli Anni 80/90 - Alla Ricerca Del Tempo Perduto	2,817	0.575%	0.29	---	244,859	-0.01% -19
15	Gli indimenticabili anni 80 e 90	1,867	0.406%	1.86	---	35,262	+0.35% +123

Fig. 1.2. The picture shows different stats for the top 15 pages ordered by total interactions (that is, the sum of Likes, Comments, Shares, and Reactions (Loves, Wows, Hahas, Sads, Angrys, Cares)). The growth of the Pages per week based on followers is listed in the last column. The picture is a screenshot of the CrowdTangle dashboard taken on February 9, 2022.

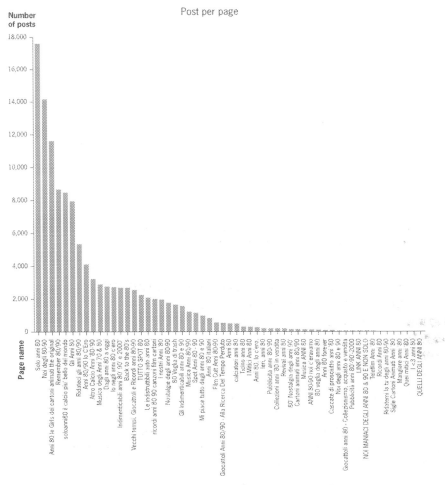

Fig. 1.3. The graph shows the distribution of posts segmented by Pages.

are nonetheless the proxy of a high level of active participation by the users following these Pages. This may be read in parallel with the total number of followers of the 63 Pages – 3,986,05 – which means an average of 63,270.65 of followers per Page – an indicator of users' strong interest in the '80s. Another interesting reflection on followers' and users' engagement in general can be made by looking at Fig. 1.2, a screenshot of the CrowdTangle dashboard (taken on 2 February 2022) displaying the top 15 Pages by total interactions. What is interesting here is that most of these Pages are growing in terms of followers compared to the previous week. This also applies to those Pages that have an average rate of posting near to 1 or even 0. This not only confirms the general public's interest in the '80s, but it also shows that, in some cases, the fact that a Page features the phrase "the '80s" is sufficient to attract followers and attention.

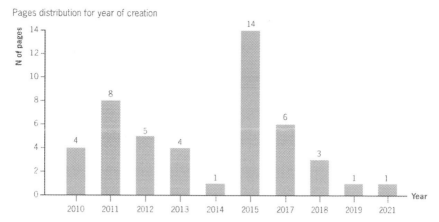

Fig. 1.4. The bar chart shows how many pages have been created in a specific year. The figure displays only 47 pages because the year of foundation was not available for all pages.

Regarding the types of content, if we look at the breakdown automatically generated by CrowdTangle (on the whole dataset) based on the total amount of 119,754 posts, we can see a prominence of Photos (53.8%), followed by Links (16.9%), YouTube videos (16.5%), and Native Videos 11% – the category Other stands at 1.8%. Of these, Status (textual status updates) are located at 1.2%. From this data, the prevalence of "visual forms of communication" among Pages is immediately visible: look, for example, at the disproportion between *photos* and *status.*

If we focus on the production of posts per Page, it is clear that not all Pages are active in the same way. As we can see from Fig. 1.3, there are about 7/8 Pages that are very active in producing posts; for the others, the distribution assumes the classical shape of a power law. This disproportion among Pages might be due to them having been started at very different times: some were founded in 2010, others in 2021. Overall, as shown in Fig. 1.4, it seems that the peak in the creation of nostalgic Pages occurred in 2015.

Descriptive as this analysis might be, it points to an interesting first insight: Facebook Pages featuring nostalgic content (in our case, about the '80s) are of great interest for a significant number of users and are able to trigger a certain level of attention and engagement.

Automated Text Analysis

Subsequently, we tried to get a bird's-eye view of these Pages' content by taking advantage of automated text analysis techniques. To do so, we performed a tf-idf analysis on posts segmented by page topics. Tf-idf is a kind

Matrix plot

Generic	Ads	Cartoons	Music	Toys	Movies	Soccer	Food	Place	Cars	Entertainment	TV
anni	anni80	ricordate	musica	foto	fantozzi	stagione	grazie	anni	fiat	buongiorno	serie
film	spotanni80	anni	the	buongiorno	anni80	gol	instagram	mitico	auto	buon	prima
anni80	spot	gig	anni	instagram	cult	anni	proscuitto	pubblicita	serie	buona	episodi
buon	anni90	buonanotte	anni80	altre	paolovillaggio	coppa	foto	indimenticabile	anni	anni	hazzard
oggi	pubblicitanni80	buon	sempre	ricordate	ridere	calcio	oggi	quando	romeo	serata	onda
compleanno	italiaanni80	buongiorno	love	spot	linobanfi	dopo	creazioni	ricordate	alfa	ricorda	anni
giovanni	spotanni90	quando	you	commenti	meme	serie	anni	mitica	pubblicata	sabato	stagione
ricordate	anni	oggi	pippo	anni	anni80style	italia	burro	gioco	venne	domenica	telefilm
buongiorno	pubblicitanni90	sogni	bella	carissimi	cinema	prima	serata	animato	modello	ciao	televisiva
onda	giocattolianni80	buona	buon	grazie	trash	foto	ricoprire	cartone	prodotta	venerd	stata
cinema	natale	amici	classic	solo	felicita	nazionale	trovarci	quegli	original	musica	corrida
ecco	giocattolovintage	nostalgici	grande	sempre	film	partita	aglio	ricordi	ultimi	purtroppo	quando
grande	italiaanni90	ricordi	seguono	ore	dicembre	quando	buon	film	volete	grande	catherine
auguri	nataleanni80	ricorda	piu	ricorda	natale	milan	ancora	serie	primo	pagina	canale
prima	qui	sempre	mondo	buon	renatopozzetto	grande	marco	giochi	versione	sara	italia
anni7080	giochianni80	ancora	cuore	tuttospot80	budspencer	sempre	notare	grande	oggi	ragazzi	infatti
ora	ancora	serie	fame	vecchi	pozzetto	due	matrimonio	duran	marca	solo	volta
style	anni2000	bambini	and	tempi	bud	finale	panna	mitici	vedere	virus	puntate
serie	oggi	vita	bellissima	cosa	risate	poi	scrive	giocattoli	porte	sera	produzione
pubblicita	cartonianni80	vero	grazie	venduto	boldi	gara	mai	tempi	turbo	fare	pubblico

emotional dimension   objects   products and/or brands   residual category

Fig. 1.5. The matrix plots show the top 20 keywords (extracted posts using the Tf-idf technique) segmented by page topic. Words are highlighted in different colours: purple = emotional dimension; light blue = objects; yellow = products and/or brands; white = residual category (comprising words not codable with the previous categories and/or too vague and general).

of automated text analysis that focuses on the most "characteristic" words within a given corpus of texts, against other given corpora (Qaiser and Ali, 2018) – rather than on the most recurrent terms per se. The results of our tf-idf analysis are presented in the matrix plot in Fig. 1.5, which displays the top 20 words per page topics. Words are highlighted in different colours; *green* refers to words with an emotional dimension, either generic (e.g., buongiorno/*good morning*) or nostalgic (e.g., ricorda/*remember*). *Blue* stands for words related to objects (e.g., film, spot/*ads*, foto/*photo*, etc.), while *yellow* indicates words pointing to specific products and/or brands (like, fantozzi,[4] hazard, fiat, prosciutto/*ham*, etc.).

This analysis offers a number of interesting insights. Firstly, if we look at the green words we can identify two main groups. On the one hand, we have terms that carry a nostalgic sentiment, like "mitici," "nostalgici," "ricorda" (i.e., *legendary* – a reference to the legendary '80s), *nostalgic people, remember*). On the other hand, we have phatic terms; words like "buongiorno" (*good morning*) or "buona serata" (*good night*) are typical phrases with

4   Fantozzi is a very popular (tragicomic) character played by the famous comedian Paolo Villaggio (whose name also appears in the "top 20 movies"). His movies were extremely popular in Italy during the '80s and '90s.

which administrators start or end a post. The same goes for "compleanno" (*birthday*): periodically, administrators post content that celebrates the birthday of an '80s star, either alive or dead (e.g., *Yesterday was the 93rd birthday of Marion Ross, Happy Birthday Marion!* (Marion Cunningham in Happy Days). Secondly, if we look at the blue and yellow words, we can observe that the sentiment of nostalgia tend to coalesce mostly around generic objects, like "pubblicità anni 80" (*'80s commercials*), "serie" (*TV series*), "giocattoli" (*toys*), or "film" (*movies*), and, more rarely, around specific brands or products, like "Fiat," "Duran Duran," or "Bud Spencer." Nonetheless, it seems evident that the sentiment of nostalgia pervading '80s Facebook Pages tends to converge mostly towards *consumption objects*, rather than entities or concepts that recall an indefinite long-gone past (see e.g., words like "natale" (*christmas*), "matrimonio" (*wedding*), "vita" (*life*), "bambini" (*children*), or "italia" (*italy*), which occur less frequently in the matrix plot.

Nostalgic Consumer Grammars and Vernaculars: Qualitative Analysis

Topic, Page Use, and Content Types

Building on the quantitative analysis just presented, we now turn to the more qualitative component of our exploration, looking to identify the specific grammars and vernaculars that characterise nostalgia on Facebook. To do so, we first perform a manual categorisation of Pages topic. Fig. 1.6 (below) shows that 34 of the 65 Pages taken into consideration have a generic reference to the '80s in their title, while 29 focus on different topics that are quite evenly distributed. Specifically, the most recurrent topics in our dataset are: *Ads, Cartoons, Music,* and *Toys*. Concerning "Page Use" (Fig. 1.6), the distribution is also split in two: 32 Pages feature a neutral attitude, while 31 feature some kind of attitude (Fig. 1.7). It is interesting to note that the most recurrent category is *Nostalgia*, followed by *Community*, and *Self-expression*. This suggests the existence of a tightly-knit relationship between nostalgia and identity, and points to the role of nostalgia as a shared sentiment with communitarian traits, acting as a "cultural glue" that brings together different social groups.

If we look at the distribution of topics per post (Fig. 1.8), we can see that the most recurrent category is not, as one would have expected, *Generic* (which accounts for only 6% of posts) but *Music* (28%), followed by *TV* (25%), and *Movies* (19%). This means, that notwithstanding the main theme of each Page, users tend to associate the '80s with specific cultural products. The role of material consumer goods is visible in the *Ads'* category (6%), which mainly

Topics distribution by Pages

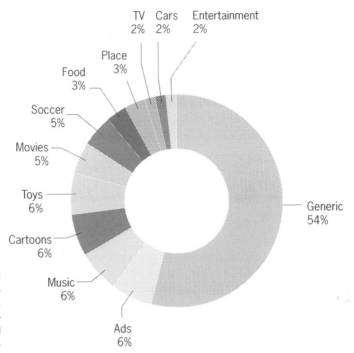

Fig. 1.6. The figure shows the distribution of topics for the 63 Pages analysed. The analysis of topics was performed manually using the Pages' titles.

Page Use distribution by Pages

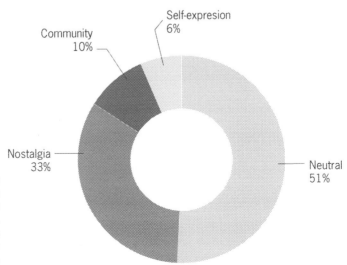

Fig. 1.7. The figure shows the distribution of the attitude towards the '80s for the 63 Pages analysed. The analysis of attitudes was performed manually using the Pages' titles.

Distribution of topics per posts

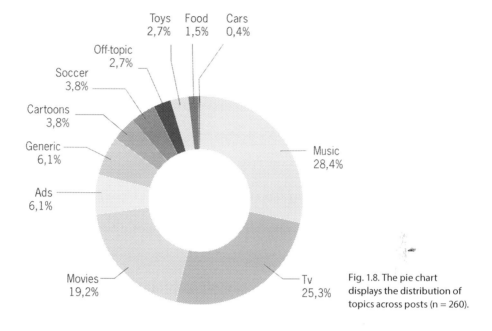

Fig. 1.8. The pie chart displays the distribution of topics across posts (n = 260).

Distribution of attitudes toward the 80s per post

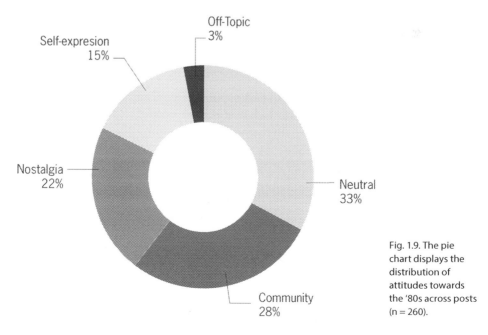

Fig. 1.9. The pie chart displays the distribution of attitudes towards the '80s across posts (n = 260).

consists of posts featuring advertisements for popular household goods and supermarket products from the 1980s. Looking at "Page Use" (Fig. 1.9), we can see that, after *Neutral*, the most recurrent category is *Community* (28%). This is not surprising, since posts in Pages are usually created by administrators who tend to engage participants by eliciting a sense of belonging and we-ness. As an example, see this post with the following text: "40 anni per la rivista [*Cioè*[5]] che ci ha accompagnato per tutta l'adolescenza ... Con un numero speciale tutto dedicato agli anni 80 ... CHE RICORDI AVETE?"/ "[Cioè] *turns 40, this is the magazine that was with us for our whole adolescence, plus an issue totally dedicated to the '80. What memories do you have about* Cioè?)." This topic and page use analysis further confirm what emerged (more generically) in the previous automated text analysis: on Facebook Pages, nostalgia tends to be structured and organised around specific consumption objects, mostly related to the cultural industry (e.g., movies, songs, TV series, etc.). It is precisely this "consumeristic imaginary" that is able to instil a sense of community amongst followers and administrators. Apparently, for our users, the '80s and the related sentiment of nostalgia seem to be meaningful mostly in terms of consumption; what they seem to miss the most is not their lost childhood/teenagehood, but rather old TV series, ads, toys, etc.

Visual Analysis

The qualitative visual analysis conducted on a random sample of 260 posts shows the existence of a number of nostalgic grammars that emerge across the Pages considered here. Grammars, here, refers to the visual content production choices made by administrators in their selection of posts published on Pages, and how these reveal different interpretations of nostalgia for the '80s. An ethnographic and grounded approach to study visual content (as opposed to the systematic counting of visual occurrences in pictures) has been employed for this analysis. This enables the observation of how visual content serves the specific purpose of producing a nostalgic imaginary, as well as of how Facebook affordances contribute to organising and structuring this nostalgic discourse. We focus specifically on the role consumption plays as a device that is instrumental to the production of the nostalgic imaginary, and what (material and cultural) consumer goods are used for this purpose. In other words, in this instance, we are not so

---

5   *Cioè* was a teen magazine, published on a weekly basis, extremely popular in Italy during the '80s and '90s.

much interested in knowing which of these grammars and objects are most recurrent in the content analysed, but rather in the variety of elements and discourses that constitute the nostalgic imaginary around consumption in the '80s.

Overall, most of the images included in our sample tend to be rudimentary and lo-fi. There seems to be little cultural work (or re-work) involved in these images, which often tend to be a mere repost of pictures found online. Thus, their visual composition is quite bleak and simple. This is interesting, on the one hand, because it adds to the dimension of authenticity that these images portray. On the other hand, this points to the idea that the users most commonly producing content for the Pages observed here may be from the Baby Boomer generation, i.e., less accustomed to the production of aesthetics that conform to digital trends and visual norms compared to younger cohorts (Giorgi, 2022). This is not surprising given that Baby Boomers were young adults during the 1980s, so they likely maintain a lived memory of the decade, as opposed to Millennials, who tend to idealise the 1980s but who, at best, were infants during this period, thus displaying what Appadurai (1996) calls "imagined nostalgia."

Among the objects portrayed, the primacy of cultural products such as movies, film, and TV is evident. This combines with the aforementioned role of nostalgia as a cultural glue to bring about a first common grammar, which we can call *celebration*. This essentially consists of posts that celebrate an idol of the '80s, either with a picture from the decade in question or in a collage that brings together a picture from the past and one from the present day. As an example, take the picture below (Fig. 1.10), which shows actors Harry Winkler and Ron Howard from the TV series Happy Days, a landmark product of Italian pop culture in the early 1980s. The picture is accompanied by the caption "Il tempo passa per tutti … mitici … ♥♥♥♥♥ 😎♥♥♥♥😎😚" (*Time goes by for everyone … Legendary …*).

A second common nostalgic grammar consists of what we may call *memorialisation*. This extends the notion of celebrating cultural products to the lived experience of their fruition. Take, for instance, Fig. 1.11, which portrays Italian TV personality Corrado, who used to host a popular lunchtime programme in the 1980s and early 1990s. The post description and the commenters associate Corrado with the experience of food in their youth, and the result is a moment of collective reminiscing (more on this later).

The third most common nostalgic grammar may be described as *techno-longing*. This materialises the feeling that things were better in the past, and that certain innovations have been no good for culture and society.

Fig. 1.10. Grammar of celebration.

Fig. 1.11. Grammar of memorialisation.

Fig. 1.12. Grammar of techno-longing.

We can see an example of this grammar n Fig. 1.12 (below), a picture of a pinball machines accompanied by the text "Let's put pinballs back in cafés, instead of slot machines. Pinballs never ruined anybody."

Albeit not majoritarian in terms of content, the presence of material consumer goods tends to cut across all these grammars. An example of the memorialisation grammar in this sense is given by Fig. 1.13, which displays chocolate Christmas-themed sweets that could be hung on Christmas trees, accompanied by the text "Chocolate Christmas decorations: do you remember them?"

This analysis confirms the insight that nostalgia for consumer goods in the '80s does not amount to an indistinct magma of memories but is articulated through specific discourses and objects across online spaces, with a clear primacy of cultural content. Facebook affordances enable the sharing of memories and facilitate the production of a nostalgic imaginary that many users participate in and whereby (material and cultural) consumer goods become a focus of attention, interaction, and engagement. Interestingly, these grammars of nostalgia also emerge because of the intersection between Page

Fig. 1.13. Material consumer nostalgia (example).

administrators' practices of content selection and sharing and Facebook affordances that incentivise memorialisation and celebration and tend to reward emotionally driven content (Geboers et al., 2020). Contextually, ordinary users produce vernacular accounts of their memories that closely follow the grammars described here. We can observe them in greater detail in the section below, through a narration analysis of comments.

Narration Analysis: Comments

To analyse the vernacular narrations expressed by users through comments to nostalgic posts, we undertook a narration analysis. In coherence with the visual analysis presented earlier, this method allows the researcher to ethnographically investigate, in a grounded way, the shared viewpoints and positionings of users in relation to a given focus of attention (Caliandro and Gandini, 2017). It is therefore perfectly suited for the study of the nostalgic attitudes of users. To conduct this analysis, we extracted the ten most-commented posts in the dataset: we deemed these to be the content that provides a better glimpse into the conversations around nostalgia for the 1980s taking place on the Facebook Pages considered here.

A first dominant narration across all types of posts, especially (albeit not exclusively) those in the grammar of "techno-longing," is what can be defined as a *reminiscent* one. This is characterised by a prominence of comments about life and culture in the 1980s with an implicit, regressive subtext, i.e., "things were better" in the past. See, for instance, this excerpt from the second post as per Total Interaction Rate in this category:

> I remember happiness. It was made up of workers who went to the sea in August. Cars without air conditioning, with luggage racks full of suitcases and motorways without traffic. Those were the years when pensioners could afford the right reward after a life of sacrifice, those were the years of the beaches with tables, baked pastries, and refrigerated containers better stocked than supermarkets. Happiness, with those folding chairs and coffees in thermos at the end of the lunch, the photos with rolls, the conversations all together at the end of the lunch, kids being kids...

This is typical of conversations about how modern living is less authentic than the past, and that the magic of the old times has been "spoiled." Many users adhering to this narration express regret that young adults today are missing out on what they believe were "the best times." Only a small portion of comments emphasise the "bad" sides of the 1980s and its controversies, thus highlighting a key feature of nostalgia – that is, it brings back mainly positive memories, suppressing the most negative ones (Gandini, 2020).

A second common narration is akin to the *playful* nostalgia highlighted by Hartmann and Brunk (2019). This revolves around the stylistically bizarre and fun fashionable items of the '80s, such as plastic hair tongs or huge portable hi-fi systems, or some of the most renowned popular culture of those times, such as cartoons and music. Interestingly, two of the ten posts analysed feature memories of popular culture of the 1980s that are commented on by users in the form of GIFs, without any text, an element that further emphasises the playfulness of the discussion. For instance, a post that features the text "An object, just one, that immediately makes you think of the '80s. Post it in the comments below," contains a number of playful comments that reference the "quirks" of the '80s, such as jackets with shoulder pads, fluo leggings, permanent wave curly hair, and much more. This shows how narrative viewpoints do not necessarily require long chunks of text for their expression; to circulate across online spaces they can also be articulated in fragmented, open-ended, and intertextual "small stories" (Georgakopoulou, 2017).

A third prominent narration draws upon nostalgia as an *experiential* dimension. This is especially tied to cultural consumption, and music in particular, whereby songs are mentioned alongside snippets about life in those days. Song excerpts are used in this context to convey the experiential dimension of one's memories, and help users to state how these were not only nice songs but ways to capture specific moments in one's life that are gone. See, for instance, how this user describes her experience of a Phil Collins song:

> Amazing! Me and her! Hugging and kissing where we could, on the bus, near the post office, by the castle ... how many lovely memories!

Overall, this analysis confirms how (material and cultural) consumption objects represents a key device in the expression of nostalgia as a shared sentiment with communitarian traits, helping users express their feelings about the past – in our case, the '80s – and to share their experiences about a past time that they usually idealise and fetishise. The manifold ways in which Page administrators and ordinary users engage in this practice further stresses how consumer nostalgia (Cross, 2015) continues to represent a key aspect in the context of platformised consumer cultures.

Conclusion and Implications

We started this chapter questioning whether and how social media users express nostalgia in relation to consumer goods, and what the role of consumption is in the development of a nostalgic imaginary and discourse on the Facebook platform. Our analysis reveals that nostalgia on social media, in our case Facebook, is produced in the form of specific grammars and vernaculars that Facebook affordances contribute to organising and standardising, leading to a nostalgic imaginary and discourse. This does not emerge as an undistinguished magma, but rather finds expression around particular cultural and material objects (music, ads, cartoons, TV shows, movies, etc.), in our case from the '80s. In this regard, it is interesting to note that, despite the increasing importance of experiences (Pine and Gilmore, 2011) and access-based consumption (Bardhi and Eckhardt, 2012), a peculiar feature of the imaginary of nostalgia on Facebook is the persistence of references to material, consumer goods. Material objects in particular are associated with a sense of longing, emerging from the visual components of posts, and practices of reminiscence through Facebook comments. In other words, the materiality of the Facebook platform – meaning, its affordances – meets with the materiality of consumption, and its visual representation, in shaping the nostalgic discourse. Objects of consumption function as devices that are able to pin (or anchor) past experiences, emotions, feelings, etc., in users' imagination and discourse, which otherwise would have been lost in the ephemeral, chaotic, and nebulous constant flux of personal remembrance. When the flux is fixed, then the affordances of social media can make it communicable and shareable.

The presence of a communitarian dimension is surprising for online social formations, which sometimes find cohesiveness precisely around rituals and/or ceremonies of remembrance of their "founding fathers" (Muñiz and Schau, 2005). Yet, nostalgia represents an aggregator of these rituals and moments of remembrance, stimulating a variety of users' self-narrations aimed at tapping into the nostalgic imaginary. Interestingly, these are most commonly connoted by a regressive subtext (that is, a discourse that stresses how "things were better back then" (Gandini, 2020).

Limitations and Further Methodological Strategies

Inevitably, however interesting and articulated this exploration is it has some significant limitations. First, it has focused exclusively on Pages, where communication and interaction are typically vertical and engineered from the top by Page administrators. In our case, this choice proved to be a good benchmark for testing our conceptualisation of the nostalgic imaginary of the '80s as a platformised cultural entity. Further research should study Facebook Groups– where communication and interactions tend to be more horizontal and "spontaneous" – more attentively, by exploring them beyond vanity metrics (Audy Martínek et al., 2023) and taking advantage of ethnographic methods (Caliandro, 2022). Secondly, the choice of a random sample for the qualitative analysis has the advantage of diversifying the content considered but might not offer an exhaustive overview of the various interpretations of nostalgia in the sample observed. Yet, more systematic visual and text analysis, perhaps aided by image and text recognition software (such as Google Vision API, see e.g., Omena et al., 2021), could expand the sample of images, as well as the typology of grammars and vernaculars observed. This, in turn, could expand our understanding of the processes of platformisation on consumer culture on a macro level.

References

Altheide, D. (1987). Reflections: Ethnographic content analysis. *Qualitative Sociology*, *10*, 65–77. https://doi.org/10.1007/BF00988269.

Appadurai, A. (1996). *Modernity at large: Cultural dimensions of globalization.* University of Minnesota Press.

Audy Martínek, P., Caliandro, A. and Denegri-Knott, J. (2023). Digital practices tracing: Studying consumer lurking in digital environments. *Journal of Marketing Management*, 39(3/4), 244–274. https://doi.org/10.1080/0267257X.2022.2105385.

Bauman, Z. (2017). *Retrotopia.* Polity.

Bardhi, F. and Eckhardt, G. M. (2012). Access-based consumption: The case of car sharing. *Journal of Consumer Research*, *39*(4), 881–898. https://doi.org/10.1086/666376.

Bristow, J. (2016). *The sociology of generations: New directions and challenges.* Springer.

Caliandro, A. (2022). Digital ethnography. In A. Ceron (Ed), *Elgar encyclopedia of technology and politics* (pp. 122–126). Edward Elgar Publishing.

Caliandro A. and Gandini A. (2017), *Qualitative research in digital environments: A research toolkit.* Routledge.

Charmaz, K. (2000). *Grounded theory: Objectivist and constructivist methods.* In N. Denzin and Y. Lincoln (Eds.), *Handbook of qualitative research* (pp. 509–535). Sage.

Cross, G. (2015). *Consumed nostalgia: Memory in the age of fast capitalism.* Columbia University Press.

Fan, C. (2022). *Understanding and citing CrowdTangle data.* https://help.crowdtangle.com/en/articles/4558716-understanding-and-citing-crowdtangle-data.

Gandini, A. (2020). *Zeitgeist nostalgia: On populism, work and the "good life."* Zero Books.

Geboers, M., Stolero, N., Scuttari, A., Van Vliet, L., and Ridley, A. (2020). Why buttons matter: Repurposing Facebook's reactions for analysis of the social visual. *International Journal of Communication*, *14*, 1564–1585. 1932–8036/20200005.

Georgakopoulou, A. (2017). Small stories research: A narrative paradigm for the analysis of social media. In L. Sloan and A. Quan-Haase (Eds.), *The SAGE Handbook of Social Media Research Methods* (pp. 266–281). Sage.

Georgakopoulou, A. (2021). Small stories as curated formats on social media: The intersection of affordances, values and practices. *System*, *102*. https://doi.org/10.1016/j.system.2021.102620.

Giorgi, G. (2022). *Memeing generations: Studying meme cultures and generational identities.* PhD dissertation, NASP, University of Milan-Turin.

Goulding, C. (2002). An exploratory study of age related vicarious nostalgia and aesthetic consumption. In S. M. Broniarczyk and K. Nakamoto (Eds.), *ACR North American Advances* volume *29* (pp. 542–546). Association for Consumer Research.

Hartmann, B. J. and Brunk, K. H. (2019). Nostalgia marketing and (re-) enchantment. *International Journal of Research in Marketing*, *36*(4), 669–686. https://doi. org/10.1016/j.ijresmar.2019.05.002.

Holbrook, M. B. (1993). Nostalgia and consumption preferences: Some emerging patterns of consumer tastes. *Journal of Consumer research*, *20*(2), 245–256. https://doi.org/10.1086/209346.

Holbrook, M. B. and Schindler, R. M. (2003). Nostalgic bonding: Exploring the role of nostalgia in the consumption experience. *Journal of Consumer Behaviour: An International Research Review*, *3*(2), 107–127. https://doi.org/10.1002/cb.127.

Holbrook, M. B. and Schindler, R. M. (1991). Echoes of the dear departed past: Some work in progress on nostalgia. In R. H. Holman and M. R. Solomon (Eds.), *ACR North American advances in consumer research, volume 18* (pp. 330–333). Association for Consumer Research.

Integrity Transparency (2022). *How do you calculate overperforming scores?* https://help.crowdtangle.com/en/articles/2013937-how-do-you-calculate-overperforming-scores.

Krause, M. (2019). What is zeitgeist? Examining period-specific cultural patterns. *Poetics*, *76*, https://doi.org/10.1016/j.poetic.2019.02.003.

Krippendorff, K. (2012). *Content analysis: An introduction to its methodology*. Sage.

Lasaleta, J. D., Werle, C. O., and Yamim, A. P. (2021). Nostalgia makes people eat healthier. *Appetite*, *162*, https://doi.org/10.1016/j.appet.2021.105187.

Lawler, R. (2022, June 23). Meta reportedly plans to shut down CrowdTangle. *The Verge*. https://www.theverge.com/2022/6/23/23180357/meta-crowdtangle-shut-down-facebook-misinformation-viral-news-tracker.

Michael, J. (2015). It's really not hip to be a hipster: Negotiating trends and authenticity in the cultural field. *Journal of Consumer Culture*, *15*(2), 163–182. https://doi. org/10.1177/1469540513493206.

Miles, C. (2022a). What data is CrowdTangle tracking? https://help.crowdtangle. com/en/articles/1140930-what-data-is-crowdtangle-tracking.

Miles, C. (2022b). Using CrowdTangle's historical data. https://help.crowdtangle. com/en/articles/1194215-using-crowdtangle-s-historical-data.

Miles, C. (2022c). FAQ: Followers. https://help.crowdtangle.com/en/articles/4797890-faq-followers.

Muñiz, A. M. and Schau, H. J. (2005). Religiosity in the abandoned Apple Newton brand community. *Journal of Consumer Research*, *31*(4), 737–747. https://doi. org/10.1086/426607.

Niemeyer, K. (2014). *Media and nostalgia: Yearning for the past, present and future.* Springer.

Omena, J. J., Pilipets, E., Gobbo, B., and Chao, J. (2021). The potentials of Google Vision API-based networks to study natively digital images. *Diseña, 19*, 1–25. 10.7764/disena.19.Article.1.

Pine, J. and Gilmore, J.H. (2011). *The experience economy: Work is theater and every business a stage (2nd edition).* Harvard Business Review Press.

Qaiser, S. and Ali, R. (2018). Text mining: Use of TF-IDF to examine the relevance of words to documents. *International Journal of Computer Applications, 181*(1), 25–29. 10.5120/ijca2018917395.

Reynolds, S. (2011). *Retromania: Pop culture's addiction to its own past.* Macmillan.

Rogers, R. (2018). Otherwise engaged: Social media from vanity metrics to critical analytics. *International Journal of Communication, 12*, 23. 1932–8036/20180005.

Rose, G. (2016). *Visual methodologies: An introduction to researching with visual materials.* Sage.

Schiermer, B. (2014). Late-modern hipsters: New tendencies in popular culture. *Acta sociologica, 57*(2), 167–181. https://doi.org/10.1177/0001699313498263.

Scott, M. (2017). "Hipster capitalism" in the age of austerity? Polanyi meets Bourdieu's new petite bourgeoisie. *Cultural Sociology, 11*(1), 60–76. https://doi.org/10.1177/1749975516681226.

Tanner, G. (2020). *The circle of the snake: Nostalgia and utopia in the age of Big Tech.* John Hunt Publishing.

Thurlow, C., Aiello, G., and Portman, L. (2020). Visualizing teens and technology: A social semiotic analysis of stock photography and news media imagery. *New Media and Society, 22*(3), 528–549. https://doi.org/10.1177/1461444819867318.

Wilson, J. L. (2005). *Nostalgia: Sanctuary of meaning.* Bucknell University Press.

Youn, S. and Jin, S. V. (2017). Reconnecting with the past in social media: The moderating role of social influence in nostalgia marketing on Pinterest. *Journal of Consumer Behaviour, 16*(6), 565–576. https://doi.org/10.1002/cb.1655.

2. YouTube and the Radicalisation (?) of Consumption

Abstract

In this chapter, we investigate the phenomenon of radicalisation on YouTube in relation to consumption. Drawing on the analysis of 7,429 videos on vegetarianism, posted from 2006 to 2020, we question the extent to which, akin to the political context (e.g., far-right, alt-right, terrorism, etc.), the YouTube algorithm has the potential to radicalise users' consumption preferences. We show that the YouTube platform, rather than radicalising consumers towards vegetarianism, tends to "indoctrinate" them about it. Moreover, in those cases where YouTube offers consumers some possible recommendation paths to radicalise their vegetarian taste, unlike the political domain, this does not necessarily represent a negative outcome but is evidence of the relevance of the cultural setting wherein recommendation paths on social media platforms emerge.

Keywords: vegetarianism, UK, YouTube Data Tools, descriptive assemblage.

In a 2018 op-ed published in the *New York Times*, sociologist Zeynep Tufekci warned about the risk of *political radicalisation* embedded in the YouTube platform. Tufekci suggested that YouTube tends to radicalise users by pushing them to watch far-right/alt-right contents by means of its algorithmic recommender system, which suggests non-stop videos to viewers on the basis of "relatedness." In subsequent years, digital media scholars started questioning Tufekci's conception of YouTube as "The Great Radicaliser"– mainly contesting that this is based on anecdotes and self-observation, rather than empirical data. To quote a famous *Wired* headline: "If YouTube Algorithms Radicalise Users, Data Doesn't Show It" (Timmer, 2021). In fact, Munger and Phillips (2022), after analysing 1 million videos posted on YouTube between 2008 to 2018, found that the "viewership of … alt-lite and alt-right creators has actually declined since 2017" (Weiss, 2019, n.p.). A Nielsen's study led by

Caliandro, A., A. Gandini, L. Bainotti, G. Anselmi, *The Platformisation of Consumer Culture: A Digital Methods Guide*. Amsterdam: Amsterdam University Press, 2024

DOI 10.5117/9789463729567_CH02

Hosseinmardi and colleagues (2021), who had access to the browsing histories of a panel of 309,813 American YouTube users, comes to similar results. After examining 21 million YouTube videos posted between 2016 and 2019, researchers concluded that news-related content accounted for only 11% of the whole dataset and, within this small percentage, the majority of videos came from "mainstream, and generally centrist or left-leaning sources" (Hosseinmardi et al., 2021, p. 2). Moreover, the research team discovered that users in the panel had a relatively mono-modal digital diet, meaning that users do not commonly access news from diversified sources: for example, leftist users primarily tend to consume leftist content, and so on. In fact, the researchers did not observe a particular increase in consumption of extremist content during the time period they monitored, meaning that the platform appears to reinforce existing behaviours, rather than instilling new ones. Hosseinmardi and her colleagues found some patterns of consumption of far-right videos too, but they stress that "the consumption of far-right content is small in terms of both number of viewers and total watch time, where the former decreased slightly and the latter increased slightly over the observation period" (Hosseinmardi et al., 2021, p. 2). Lastly, they also noticed that far-right users have the habit of consuming a large amount of extremist content *outside* the YouTube platform (e.g. alt-right blogs): this indicates that users' radical behaviour is much more driven by their personal preferences, rather than the YouTube algorithm.

Nonetheless, it would be hasty to dismiss the "radicalisation hypothesis" as inaccurate. In fact, a number of studies have empirically identified the presence and circulation of inappropriate, problematic, and extreme content on YouTube (O'Callaghan et al., 2015; Ribeiro et al., 2020). See, for example, the study of Faddoul et al. (2020) on conspiracy theories, who, although noting a decrease in views of conspiracy videos on the platform from 2018 to 2020, still observed the presence of filter bubbles around this topic (i.e., they found a "clear positive correlation between the conspiracy likelihood of the source video and the conspiracy likelihood of the recommended video" (Faddoul et al., 2020, p. 5)). Moreover, several analysts are sceptical about YouTube's (recent) public commitment to contrast and eradicate inappropriate videos from the platform (through demonetisation as well as changes to its recommendation algorithm) (YouTube, n.d.). Although it is possible to observe a progressive drop in views of problematic content after the YouTube announcement, researchers point out that much work is still to be done in this direction (Thomson, 2020). For instance, in their longitudinal analysis of YouTube's algorithmic recommendation system, Matamoros-Fernández et al. (2021) observed that the effectiveness of YouTube moderation seems to vary significantly based on the topic taken into consideration. By following the keyword "coronavirus" from March 7, 2020 to April 22, 2020, the researchers noted that the YouTube algorithm tends (mostly) to prioritise and recommend "official" videos coming from authoritative sources (e.g., pieces of news uploaded by CNN, NBC, or BBC). Yet, the same cannot be said for keywords like "beauty" and "feminism", around which Matamoros-Fernández et al. (2021, p. 245) found clusters of "highly stereotyped, commercialised, gendered" and anti-feminist content. These results seem to suggest that, at present, the YouTube moderation system works better with hot and highly visible topics, rather than with more general and mundane ones.

Starting from this insight, in this chapter, we would like to further test the hypothesis of "radicalisation" by changing the perspective slightly; that is, by focusing on the more mundane sphere of consumption, rather than on politics. It seems reasonable that YouTube does not radicalise users' political views because it is simply not interested in doing so: ultimately, this is not what the platform is for. In fact, YouTube is a commercial platform made to connect commercial stakeholders, such as consumers, advertisers, marketers, companies, and brands (Van Dijck and Poell, 2013). In turn, it is more likely that YouTube wants users to spend as much time as possible on the platform in order to expose them not only to digital ads, but also to new cultural trends and lifestyles that can inspire them towards new consumption behaviours (and possibly stir up purchase decisions). Therefore, here, we intend "radicalisation" in an unorthodox and provocative sense, meaning the tendency of the YouTube platform to feed its users with a cultural imaginary that stimulates them to find and engage with increasingly narrower and more complex trends of consumption.

Before proceeding with the discussion of our methodology and results, two further premises must be noted. First, while we borrowed the concept of *radicalisation* from research on political content on YouTube, we do not intend this term in a necessarily negative vein. In existing research dealing with consumption of political content on YouTube, the term "radicalisation" has a definitely negative connotation, which implies that consuming radical political contents means, essentially, to get involved with far-right or terroristic videos (Rogers, 2019; Hosseinmardi et al., 2022). In our case, instead, since we employ the notion of radicalisation within the realm of consumption, and particularly in relation to the vegetarian lifestyle, we do not attach any moral judgement to it. So, for instance, we could consider veganism as a "radical" version of vegetarianism, but simply because the former is a narrower and more complex version of the latter. Nor are we to state that vegetarianism is better than veganism, or carnivorism, or whatever kind of dietary regime. Second, since a shared definition of "radicalisation of consumption" does not exist, and there is no empirical research on this topic, we had no pre-existing frames of reference to operationalise and measure such a phenomenon. What we did was to engage in an in-depth exploration of a dataset of YouTube videos, at the end of which we elaborated some insights and discussed some theoretical implications. Therefore, we consider the analysis and results presented in this chapter as experimental and the related theorisations as an intellectual exercise, and we would like to exhort the reader to do the same. That said, we do hope that our work will inspire further and more systematic research on this topic.

Research Question, Data Collection, and Techniques of Analysis

Our exploration of the radicalisation of consumption on YouTube starts from the following research questions: *Does the YouTube platform contribute to radicalising processes of consumption? If so, how and to what extent? Is YouTube pushing users to view homogeneous content that encourages them to stick with a specific consumer niche as well as funnel them towards more extreme and controversial versions of the same niche?*

In order to address these research questions, we developed a study on *vegetarianism*. We deem vegetarianism to be a suitable topic to develop an exploratory research project on radicalisation of consumption on YouTube. First, vegetarianism is a well-established niche of consumption, with recognisable dietary patterns and lifestyle habits (Janda and Trocchia, 2001). Therefore, to put it in more empirical terms, when we type the keyword "vegetarianism" on the YouTube search bar, we can be confident that we will (very likely) encounter in-topic videos (that is, videos dealing with vegetarian themes and issues, also as posted by users, interested, either in a positive or negative way, in disseminating information about vegetarianism). The same cannot be said, for example, about keywords like "music" or "movies," which tend to cross over and fork into a variety of semantic domains (Airoldi, 2021). Second, vegetarianism appears to be a suitable phenomenon to observe within a process of growing radicalisation, as intended here. In practical terms, we can imagine that, in subsequent iterations, having seen a vegetarian video the YouTube algorithm then suggests, for example, a vegan one, and then a crudist one: thus, we can argue that we are witnessing a process of radicalisation of consumption.

We devised two research strategies to explore the radicalisation of vegetarianism on YouTube, and the role played by its algorithm. For both strategies, we collected data using the *YouTube Data Tools*[1] – a free and user-friendly online software that allows users to acquire data from YouTube by interrogating the YouTube API v3 (Rieder, 2015).

Regarding the first strategy, we took advantage of the "Video List" module embedded in the YouTube Data Tools, which we set as follows:

–   search query: *vegetarianism*
–   language: *English*
–   region: *UK*[2]
–   iterations: *10* (the maximum allowed is ten, and one iteration retrieves 50 items);
–   videos ranked by: *relevance*[3]

Then, we repeated the above research query for each year from 2006 (when Google bought YouTube) to 2020. The scope was to have a comprehensive and longitudinal overview of how the YouTube algorithm organises vegetarian videos on its homepage and thus presents them to users. This way, we obtained a dataset of 7,429 videos[4] along with their related metadata (e.g., *position*, *videoId*, *videoTitle*, *videoDescription*, *viewCount*, etc.). We then integrated the longitudinal analysis of videos with a computational text analysis of video descriptions (Rieder et al., 2023). These analyses were useful for getting a glimpse of a broader grammar that orients users' behaviour on the platform.

As far as the second strategy is concerned, we took advantage of the "Video Network" module of YouTube Data Tools. This module creates a network of relations between videos, starting from a search or a list of video IDs (Rieder, 2015). A related video is one of those entities appearing in the list on the right of the YouTube interface as soon as one clicks on a video to watch it. Currently, YouTube no longer discloses how it algorithmically defines and displays a list of related videos (Rieder, 2023) – thus secluding key

---

1   The link to YouTube Data Tools: https://tools.digitalmethods.net/netvizz/youtube/index.php. The reader can find a tutorial to get acquainted with the tool, featuring the developer of it (Bernhard Rieder) at the following link: https://www.youtube.com/watch?v=TmF4mWZYnbkandt=39s.
2   We decided to focus only on English content within the UK region for pragmatic reasons, to avoid the multiplication of keywords, languages, and topics.
3   Simply put, on YouTube relevance is decided by the title, description, tags, and keywords applied by the user who uploaded a video (Airoldi et al., 2016).
4   Consider that the tool does not necessarily retrieve 500 videos for each query, it depends on how many "relevant" videos the YouTube API makes available for a specific keyword and/or time range selected. For example, in our case, the tool retrieved only 480 videos for 2006.

information on a crucial component of the platform: the recommendation system. In any case, drawing on the most recent information available, we know that a video list should comprise videos that are usually watched in sequence (Airoldi et al., 2016; McLachlan and Cooper, 2023). Therefore the "video network" module might not give us a clear understanding of the algorithmic functioning of the YouTube recommendation system, but it does, at least, give us a glimpse into users' co-view habits (Rieder, 2023). This is more than sufficient for our research scopes, since we are interested in exploring possible patterns of radicalisation of vegetarianism, rather than uncovering the functioning of the YouTube algorithm per se.

The technical procedure we applied is as follows. First, we took the top 20 videos on vegetarianism of 2020 (as retrieved through the "Module List" function) and then put them into the "Video Network" module. In order to keep things simple, we set the module at iteration "1," meaning we extracted all the related videos of the initial 20 seeds. To analyse and visualise the video network, we used the open-source software Gephi (Bastian et al., 2009). Specifically, we took advantage of the Gephi's algorithm of community detection, which identifies and clusters together node groups that (statistically) tend to be more connected. Then, using Gephi's "Modularity" function, we estimated that our network was composed of ten clusters, each of which aggregating a similar number of videos (between 10% and 8%). To visualise the network, we used the ForceAtlas2 layout (another default command of Gephi). ForceAtlas2 is a force directed layout that "simulates a physical system in order to spatialise a network" (Jacomy et al., 2014, p. 2); this is very useful for visualising nodes and clusters as well as their relations within a network. The goal of this analysis was to obtain a quick overview on the different patterns of consumption that YouTube offers to a user who navigates the platform searching for content on vegetarianism. This analysis was also useful for observing the kinds of vernaculars users built on top of the grammar we observed in strategy 1.

This two-step research strategy allowed us to simulate (and repeat on a larger scale) the user experience of an ordinary person who accesses YouTube to look for information about vegetarianism, and so, s/he is first presented with the platform home page, and then (after clicking on a given video) a list of related videos.

Finally, to observe if and to what extent the YouTube algorithm is able to "radicalise" vegetarian consumption, we followed Rieder et al.'s (2018) approach of studying algorithmic outcomes through description, instead of aiming at identifying "hard moments of causality" (Matamoros-Fernández et al., 2021, p. 53). That is, we drew on what Rieder et al. (2018) call *descriptive assemblage* (Savage, 2009), an analytical approach "where processes of creativity, conceptual innovation, and observation can be used to mobilise novel insights" (Matamoros-Fernández et al., 2021, p. 170).

Strategy 1: Exploring YouTube's Video List Results over Time

As a first step, we performed a manual analysis of some of the metadata released by the YouTube API v3, specifically: *Licensed Content*, and *Video Category Label*. This had the scope of obtaining a general overview of the grammar of the vegetarian ecosystem on YouTube and exploring how it evolves overtime. For this kind of analysis, we focused on the first ten videos retrieved by YouTube Data Tools for each of the 15 years taken into account – 140 posts in total. We kept the first ten posts because of the well-known tendency of internet users to not scroll beyond the tenth result when confronted with SERP outputs (Spink and Jansen, 2004).

Firstly, we focused on *Licensed Content* (hereafter, LC); this label indicates that the user who uploaded the video chose to attach to it "either the Creative Commons licence or the standard YouTube licence" (YouTube, n.d.). Usually, professional content creators attach a licence to their posts, in order to protect their intellectual property (Mittiga, 2022). Thus, the metadatum "*LC*" can be considered as a proxy of professionalisation of content production on YouTube. Turning to our exploration, as one can see from Fig. 2.1, there is an exponential increase of LCs from 2006 to 2020, which tend to occupy the first positions of the top 10 (in 2018, the top 10 is almost exclusively comprised of LCs). Overall, we notice that, over the years, the production of videos on vegetarianism undergoes a process of progressive professionalisation. Considering this result, we would have expected a proliferation of "commercial-like" posts; that is, videos dealing with recipes or dietary advice, i.e., the kind of "trivial" content that makes it easier for content creators to get visibility (Bishop, 2019). However, this is not the case according to our data. Looking at Fig. 2.2 (based on the metadatum "Video Category Label"), videos categorised by YouTube as "How to and Style" do not monopolise the distribution (even though they seldom rank as number one in the top 10, see 2010, 2012, 2019, 2020). In fact, the categories visualised in the Matrix Plot are diverse and heterogeneous: see, for example, the large diffusion of categories such as "Nonprofits and Activism," "Pets and Animals," "Science and Technology," "Education," "People and Blogs," and "Entertainment." To provide a clearer context around these labels, as well as a better understanding of what kinds of specific content such labels refer

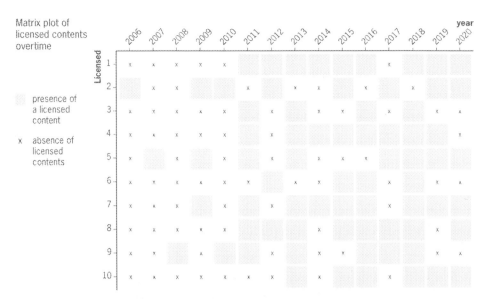

Fig. 2.1. The graph shows the progression of licenced contest over 15 years.

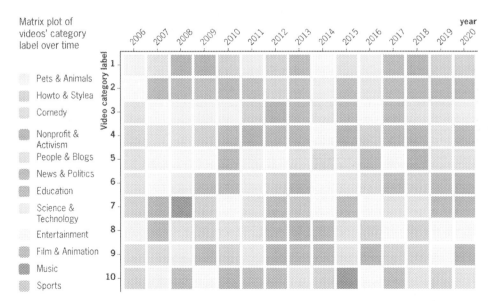

Fig. 2.2. The graph shows the progression of videos' label category over 15 years. The categories are automatically assigned by YouTube.

to, we performed an ethnographic content analysis (Altheide, 1987) of the 140 videos in our dataset. The content analysis was based on the watching of the videos as well as on the close reading of videos' descriptions; we focused on the topic of the video and its sentiment. In so doing, we identified eight main topics: "Advocacy" (videos that explain what is vegetarianism and why it is important to be a vegetarian: for the animals, the planet, the body, the soul, etc.); "Food and Diet" (videos about recipes and/or dietary tips); "Storytelling" (videos in which someone talks about their personal experience of being vegetarian and/or expressing their personal opinion on vegetarianism); "Health Dissemination" (videos in which medical experts talk about vegetarianism); "Comedy" (mostly parodies on the vegetarian lifestyle); "News" (informational content about vegetarianism taken from or uploaded by mainstream media channels); "Other" (residual category). The sentiment was segmented into its three usual categories: "Positive" (videos putting vegetarianism on a positive light); "Negative" (videos putting vegetarianism on a negative light); "Neutral" (videos whose attitude towards vegetarianism is neither positive nor negative) (Caliandro and Gandini, 2017).

The results of our ethnographic content analysis are more insightful and specific than those of the Video Category Labels. As shown in Fig. 2.3, the videos that we categorised as "Advocacy" are definitely the most diffused ones, as they take the first spots the top 10 (the distribution of 2020 essentially comprises only "Advocacy" videos). The Diet category also has a good diffusion, albeit this is not comparable to that of "Advocacy." Likewise, the sentiment analysis provides quite interesting insights; the vast majority of videos in the dataset have a positive attitude towards vegetarianism (see Fig. 2.4). By contrast, videos that portray vegetarianism negatively, such as "Problems Being a Vegetarian – Dr. Berg on Downsides of Vegetarian Diets" or "Is Vegetarianism Bad for Your Brain? (Re: The Scary Mental Health Risks of Going Meatless)" tend to be quite popular: the former scored 25,5490 views in 2014 and the latter 39,144 in 2015. Both appear in the first place of the top 10, but have a very small diffusion over time.

This brief and simple analysis already provides us with very interesting insights, which (partially) allow us to address our research question. At this stage of the analysis, it is not possible to speak of any radicalisation with respect to vegetarianism on YouTube or of commercialisation of vegetarian culture. Nevertheless, something equally relevant seems to emerge: even though we did not observe any process of radicalisation, we did observe the emergence of a "grammar of indoctrination." In fact, over 15 years, those videos categorised as "Advocacy" are largely the most diffused and they always tend to appear in the first places of the top 10. Moreover, the vast majority of these videos lack heterogeneity in terms of diversity of point of views, in the sense that they always tend to show a positive attitude towards vegetarianism.

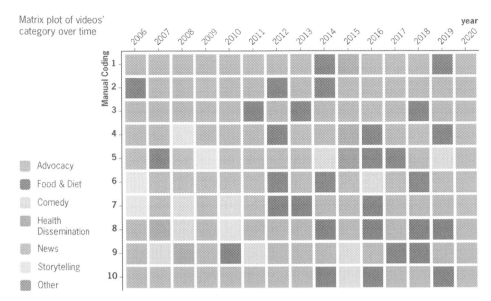

Fig. 2.3. The graph shows the progression of videos' category over 15 years. These categories are the results of a qualitative content analysis.

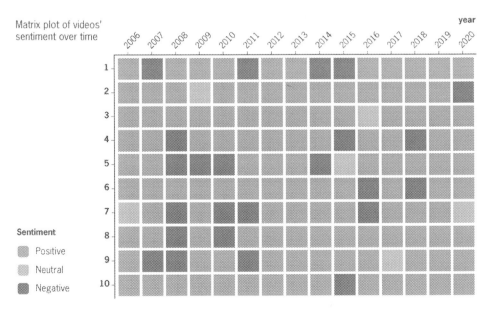

Fig. 2.4. The graph shows the progression of videos' sentiment over 15 years.

To conclude our first research strategy, we developed a further quantitative analysis. Here, we tried to explore the content of the videos on a macro level, in order to check for the presence of some radicalisation trends that we might

Automated keyword analysis of videos' captions over time

2006	2007	2008	2009	2010	2011	2012	2013	2014	2015	2016	2017	2018	2019	2020
university	teaspoon	recipe	recipe	recipe	recipe	recipe	recipe	recipe	recipe	recipe	recipe	recipe	recipe	recipe
health	cup	food	health	health	food	vegan	food	food	tbsp	tsp	food	food	food	food
show	recipe	meat	easy	meat	meat	diet	diet	indian	tsp	vegan	diet	diet	diet	diet
meat	oil	josiah owen	food	diet	health	meat	cup	vegan	food	food	vegan	tsp	vegan	tsp
maharishi	ingredients	free	people	vegan	cooking	health	cooking	sauce	vegan	protein	cup	cup	indian	tbsp
new	chopped	expert	indian	food	vegan	food	salt	tsp	chopped	cup	oil	vegan	english	powder
recipe	salt	teaspoon	meat	animals	diet	cup	oil	easy	cup	tbsp	cooking	oil	dixtt	oil
food	tsp	vegan	protein	cooking	free	salt	chopped	rice	oil	diet	meat	sauce	healthy	cup
music	cumin	cup	diet	animal	tsp	minutes	tsp	ingredients	sauce	asian	music	salt	meal	day
students	water	animals	vegan	teaspoon	animals	ingredients	meat	cooking	ingredients	salt	sauce	chopped	meat	easy
time	powder	diet	quick	people	world	free	garlic	diet	salt	meat	plan	water	cup	salt
pig	dish	ingredients	great	world	great	teaspoon	vegan	meat	powder	oil	powder	ingredients	protein	healthy
festival	tbsp	rice	foods	easy	water	protein	healthy	oil	garlic	chopped	meal	garlic	tsp	sauce
live	green	bio	step	life	oil	delicious	protein	chopped	cooking	sauce	tsp	pepper	weight	ingredients
life	food	filmmaker	beans	meal	indian	pepper	water	cup	water	cooking	free	tbsp	music	vegan
film	cooking	years	dish	show	people	cooking	powder	salt	meat	garlic	healthy	healthy	oil	meat
cause	dal	people	animals	protein	ingredients	oil	pepper	tbsp	indian	ingredients	salt	cooking	salt	teaspoon
meals	coriander	salt	free	free	animal	meal	beans	health	easy	cheese	easy	powder	keto	music
chicken	seeds	indian	cuisine	cup	taste	animal	easy	pepper	taste	water	day	indian	cheese	indian
college	flour	chef	spicy	love	meal	rice	ingredients	cheese	dish	pepper	kitchenaid	curry	ingredients	chopped

Recipe · Vegan · Indian/Asian cuisine · Keto diet

Fig. 2.5. The graph shows the results of the automated keyword analysis that we developed on videos' captions over time. The figures show the top 20 keywords for each year. To create the top 20 and make it more readable and meaningful, we eliminated redundant words, such as "vegetarian" (which, of course, was always present in the dataset and always in the top positions), stop words (e.g., and, or, etc.), words related to the platform vernacular (e.g., YouTube, Facebook, like, subscribe, etc.), verbs (anything related to cooking and eating activities, "make," "cook," "eat," "drink," "prepare"). We also merged similar words and/or synonyms like "recipe" and "recipes" or "health" and "healthy."

have missed in the qualitative analysis. To do so, we performed an automated text analysis of video descriptions for the whole dataset (7,429 entries). We implemented a very simple keyword count, useful for spotting the most recurrent terms within a corpus of texts (Krippendorff, 2002); in our case, this method was very useful for making quick comparisons across years.

Firstly, looking at Fig. 2.5 (that shows the top 20 keywords for each year), we can see that – in contrast to what emerged earlier – in the whole dataset there is a predominance of recipe videos (as indicated by keyword *recipe*, which was always in the first position in the top 20 from 2008, as well as other related words, such as *food, ingredients, cooking, oil, cup, chopped, salt*, etc.). It is also interesting to see the steady presence of the keywords "meat" and "protein." Yet, these keywords do not account for "diversity" in the dataset; in fact, these words are not associated with posts encouraging people to eat meat. On the contrary, they refer to videos explaining how to *substitute* meat and animal proteins with vegetables or that promote living *without* eating meat. See, for example, the following excerpt from the description of a video called "Complete Proteins – Vegetarian Diet and Myths about Plant Proteins": "For years I thought that you need to eat meat to obtain complete proteins and thus I thought it must be hard for vegetarians or vegans to live a healthy lifestyle. In fact it was quite the opposite. If you have ever considered the vegetarian diet or wanted to cut down on the amount of meat you ate while still be healthy then this video is a must watch."

However, if one wants to search for clues that point towards the radicalisation of vegetarian consumption, it is possible to find some. First, we can observe that, in 2008, the keyword "vegan" appears in the top 20 and remains there until 2020 – almost always occupying one of the highest positions. This trend seems to point to some sort of radicalisation: starting from watching vegetarian videos, the user is "encouraged" by the YouTube platform to explore a more "radical" version of it, that is "veganism," In fact, veganism, similarly to vegetarianism, rejects the consumption of meat broadly intended (i.e., red meat, poultry, seafood, and other animals); but it goes beyond it, also excluding any food products derived from animal exploitation (e.g., eggs, dairy products, honey, etc.). In this fashion, veganism is more of a "philosophy" than a simple dietary regime (Greenebaum, 2012). A second clue to radicalisation comes from the emergence of keywords related to Indian cuisine and culture. In the graph, this is immediately visible from the presence of the keyword "Indian," which appears in 2008 and maintains a steady presence in the dataset from 2014 to 2020 (with the exception of 2016, where we see the word "Asian" instead). Along with the keyword "Indian," we can notice the emergence of other words related to Indian cuisine, such as *curry, cumin, coriander, dal* (which are "dried, split pulses (e.g., lentils, peas, and beans)"). It is no surprise that a dataset on vegetarianism features words related to Indian food; in fact, Indian cuisine has plenty of delicious vegetarian dishes. Looking closely into the dataset, one can see that the term "Indian" does not refer uniquely to food matters. On the one hand, of course, there are videos featuring recipes, such as: "High Protein Diet Plan for Weight Loss – Indian Protein Recipes Vegetarian." On the other hand, it is possible to find videos that tend to mix vegetarian cuisine with more general elements of Indian culture; see, for example, this post: "What can we learn from Indian vegetarianism?," whose description is quite eloquent: *Is it enough the ideology of "not to drink milk," "not to eat meat" or "not to consume garlic and onions" to divide whole societies? The Ayurveda doctor and Indian researcher Vijayendra Murthy proposes an harmonious, peaceful and efficient development of the vegetarian and vegan currents in India and in the world.*

Remaining in the realm of Indian culture, it is also interesting to notice the presence of the word "Maharishi" (2006), which stands for "Maharishi International University." The Maharishi International University is an academic institution that, along the "classical" courses in "Business" or "Computer Science," offers programs in "Ayurveda Wellness and Integrative Health" or "Yoga and Ayurveda," The university is also committed to offering its students fresh and "organic vegetarian meals" daily [5]

Finally, it is worth mentioning a last example, which is definitely interesting and quite odd, but admittedly minoritarian (since it occurs only once). Specifically, in 2019, we can see the appearance of the term "keto," meaning "ketogenic diet," which, according to Mawer (2023), consists of a "very low carb diet … that involves *drastically* reducing carbohydrate intake and replacing it with fat." Considered in this fashion, the ketogenic diet is the opposite of vegetarianism, since, usually, one gets "fats" from meat. Anyway, this term appears in our dataset because of some videos that introduce viewers to the "vegetarian ketogenic diet," a kind of ketogenic diet where "fats" are obtained from eggs and cheese, instead of red meat, fish, or poultry (as explained, for example, by the video "Guide to the Vegetarian Keto Diet"[6]). Again, we can see videos that encourage users to explore a narrower and more complex version of vegetarianism.

Undoubtedly, this further quantitative analysis helped us to spot trends related to the radicalisation of vegetarian consumption that we missed in the qualitative research. Certainly, we can argue that, according to our data, radicalisation of consumption is not necessarily a negative process; or, at least, it can be framed as a neutral one. In fact, we identified three elements pointing towards a possible radicalisation of vegetarianism: *veganism, keto vegetarianism, Indian cuisine and culture*; that is, three specific trends that exhort users to explore narrower and more complex versions of vegetarianism, which go beyond a simple meatless dietary regime. From this perspective, it would be difficult to maintain that "contaminating" a vegetarian dietary regime with elements of veganism as well as Indian cuisine and culture would be something detrimental for consumers' lifestyle, health, or worldview. Therefore, we can conclude that the YouTube platform does not offer users solely a grammar of indoctrination towards vegetarianism, but rather some possible path to radicalise their vegetarian taste. These paths will become clearer in the section, which explores users' vernaculars.

5   https://www.miu.edu/.
6   https://www.healthline.com/nutrition/vegetarian-keto-diet-plan.

Strategy 2: Exploring YouTube's Video Network

The second strategy devised for this chapter was aimed at mapping, visualising, and describing the different patterns of consumption that YouTube
suggests to users interested in vegetarian topics. To do so, we built a network
of related videos. This strategy allowed us to observe several vernaculars
emerging on top of the grammar we encountered in the previous section. In
fact, on top of a "grammar of indoctrination" towards vegetarianism, users
seem to build their own vernaculars; that is, very specific ways to decline
the vegetarian diet, cuisine, and culture that users cocreate through their
collective viewing habits and interactions with the algorithm. As shown
in Fig. 2.6, eight clusters out of ten in the network aggregate a significant
number of videos. It is also worth noticing that most of the clusters revolve
around a single channel that generates almost all the videos included in
the cluster. This likely reflects the tendency of the YouTube algorithm to
suggest users videos from the same channel, once a viewer (more or less
randomly) lands on it (Rieder et al., 2020). In any case, the network has
eight main clusters:

-   Cluster 1 (n°4, 10.48%): We called this one the *Gordon Ramsay* cluster. It
    aggregates videos mostly coming from the "Gordon Ramsay" channel or
    similar entertainment channels, such as "Food Network UK," "Kitchen
    Nightmares," or "MasterChef World." Most of the videos feature chef
    Gordon Ramsay engaging with vegetarian or Indian cuisine; see e.g.,
    these two videos: "Indian Guru Tries To Convince Gordon Ramsay To
    Be Vegetarian: Gordon's Great Escape"; "Gordon Ramsay Cooks Indian
    Street Food For Locals."
-   Cluster 2 (n°0, 10.08%): *Araathi* cluster. All the videos that compose
    this cluster are posted by the same channel: "Araathi," a channel that
    YouTube classifies as "entertainment." In fact, Araathi is an Indian
    female youtuber offering funny sketches, videos, and web series. Specifi-
    cally, most of the videos that form Cluster 2 are ironic videos set in the
    context of the everyday life of a young Indian girl, such as: "Types of
    Selfie Pullingo." In general, these videos make fun of specific aspects
    of Indian culture and lifestyle. More rarely, posts appear dealing with
    vegetarianism ("Purattasi Atrocities: Struggles of Every Non-vegetarians"
    or Indian cuisine ("Types Of Eaters in Restaurant").
-   Cluster 3 (n°5, 10.08%): we called this the *Traditional Indian* cluster.
    All the videos in the cluster come from the same channel: "Village
    Cooking Channel," a channel featuring traditional Indian food, as it

is cooked in rural villages and country areas. The videos fall into two categories: vegetarian Indian recipes ("Vegetable Biryani: Biryani Recipe for Vegetarians") and non-vegetarian Indian recipes ("Butter Chicken: Delicious Healthy Country Chicken Recipe").

- Cluster 4 (n°7, 10.08%): *ASMR* cluster. This is exclusively composed of videos produced by the following channel: "Spice ASMR." The owner of the channel is an Indian girl performing a practice called ASMR, which, according to Fredborg et al. stands for "Autonomous Sensory Meridian Response, [that is] a perceptual condition in which the presentation of particular audio-visual stimuli triggers intense, pleasurable tingling sensations in the head and neck regions, which may spread to the periphery of the body" (2017, p. 1). Spice ASMR performs this practice mostly by binge-eating spicy Indian food. See e.g., the post: "ASMR: Chole Bhature *recipe*+ eating Chole Bhature (street food) vegetarian food Mukbang."[7]
- Cluster 5 (n°8, 10.08%): the *Tex-Mex* cluster. This is miscellaneous in terms of channels posting videos but coherent in terms of contents. Similar to Cluster 3, this includes two kinds of posts: videos featuring vegetarian Tex-Mex recipes ("Vegetarian Chili"), and videos featuring non-vegetarian Tex-Mex recipes ("How to Make the Absolute Best Ground Beef Chili").
- Cluster 6 (n°9, 10.08%): *Indonesian* cluster. This includes videos featuring vegetarian Indonesian recipes (see for example "Mask salmon vegetarian untuk kakak tercinta" or "Mask telor[8] vegetarian untuk kakak tercinta"), all posted by Jessica Jane, a young Indonesian youtuber.
- Cluster 7 (n°1, 9.88%): the *Gaming* cluster. This can be considered an off-topic cluster; in fact, all the videos come from "Mythpat" (an Indian gamer). In the videos included in this cluster, words like "vegetarian" or "Indian" appear only occasionally and a bit out of context ("DO NOT become VEGETARIAN in Minecraft (Part 6)").
- Cluster 8 (n°2, 9.88%): the *Entertainment* cluster. Most of the videos included in this cluster are posted by JaiPuru (an Indian duo) and feature funny sketches on vegetarianism (e.g., "Vegetarian v/s Non-Vegetarian") and Indian lifestyle (e.g., "Indians during summer").

---

7   The term Mukbang comes from "the Korean word 먹방, (meokbang), which combines the Korean words for 'eating' (먹는 meongneun) and 'broadcast' (방송 bangsong). [It] is a live-streamed video where viewers watch the host eat. Mukbang is characterised by the copious amount of food consumed during the streaming" (Lawrenson, 2023).
8   Egg.

Cluster of related videos

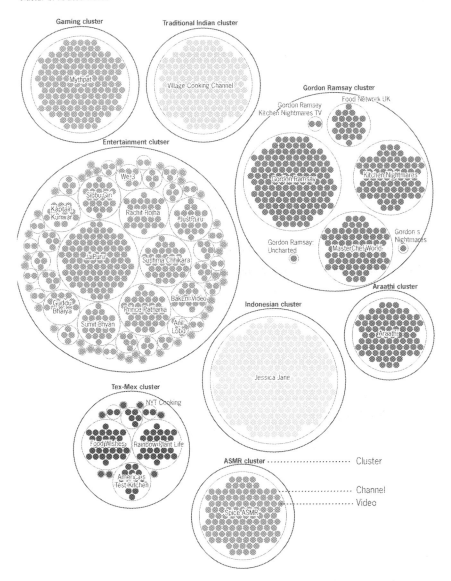

Fig. 2.6. The circles represent the clusters identified by Gephi's algorithm of community detection. The coloured dots represent the videos belonging to each cluster. For some clusters, dots are included in ad hoc sub-circles, which represent the YouTube channels they belong to.

Although we did not find a specific "Vegan" cluster (which we had, in fact, expected), this network analysis largely confirms the results that emerged in the previous keyword analysis. Specifically, the cluster analysis shows that YouTube offers different and variegated venues through which users can "radicalise" their vegetarian teste. Far from proposing a plain meat-less dietary regime and a generic healthy lifestyle, the YouTube platform encourages users to explore Indian, Indonesian, and Tex-Mex cuisine, along with some specific aspects of these cultures. In one case, the platform even proposed a quite extreme way to experience vegetarianism and Indian food: the binge-eating featured by ASMR videos. However, it is also important to highlight that YouTube also offers paths to escape from vegetarianism, see for example Gordon Ramsay's videos or the non-vegetarian recipes featured by Village Cooking Channel or videos composing Cluster 5.

Conclusion and Implications

This brief inquiry into vegetarian culture on YouTube provided us with some interesting insights on the processes of radicalisation of consumption unfolding within the platform. Overall, the data presented in this chapter does not allow us to affirm, definitively, that the YouTube platform is meant to radicalise users and their consumption preferences. Nevertheless, our analysis pointed to several insights that do permit us to argue that some aspects of the YouTube *grammar* and *vernaculars* can favour some processes of radicalisation of vegetarian consumption. First, we observed the emergence of a "grammar of indoctrination" that drives users towards certain patterns of video consumption; that is, we saw that, over 15 years, the YouTube homepage tends to consistently push videos that frame veg-etarianism in a positive way to users. Then, through a further quantitative analysis of the video descriptions, we also noticed that YouTube offers users possible paths to explore more "radical" versions of vegetarianism, namely, veganism, keto vegetarianism, Indian cuisine, and culture. Lastly, the video network analysis permitted us to identify some specific vernaculars; that is, specific ways through which users decline vegetarianism and possibly radicalise it – by, for example, contaminating it with rural Indian cuisine, Indonesian cuisine, vegetarian Tex-Mex cuisine, and even binge-eating practices.

These results led us to a first interesting reflection. We can argue that the process of radicalisation of consumption on YouTube is not necessarily a negative one, or at least may be framed as a neutral one. In fact, with the exception of binge-eating, it is not necessarily detrimental for a vegetarian to "contaminate" her dietary regime and lifestyle with elements of veganism, Indian, Indonesian, and Tex-Mex cuisine as well as Eastern culture – the opposite may be true in fact.

Nonetheless, as said earlier, we identified a significant share of videos that do not point towards radical versions of vegetarianism (see the wide recurrence of generic keywords like "healthy," "diet," "oil," "salt") or even push users away from vegetarianism (see those videos portraying vegetarianism negatively or those featuring non-vegetarian recipes). This last point is crucial since it allows us to draw two key lessons: one theoretical and the other methodological.

Theoretically, the fact that the YouTube platform offers users simultaneous paths to both radicalise and de-radicalise their consumption behaviours, echoes Airoldi and Rokka's theory of "algorithmic articulation" (2022). Airoldi and Rokka establish a dialect relation between algorithmic power and consumer agency; that is, algorithms endow technical features that constrain consumers' activities but, at the same time, consumers manipulate those very features to achieve their own goals. In our case study, we witnessed the same dynamic, but at a (macro) platform level. That is, here we have the platform itself constraining users' behaviours and providing them the means to elude such constraints at once. It is like the YouTube platform incorporates a tension between datafication and liquification (Airoldi and Rokka, 2022[9]): on the one hand, the platform needs to standardise consumer behaviours to more efficiently surveil them; on the other hand, it needs consumer behaviours to be free, unexpected in some way – to encourage users to keep coming back and not to abandon the platform. Therefore, further studies on radicalisation of consumption should explore this aspect more. That is, by using the theme of radicalisation (possibly scaled on different and more heterogeneous consumer topics), scholars should try to better investigate such platform tension between datafication and liquification, and, possibly, ask themselves: which of the two aspects is predominant over the other? Why? Does it depend on the topic of research chosen or on other variables (e.g., the time frame of analysis)? How does this tension impact consumers' imaginary?

Finally, from a methodological point of view, we can conclude that radicalisation of consumption cannot be studied in a *techno-deterministic* way, that is, by implying the existence of some sort of straightforward algorithmic mechanism that, once cracked, allows us to discover causal relations: given the input X (a vegetarian video) we always get the output Y (a video showcasing a more extreme version of vegetarianism). Instead, processes of radicalisation on YouTube must be addressed by employing an holistic approach: the YouTube platform is made by a heterogeneous

9   As mentioned in the Introduction, Airoldi and Rokka identify this tension in the broader consumer culture literature on digitisation.

set of actors, logics, technical features, and users' practices that, together, converge to provide users with certain content, clues, and paths that, under certain circumstances, could drive them to radicalise their consumption tastes. The platform does not oblige users to take the radicalisation path, it simply gives them the opportunity and the instruments to enter the "rabbit hole" of radicalisation of consumption; a path that they will follow only if they are willing to do so

Limits and Further Methodological Strategies

In the end, it is necessary to stress the methodological limits of our research project, too. What we have presented here is a simple exercise; if scholars want to systematically study radicalisation of consumption on YouTube, they definitely need more data and more case studies – for example, by exploring more keywords and topics pointing to different consumption domains. Moreover, a cross-linguistic analysis would be needed to get more refined and accurate results (Moe, 2019); for example, in our case, it is undeniable that the large share of data related to Indian cuisine and culture was determined by our methodological choice to set the region parameter of the YouTube Data Tool as "UK" – a country where the Indian community accounts for 1.4 million people (equating to around 2.5% of the population) (BBC, 2020). Therefore, a cross-linguistic analysis of YouTube could establish whether the link between vegetarianism and Indian cuisine/culture is typical of vegetarian culture or it is a byproduct of our dataset. Finally, to scale up the study of radicalisation of consumption on YouTube, it could be useful to employ a mixed-method approach, in order to try to better understand users' reactions to "radical" contents – for instance by combining digital methods with face-to-face interviews or the monitoring of the browsing history of a panel of participants (Romano et al., 2022).

References

Airoldi, M., and Rokka, J. (2022). Algorithmic consumer culture. *Consumption Markets and Culture*, 25(5), 411–428. https://doi.org/10.1080/10253866.2022.2084726.

Airoldi, M. (2021). The techno-social reproduction of taste boundaries on digital platforms: The case of music on YouTube. *Poetics*, *89*, https://doi.org/10.1016/j.poetic.2021.101563.

Airoldi, M., Beraldo, D., and Gandini, A. (2016). Follow the algorithm: An exploratory investigation of music on YouTube. *Poetics, 57*, 1–13. https://doi.org/10.1016/j. poetic.2016.05.001.

Altheide, D. (1987). Reflections: Ethnographic content analysis. *Qualitative Sociology, 10*, 65–77. https://doi.org/10.1007/BF00988269.

Bastian, M., Heymann, S., and Jacomy, M. (2009). Gephi: An open source software for exploring and manipulating networks. In Proceedings of the international AAAI conference on web and social media (vol. 3, no. 1, pp. 361–362).

BBC (2020). BAME we're not the same: Indian. https://www.bbc.co.uk/creative-diversity/nuance-in-bame/indian/#:~:text=Made%20up%20of%201.4%20million,within%20the%20global%20Indian%20diaspora.

Beer, D. (2017). The social power of algorithms. *Information, Communication and Society, 20*(1), 1–13. https://doi.org/10.1080/1369118X.2016.1216147.

Bishop, S. (2019). Managing visibility on YouTube through algorithmic gossip. *New Media and Society, 21*(11/12), 2589–2606. https://doi.org/10.1177/1461444819854731.

Caliandro A. and Gandini A. (2017). *Qualitative research in digital environments: A research toolkit*. Routledge.

Faddoul, M., Chaslot, G., and Farid, H. (2020). A longitudinal analysis of YouTube's promotion of conspiracy videos. *ArXiv*. http://arxiv.org/abs/2003.03318.

Fredborg, B., Clark, J., and Smith, S. D. (2017). An examination of personality traits associated with autonomous sensory meridian response (ASMR). *Frontiers in Psychology, 8*(247). https://doi.org/10.3389/fpsyg.2017.00247.

Greenebaum, J. (2012). Veganism, identity and the quest for authenticity. *Food, Culture and Society, 15*(1), 129–144. https://doi.org/10.2752/175174412X13190510222101.

Hosseinmardi, H., Ghasemian, A., Clauset, A., Mobius, M., Rothschild, D. M., and Watts, D. J. (2021). Examining the consumption of radical content on YouTube. *Proceedings of the National Academy of Sciences, 118*(32), e2101967118. https://doi.org/10.1073/pnas.2101967118.

Jacomy, M., Venturini, T., Heymann, S., and Bastian, M. (2014). ForceAtlas2, a continuous graph layout algorithm for handy network visualization designed for the Gephi software. *PloS one, 9*(6), e98679. https://doi.org/10.1371/journal. pone.0098679.

Janda, S. and Trocchia, P. J. (2001). Vegetarianism: Toward a greater understanding. *Psychology and Marketing, 18*(12), 1205–1240. https://doi.org/10.1002/mar.1050.

Krippendorff, K. (2012). *Content analysis: An introduction to its methodology*. Sage.

Lawrenson, E. (2023, June 13). What is mukbang? And why is it so popular? https://www.qustodio.com/en/blog/what-is-mukbang/.

Matamoros-Fernandez, A., Gray, J. E., Bartolo, L., Burgess, J., and Suzor, N. (2021). What's "up next"? Investigating algorithmic recommendations on YouTube across issues and over time. *Media and Communication*, 9(4), 234–249. https:// doi.org/10.17645/mac.v9i4.4184.

Mawer, R (2023, November 7). The ketogenic diet: A detailed beginner's guide to keto. https://www.healthline.com/nutrition/ketogenic-diet-101#:~:text=%3E-,Keto%20 basics,a%20metabolic%20state%20called%20ketosis.

McLachlan, S. and Cooper, P. (2023, April 18). How the YouTube algorithm works in 2023: The complete guide. Hootsuite. https://blog.hootsuite.com/ how-the-youtube-algorithm-works/.

Mittiga, C. (2022, November 16). Copyright protection: A content creator's guide to YouTube. https://legalvision.com.au/content-creators-guide-youtube/.

Moe, H. (2019). Comparing platform "ranking cultures" across languages: The case of Islam on YouTube in Scandinavia. *Social Media+ Society*, 5(1), https://journals. sagepub.com/doi/full/10.1177/2056305118817038.

Munger, K. and Phillips, J. (2022). Right-wing YouTube: A supply and demand perspective. *The International Journal of Press/Politics*, 27(1), 186–219. https:// doi.org/10.1177/1940161220964767.

O'Callaghan, D., Greene, D., Conway, M., Carthy, J., and Cunningham, P. (2015). Down the (white) rabbit hole: The extreme right and online recommender systems. *Social Science Computer Review*, 33(4), 459–478. https://doi. org/10.1177/0894439314555329.

Ribeiro, M. H., Ottoni, R., West, R., Almeida, V. A. F, and Meira, W. (2020). Auditing radicalization pathways on YouTube. In M. H. Ribeiro, R. Ottoni, R. West, and V. A. F. Almeida, W. Meira (Eds.), *Proceedings of the 2020 conference on fairness, accountability, and transparency* (pp. 131–141). ACM.

Rieder, B. (2015, May 4). Introducing YouTube Data Tools: The politics of systems. http://thepoliticsofsystems.net/?s=youtube.

Rieder, B. (2023, May 3). YouTube Data Tools – Overview (May 2023). https://www. youtube.com/watch?v=TmF4mWZYnbkandt=39s.

Rieder, B., Matamoros-Fernández, A., and Coromina, O. (2018). From ranking algorithms to "ranking cultures": Investigating the modulation of visibility in YouTube search results. *Convergence*, 24(1), 50–68. https://doi.org/10.1177/1354856517736982.

Rieder, B., Coromina, Ò., and Matamoros-Fernández, A. (2020). Mapping YouTube: A quantitative exploration of a platformed media system. *First Monday*, 25(8). https://doi.org/10.5210/fm.v25i8.10667.

Rieder, B., Borra, E., Coromina, Ò., and Matamoros-Fernández, A. (2023). Making a Living in the creator economy: A large-scale study of linking on YouTube. *Social Media+ Society*, 9(2), https://doi.org/10.1177/20563051231180628.

Rogers, R. (2019). *Doing digital methods*. Sage.

Romano, S., Polidoro, A., Corona, G, Kerby, N., Rama, I., and Giorgi, G. (3 July 2022). Non-logged-in children using YouTube: How does YouTube use data about non-logged-in under 18 users? What adverts, and potentially harmful content, are they exposed to? Tracking Exposed Special Report. https://tracking.exposed/ pdf/youtube-non-logged-kids-03July2022.pdf.

Savage, M. (2009). Contemporary sociology and the challenge of descriptive assemblage. *European Journal of Social Theory*, *12*(1), 155–174. https://doi. org/10.1177/1368431008099650.

Spink, A. and Jansen, B. J. (2004). *Web search: Public searching of the web*. Springer Netherlands.

Thomson, C. (2020, September 18). YouTube's plot to silence conspiracy theories. https://www.wired.com/story/youtube-algorithm-silence-conspiracy-theories/.

Timmer, J. (2021, August 8). If YouTube algorithms radicalize users, data doesn't show it. https://www.wired.com/story/youtube-algorithms-radicalization-data-doesnt-show-it/.

Tufekci, Z. (2018, March 10). YouTube, the great radicalizer. *New York Times*. https:// www.nytimes.com/2018/03/10/opinion/sunday/youtube-politics-radical.html.

Van Dijck, J. and Poell, T. (2013). Understanding social media logic. *Media and Communication*, *1*(1), 2–14. https://ssrn.com/abstract=2309065.

Weiss, G. (2019, October 23). Penn State study posits YouTube's algorithm isn't to blame for far-right radicalization. https://www.tubefilter.com/2019/10/23/ penn-state-study-youtube-algorithm-isnt-to-blame/.

YouTube. (n.d.). How does YouTube provide more quality information to users? https://www.youtube.com/intl/ALL_au/howyoutubeworks/our-commitments/ fighting-misinformation/#raising-quality-info.

YouTube (n.d.). Search: list. https://developers.google.com/youtube/v3/docs/search/ list.

3. The Platformisation of Music Genres on Spotify

Abstract

Existing research on music consumption suggests that, in recent years, the preferences of music listeners have shifted from a genre-based kind of consumption, where listening habits are shaped around typical music styles (e.g., rock, pop, metal, folk, etc.), to "situational" forms, where moods and the social context wherein music is listened to play a more important role than the adherence to a particular genre. In this chapter we employ the newly created SpotiGem tool to query the Spotify API and thus analyse a set of genre-based playlists vis-à-vis mood-based ones, to observe the extent to which playlist composition has shifted away from genre-specific boundaries. We show that genre consistency still maintains significant relevance in playlist construction, for both users and the Spotify platform, and that even in "mood-based" or "situation-based" playlists there tends to be a certain convergence towards a small number of genres, as opposed to an increase in heterogeneity.

Keywords: genre, mood, playlists, situational consumption, SpotiGem

Music listening – a quintessential instance of cultural consumption – has been heavily subjected to the logics of platformisation. This should be read in the context of the wider process of "liquidisation" of consumption fostered by digital media (Bardhi and Eckhardt, 2016), which has inevitably involved music too. Beginning in the late 1990s with the diffusion of the internet, the popularisation of digital media radically overturned the music business as a whole. Before then, music consumption was mainly centred around the ownership of physical records – vinyl and, later, CDs. The invention and subsequent popularisation of the MPEG encoding format – the technical baseline of the MP3, today's commonplace standard for digital music files – significantly reduced the file size of music tracks, paving the way for their

Caliandro, A., A. Gandini, L. Bainotti, G. Anselmi, *The Platformisation of Consumer Culture: A Digital Methods Guide*. Amsterdam: Amsterdam University Press, 2024
DOI 10.5117/9789463729567_CH03

unregulated circulation across digital peer-to-peer services – particularly, Napster (Gandini, 2021). At the turn of the century, this produced a significant economic downturn for the entire sector, as traditional pathways to profit were substantially upended. It is estimated that music sales experienced a shrinkage of about 53% worldwide in the early 2000s, while record labels, artists, and other actors involved struggled to adapt to the incipient digital ecosystem (for a discussion on the transition towards digital music, see Arditi, 2015).

From this transition phase, the platform model emerged as that around which the music industry as a whole ultimately coalesced. Since its foundation in 2005, YouTube has been the go-to social media for free music listening and it remains broadly relevant for this purpose. Yet, the process of platformisation of music listening essentially became synonymous with the rise of Spotify. Founded in 2006, in Sweden, Spotify launched in the US in 2011 – and internationally soon thereafter – explicitly branding itself as the new standard for legal digital music streaming. Spotify promoted a model of "freemium" music access, whereby consumers could either browse a large catalogue for free, subject to advertising exposure, or pay a monthly subscription to obtain advertising-free access to music and enjoy extended features (see Eriksson et al., 2018). At the time of writing, Spotify accounts for about 30% of the global market share of digital music platforms, followed by Apple Music (15%), Amazon Music and Tencent, both at 13% (Mulligan, 2022).

Paraphrasing Bardhi and Eckhardt (2012) it may be said that, over the short span of 20 years, everyday music listening practices shifted almost entirely from an ownership-based to an "access-based" consumption practice. Throughout this process, platforms were successful in remediating and newly ring-fencing listening practices within a single socio-technical environment. In so doing, they enabled the large-scale collection of data about individual music listening preferences and their subjection to profit-making activities (Hesmondhalgh and Meier, 2018). From the consumers' side, this was accompanied by a new set of everyday listening habits. In particular, algorithmic recommender systems (Airoldi et al., 2016; Seaver, 2018; Prey, 2019) have come to represent a significant element of novelty in this context. As a key affordance of music platforms, algorithmic recommender systems present users with automatic, data-driven music suggestions, learning from an individual's existing patterns and preferences (Airoldi, 2021). Yet, as with other platform environments, we know little about the ways in which music recommendations are algorithmically produced and proffered to users on Spotify and similar services, as these algorithms remain "black boxed" and often observable solely via "reverse engineering," i.e., monitoring the outputs of the algorithmic processes by controlling the input without knowing the actual steps occurring in between (cf. Pasquale, 2015). Moreover, the strategies deployed by platforms while developing these algorithms are also "black-boxed" as software developers are often required to sign non-disclosure agreements and are prevented from discussing such matters with researchers (Bonini and Gandini, 2020).

Specific to the music setting, the combination of increased access to content and algorithmic forms of recommendation has led to the diffusion of consumption practices that actually signal a move away from consumer preferences based on music genres, in favour of more diversified habits. Contextually, we have seen the concomitant rise of "situational" practices of consumption, whereby moods and the social context of listening become more important than adherence to a certain stylistic canon, or belonging to a given subcultural milieu (Airoldi et al., 2016; Airoldi, 2021). This is so relevant that, since February 2021, Spotify has permitted users to organise their Liked Songs library distinguishing by genre or mood (Newsroom Spotify, 2021). This shift also coincides with the growing centrality of playlists in digital music streaming practices. Marked by a blend of editorial and algorithmic logics (Bonini and Gandini, 2019), during the 2010s, playlists affirmed themselves as the main means of platform music consumption, allegedly assuming primacy over albums as a more dynamic and flexible affordance, which allows for greater personalisation (Prey et al., 2022).

Consequently, playlists represent a natural point of entry for a digital methods inquiry on the study of platformised music consumption. In this chapter, we employ digital methods to query the Spotify API and qualitatively investigate the grammars and vernaculars concerning the composition of playlists on Spotify. In doing so, we focus on three types of playlists: genre-based, mood-based, and situation-based, to observe the extent to which playlist composition might provide evidence of a move away from genre-based practices of listening. In particular, we ask: *what role does genre play in playlist composition on Spotify? To what extent do Spotify-created playlists based on moods and situations entail genre in their composition? To what extent do user-created playlists based on moods and situations entail genre in their composition?*

The Tool: SpotiGem Hub

To do so, we employ *SpotiGem Hub* (https://spotigem.lim.di.unimi.it). This is the outcome of a collaboration between researchers at the Departments of Social and Political Sciences, Informatics, and Cultural and Environmental

Heritage, at the University of Milan. First released in October 2021, SpotiGem Hub (hereafter, SpotiGem) is a tool that allows us to query the Spotify API for all publicly available data on playlists hosted on the platform. This includes the genre associated with each artist in the playlist, together with basic song data as well as a variety of audio features, such as key, tempo, "danceability," and "loudness," among others. SpotiGem obviously relies on the (huge) genre taxonomy produced by Spotify, which is the result of editorial and data-driven elaborations derived from *The Echo Nest*, a music intelligence and data platform acquired by Spotify itself in 2014. A constantly updated rendition of genre taxonomies employed by Spotify can be found on the website *Every Noise At Once* in the form of an algorithmically generated, readability-adjusted scatter plot based on Spotify data and tracked and analysed for genre-shaped distinctions.[1] Spotify playlists can be searched on SpotiGem via the playlist ID, which is what follows the standard url root: https://open.spotify.com/playlist/ in any playlist url, and which can be retrieved from Spotify itself. Like other API-calling digital methods tools, SpotiGem requires the researcher to log into Spotify in order to produce its calls. This does not affect the validity of data collection, as the search is based on individual playlists and not on algorithmically recommended data (more on this later in the chapter). Data collected via SpotiGem can also be downloaded as a .csv file for further elaboration.

Data Collection

As a first step, we started by querying different types of playlists based on a conventionally established music genre. This has the important advantage of countering the potentially "obvious" result that, in absolute terms, genre-based playlists are less diverse in terms of genre composition than mood-based and situation-based ones, if randomly chosen. We can reduce this potential bias by searching for different types of playlists within the same genre pool.

To select these playlists, and in order to circumvent Spotify's personalisation algorithms, which learn from a user's listening habits to tailor personalised content recommendations, we relied on Chosic,[2] a website that, among other things, categorises Spotify playlists on the basis of parameters that are not available from the main Spotify platform – for instance, ordering the most followed playlists by genre. Thus, we used Chosic to search for the

1   See: https://everynoise.com and https://artists.spotify.com/en/blog/how-spotify-discovers-the-genres-of-tomorrow.
2   See: https://www.chosic.com/best-spotify-playlists/.

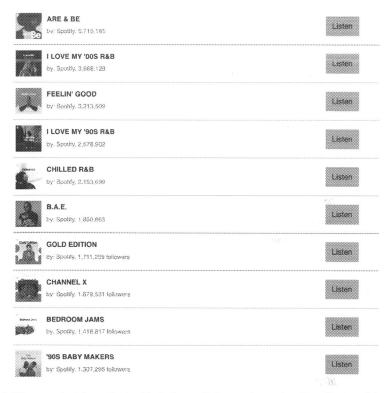

Best Rnb playlists on Spotify

If somebody in R&B is doing something that matters right now, you'll find it here.

ARE & BE
by Spotify, 5,715,185
Listen

I LOVE MY '00S R&B
by Spotify, 3,666,128
Listen

FEELIN' GOOD
by Spotify, 3,213,509
Listen

I LOVE MY '90S R&B
by Spotify, 2,678,902
Listen

CHILLED R&B
by Spotify, 2,153,699
Listen

B.A.E.
by Spotify, 1,850,663
Listen

GOLD EDITION
by Spotify, 1,711,259 followers
Listen

CHANNEL X
by Spotify, 1,679,531 followers
Listen

BEDROOM JAMS
by Spotify, 1,416,817 followers
Listen

'90S BABY MAKERS
by Spotify, 1,307,295 followers
Listen

Fig. 3.1. This screenshot shows the top 10 playlists on RnB appearing on Spotify at the time of the search, according to the Chosic ranking.

top 10 playlists ranked by followers, based on a conventional genre: in our case, RnB (see Fig. 3.1). From this search, the playlist "Are and Be" emerges as the one with the largest follower count (more than 5 million users on the date of data collection). Interestingly, we can see that mood-based and situation-based playlists are also present in this ranking. See, for instance, the playlist entitled "Feelin good" (position 3), or "Chilled rnb" (position 5), which are clearly driven by mood, or "Bedroom Jams" (position 9), which makes explicit reference to the social situation of "jamming" songs in one's bedroom. We can also observe the presence of generational playlists, which enlist music by decades, at positions 2 ("I love my '00s RnB") and 4 ("I Love my '90s RnB"), respectively. This suggests that listeners of RnB on Spotify are mainly interested in RnB music originating from these decades. Finally, the

Fig. 3.2. This screenshot shows the SpotiGem interface when searching for a Spotify playlist.

playlist entitled "90s Baby Makers," at position 10, is also interesting, since it blends the generational element with a reference to a social situation, nodding at an intimate and romantic setting.

Based on this preliminary search, we decided to focus on "Are & Be" as a genre-based playlist, "Chilled R&B" as a mood-based playlist, and "Bedroom Jams" as a situation-based playlist. These are all generated by Spotify, and have the same number of songs (50). This allows us to investigate platform grammars in playlist composition styles in a consistent way, and thus question the extent of their diversification on the basis of playlist type.

We begin with Are and Be. After inserting the playlist ID into SpotiGem, we are taken to a dashboard that contains clickable information about each song and features a button that allows for the downloading of the full .csv file (Fig. 3.2). Moving down the page, we find an interactive visualisation tool, which displays genre breakdown by song.[3] This feature can also be used to navigate other song parameters, such as "key," "tempo," and much more. We perform this operation for all the three playlists selected and download the .csv file for each of them, so that we can proceed with more elaborate analyses if we want to.

Platform Grammars/1: Playlist Composition within the Same Genre

Table 3.1 reports a breakdown of the top unique artists (also considering collaborations) that appear in the "Are & Be" playlist. We can see that the band The Weeknd appears four times, followed by Muni Long, Silk Sonic (a

---

3   Commonly, each song on Spotify has more than one genre appended to it. The SpotiGem tool separates individual genres appended to each song, and calculates their frequency.

collaboration between Anderson.Paak and Bruno Mars), and Kehlani, all appearing three times. Five other artists appear twice.

Table 3.1. "Are & Be," unique artists

Artist	Frequency
The Weeknd	4
Muni Long	3
Silk Sonic	3
Kehlani	3
Lucky Daye	2
Jazmine Sullivan	2
Ella Mai	2
Chris Brown	2
Syd	2

If we look at the genre breakdown for this playlist (Fig. 3.3) as elaborated through the SpotiGem dashboard, there seems to be a convergence towards two main genres: "pop" and "r&b", followed by "dance pop" and "urban contemporary."

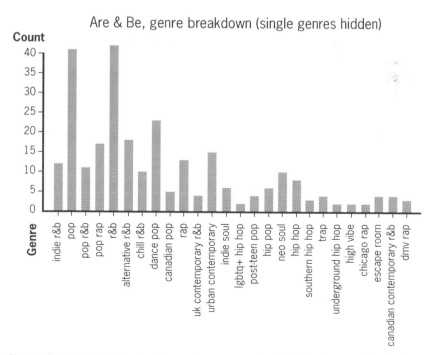

Fig. 3.3. This image shows the breakdown of genres appearing in the Spotify-created playlist "Are and Be," elaborated by SpotiGem.

The playlist "Chilled R&B" features a similar set of artists (Table 3.2). Here, Lucky Daye appears four times, while seven other artists appear twice.

Table 3.2.   "Chilled R&B," unique artists

Artist	Frequency
Lucky Daye	6
Kehlani	2
Summer Walker	2
The Weekend	2
Safe	2
Kenyon Dixon	2
Eric Bellinger	2
Jojo	2

If we look at the genre breakdown for this playlist (Fig. 3.4), we can see a similar prevalence of two main genres: "pop" and "r&b". Yet, we can also see the growth of "alternative r&b" and "indie r&b," which signals an attempt to diversify the playlist towards a more specific public. Greater genre variation could be expected here; however, as in the case of "Are & Be," we can observe a

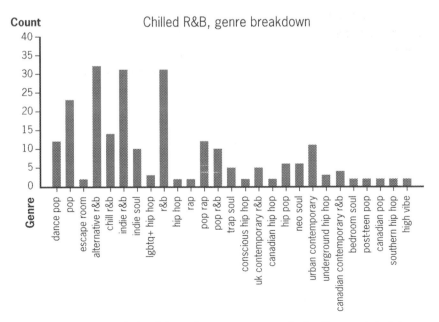

Fig. 3.4. This image shows the breakdown of genres appearing in the Spotify-created playlist "Chilled R&B," elaborated by SpotiGem.

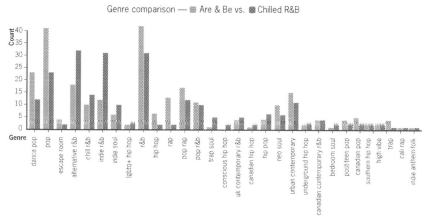

Fig. 3.5. This image shows the comparison of genres appearing in the Spotify-created playlists "Are and Be" (green) and "Chilled R&B" (purple), elaborated by SpotiGem.

certain genre consistency around a handful of specific labels. We can further appreciate this insight if we contrast the two playlists via the Compare Playlists feature of SpotiGem (Fig. 3.5). While genre-specificity decreases slightly, our mood-based playlist mainly revolves around a small number of genres.

The situation-based playlists "Bedroom Jams" (Table 3.3) taps into a specific listening context, a nod to the DJ figure who "jams" records on her decks in the intimate setting of the bedroom. We can see that the artists featured in this playlist are very similar to those included in the previous ones, albeit with some important differences, which point to a further refinement of the type of music included in this collection. This is seemingly more focused on alternative, young artists.

Table 3.3.   "Bedroom Jams," unique artists

Artists	Frequency
Lucky Daye	4
Tanerelle	2
Snoh Aalegra	2
LAYA	2
Syd	2
Shelley FKA DRAM	2
Femme It Forward	2

This insight is confirmed by the analysis of genre composition (Fig. 3.6), where "alternative r&b" takes primacy. Yet again, a certain genre consistency

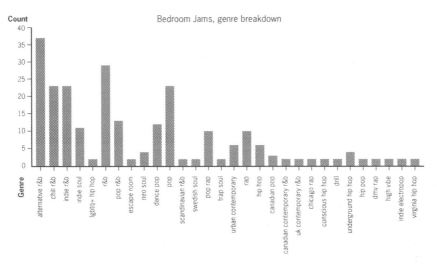

Fig. 3.6. This image shows the breakdown of genres appearing in the Spotify-created playlist "Bedroom Jams," elaborated by SpotiGem.

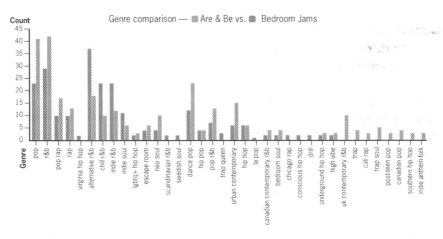

Fig. 3.7. This image shows the comparison of genres appearing in the Spotify-created playlists "Are & Be" (green) and "Bedroom Jams" (blue), elaborated by SpotiGem.

can be observed around a small number of genre labels. This can be fully appreciated in Fig. 3.7, which presents a comparison between "Are and Be" (our main playlist) and "Bedroom Jams."

This analysis suggests that, while we can see a tendency towards increased diversification of genres in mood-based and situation-based playlists, a certain genre-centrality continues to exist in playlists that are principled on a certain mood or situation. While this insight cannot be generalised, it nonetheless suggests that playlist composition practices by Spotify tend to prioritise a small number of genre labels for consistency purposes, so as to address a specific public. We may ask what changes if the starting point of the consumption experience is not a conventionally defined music genre, such as r&b, but is instead the mood or the situation itself, and whether greater diversification in genre labels can actually be observed in such cases.

Platform Grammars/2: Playlist Composition across Genres

To this end, using the same procedure illustrated earlier, we collected and analysed data related to a situation-based set of playlists: those revolving around "workout." Here, however, we decided to take three Spotify-created playlists that include our search term – "workout" – in their title. Specifically, these are: "Workout," which features around 4.6 million followers at the time of writing, and includes 100 songs; "Workout Beats," which has around 1.1 million followers and 40 songs; and "Workout Hits," which has around 420,000 followers and 60 songs. Like the RnB playlists previously analysed, these are all created by Spotify. Given their taxonomic similarity, it seems interesting to investigate how they differ in terms of genre composition with a view to questioning why Spotify gets to create different products with essentially the same name.

Beginning with "Workout," Table 3.4 (below) provides an overview of the unique artists appearing more than once in the playlist. Dua Lipa and Griff top this chart with four songs, either alone or in collaboration with others. Looking at the genre breakdown (Fig. 3.8), this shows a comprehensively greater diversification in the "long tail" of genres when compared to the previously observed r&b playlists. Yet again, this mood-based playlist seems to be centred around a handful of main genres – in this case, "pop," "electropop," and "dance pop." It appears as though the "Workout" playlist, while, at first glance, is more heterogeneous, still maintains a significant genre consistency.

Table 3.4.   "Workout," unique artists

Artists	Frequency
Dua Lipa	4
Griff	3
bülow	3
Years and Years	3
Lights	2

Artists	Frequency
Charli XCX	2
The Weeknd	2
Sigrid	2
MØ	2
Miley Cyrus	2
Conan Gray	2
Twenty One Pilots	2
Bastille	2
Adele	2
Majid Jordan	2
Lizzo	2

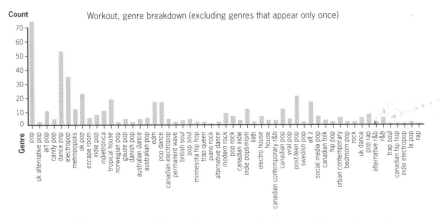

Fig. 3.8. This image shows the breakdown of genres appearing in the Spotify-created playlist "Workout", elaborated by SpotiGem.

Concerning "Workout Beats" (Table 3.5), while some artists who feature in "Workout" (e.g. Years and Years, Charli XCX) are included, overall it includes a different set of performers. The genre breakdown (Fig. 3.9) confirms that this playlist is more diverse in terms of genre composition than "Workout." Alongside "pop" and related sub-genres, here we also find genre labels such as "edm," "house," and related sub-genres (e.g. "deep house"), which signals a clearer interest in engaging with diversified publics.

Table 3.5. "Workout Beats," unique artists

Artists	COUNTA di Frequency
Fatboy Slim	4
Charli XCX	3

Artists	COUNTA di *Frequency*
RÜFÜS DU SOL	2
Mylo	2
Years and Years	2
Sofi Tukker	2
Roger Sanchez	2
Purple Disco Machine	2
Nina Simone	2
Miley Cyrus	2
Cosmo's Midnight	2
AlunaGeorge	2
Aluna	2

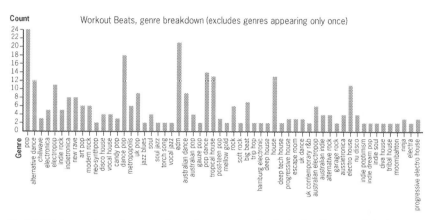

Fig. 3.9. This image shows the comparison of genres appearing in the Spotify-created playlist "Workout Beats," elaborated by SpotiGem.

Concerning "Workout Hits" (Table 3.6), we can see that the set of unique artists included in this playlist is notably different from both "Workout" and "Workout Beats." The genre breakdown (Fig. 3.10) graph confirms that we are confronted with a playlist that clearly revolves around two main genres: dance and house music. Qualitatively, this playlist seems to be akin to "Workout Beats" as it features a rather coherent set of dance and house songs. However, while diversification increases, only a handful of genres are prominent. This confirms the insight that mood-based and situation-based playlists created by Spotify, albeit more diverse overall than genre-based ones, are still built around a small number of genres. In particular, these playlists seem to differ from one another mostly as an attempt to tap into different music publics, aiming at engaging users who relate to the same social situation but whose music taste varies across the high-tempo and danceability spectrum.

Table 3.6.   "Workout Hits," unique artists

Artists	Frequency
Tiësto	3
Alesso	3
VIZE	2
MEDUZA	2
LIZOT	2
Gabry Ponte	2
Armin van Buuren	2
Alok	2
ACRAZE	2
Cherish	2

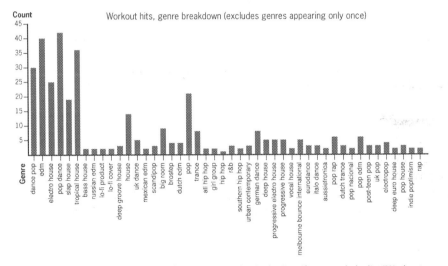

Fig. 3.10. This image is a comparison of genres appearing in the Spotify-created playlist "Workout Hits," elaborated by SpotiGem.

To corroborate this latter hypothesis, we extracted data about these playlists concerning "tempo," which identifies how fast a certain song is, and "danceability," which is a statistical elaboration (based on undisclosed parameters) that approximates how much one is likely to dance to a certain song on a range between 0 (minimum) and 1 (maximum).[4] For "Workout," we can see that this has a danceability measure around 0.679, which is the benchmark value. If we look at "Workout Beats" instead, we note that the "tempo"

4   Interestingly, both "tempo" and "danceability" are classified by Spotify as "mood" measures, see: https://developer.spotify.com/discover/.

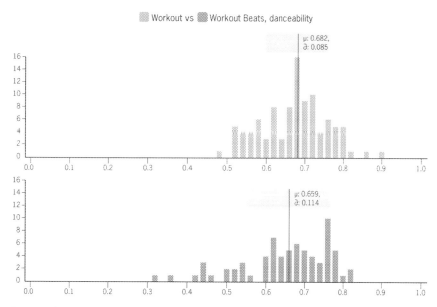

Fig. 3.11. This image shows the comparison of "danceability" parameters between the Spotify-created playlists "Workout" (grey) and "Workout Beats" (orange), elaborated by SpotiGem.

increases slightly when compared to "Workout," as does the "danceability" measure (Fig. 3.11). This reveals a comprehensively more "dynamic" playlist. Fig. 3.12 below accounts shows the danceability comparison.

Regarding "Workout Hits," we can see that its emphasis on dance and house music is clearly reflected in the average tempo, as songs included in this playlist have a greater number of beats per minute (bpm) when compared to the others observed here. Interestingly, the "danceability" chart is more mixed, with greater internal diversification in relation to this parameter when playlists are compared. Overall, these graphs closely mirror the compositional features of each of these playlists, and reflect their specificities. Fig. 3.13 visualises a comparison between "Workout" and "Workout Hits."

Overall, these elaborations seem to corroborate the hypothesis that, despite the popularity of situation-based and mood-based playlists, which suggests a move away from genre-based music consumption, Spotify-created playlists remain constructed around a remarkable genre coherency and consistency. While, obviously, many other examples of playlists can (and ought to) be analysed in order to fully corroborate this insight, it can be argued that genre remains an important dimension in the grammars of playlist composition by curators of the Spotify platform. Genre emerges from this account as an ever-important axis for the organisation and coordination of listening practices by

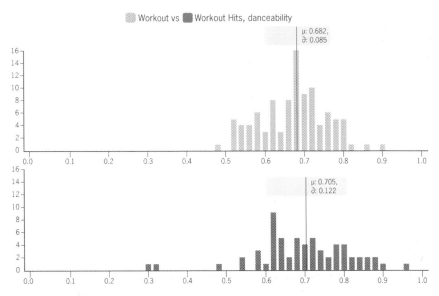

Fig. 3.12. This image is a comparison of "danceability" parameters between the Spotify-created playlist "Workout" (grey) and "Workout Hits" (pink), elaborated by SpotiGem.

music streaming platforms such as Spotify. While algorithms and data-driven processes substantially influence decision-making processes (Bonini and Gandini, 2019), these results suggest that playlist curation practices on Spotify continue to take into consideration the genre variable, which obviously affects the inclusion of certain artists in given playlists and their juxtaposition with others. The persistent centrality of genre in the grammars of composition of Spotify-created playlists leads us to the conclusion that music streaming platforms continue to see genre as an important cultural mediator between, on the one hand, users' listening cultures, which platforms must organise and coordinate for data collection purposes, and algorithmic optimisation (Prey et al., 2022). In particular, the different workout playlists examined here evidence that, even when looking at very similar digital objects, the grammars of playlist composition can differ greatly, as a result of the intention to target different publics interested in the same social situation (see Airoldi, 2022).

On the Consumer Side: Genre and Platform Vernaculars in User-Created Playlists

In order to investigate platform vernaculars concerning playlist composition, we need to look at user-created playlists on Spotify and compare these with the grammars of Spotify-created playlists. To this end, we turned again to the SpotiGem tool. Among its features, SpotiGem also permits the collection and analysis of playlist consumption and production by a single user if s/he logins into SpotiGem with their own Spotify credentials. For this purpose, we assembled a set of 25 research participants[5] who, having given their informed consent, logged onto the SpotiGem platform and had their playlist consumption and production monitored for a period of one month. This allowed us to collect data about which playlists users liked and created on the platform during this period, and thus investigate the cultural logics that characterise them. The users involved in this component of the research are between 19–25 of age and based in Italy. Of these, 14 are men and 11 are women. Only two of them do not have any university education; all the others either have a university degree or are studying to obtain one. Prior to the tracking of their playlist consumption and production, participants attended a focus group discussion, through which we collected self-reported data about their music preferences, playlist curation, and listening practices.

Overall, the playlists created by our participants are a diverse mix of situation-based, mood-based, genre-based, and artist-based ones. For the purposes of this chapter, we analysed three playlists created by three differ-ent users with different music preferences. The first one is a situation-based playlist created by a user with a self-described "diverse" taste, who reports listening habits that regularly adapt to the situation s/he is involved in. This playlist features 29 songs, and its title references a romantic dinner (actual playlist titles are omitted for anonymisation purposes). A list of unique artists included in this playlist is presented in Table 3.7, below. This is consistent with the self-description of an eclectic music listener whose main taste is anchored in Italian music, but it reveals a degree of temporal and genre variety.

Table 3.7.   Situation-based playlist, user-created, unique artists (appearing more than once)

Artists	Frequency
Fred again	4
Motta	3
Woodkid	2
Venerus	2

5   Research participants were recruited by means of an open call, circulated online, which asked for volunteers to participate in a study on the relevance of music genres in digital music consumption. Information is available at: https://spotigem.unimi.it.

Artists	Frequency
MACE	2
Negramaro	2
Liberato	2
Kings of Convenience	2
James Blake	2

The genre breakdown (Fig. 3.14) of this playlist shows a significant diversi-fication of styles. Different from the Spotify-created playlists seen earlier, a variety of genres appear more than once. Among them, genres related to Ital-ian music, such as "Italian indie pop" and "pop," feature more prominently, together with a set of diverse labels, such as "Italian hip hop" and "Italian rnb." This playlist seems to be quite diverse in terms of composition, which may be indicative of a user who actually moves across different genre labels, albeit within the broad context of Italian music.

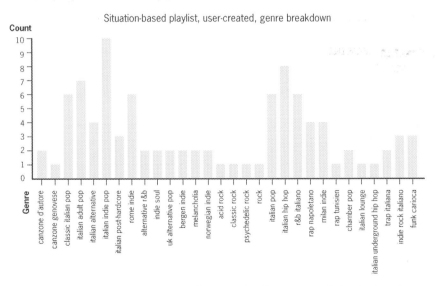

Fig. 3.13. This image shows the breakdown of genres within the user-created, situation-based playlist examined, elaborated by SpotiGem.

Then, we observe a genre-based playlist, created by a user who self-describes as a listener who is primarily interested in the most popular tracks of the moment. In particular, we focus on a playlist with a title that refers to '90s dance music, thus showing a generational-based and genre-based selection. The playlist contains 100 songs. Table 3.8 (below) shows a list of artists who appear in it more than once.

Table 3.8.   Genre-based playlist, user-created, artist breakdown

Artists	Frequency
Eiffel 65	8
Gabry Ponte	6
Gigi D'Agostino	2
Raffaella Carrà	2
Prezioso/Marvin	2
Miani/Godzilla	2
Il Pagante	2
Finley	2
DJ Ross	2
Dari	2
Articolo 31	2

While the artists included in this playlist seem to be quite coherent with its title, some outliers also stand out. Raffaella Carrà, for instance, is an Italian pop and dance artist who was active across three decades, starting

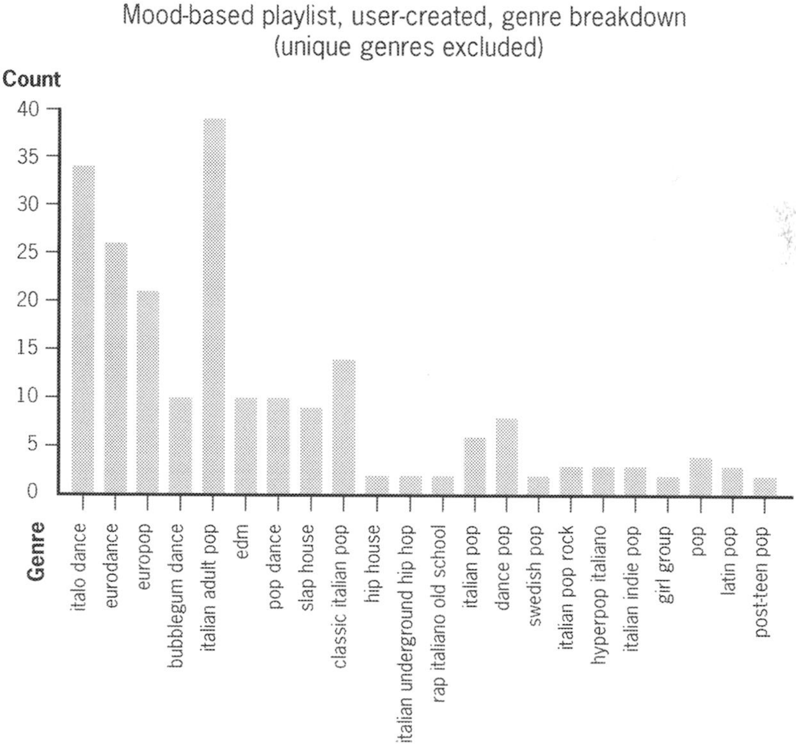

Fig. 3.14. This image shows the breakdown of genres within the user-created, genre-based playlist examined, elaborated by SpotiGem.

from the 1960s, and her songs included in this playlist do not belong to the 1990s. The artist Il Pagante appears twice despite only being active since the 2010s. Articolo 31, who have been quite eclectic across their career, are commonly considered a rap act (albeit from the 1990s). The genre breakdown of this playlist (Fig. 3.15) reveals a consistent composition style around dance-related genres; yet, it presents signs of diversification and genre multiplication, also including genres such as "classic Italian pop" and "Italian underground hip hop," despite its main focus being on a "traditional" genre category (dance).

Lastly, we take a playlist from a self-described "subcultural" user who has a strong preference for rock and alternative rock music. In this case, we have a mood-based playlist containing 138 songs, with a title that refers to "sadness." From the artist breakdown (Table 3.9), we can see a good correspondence between their self-described taste and the composition of this playlist, which features a set of alternative international rock artists. Genre breakdown (Fig. 3.15) shows a fair degree of diversification despite their self-reported subcultural taste. While the most recurrent genre labels sit coherently within the broad genre category of rock and alternative rock, this user's composition of a "sad" playlist shows clear signs of a diversified approach, which takes her favourite genre as a main point of reference but is open to including other types of music.

Table 3.9.   Mood-based playlist, user-created, unique artists (appearing only once)

Artists	Frequency
Metallica	9
Linkin Park	8
My Chemical Romance	5
Lady Gaga	5
Slipknot	4
Five Finger Death Punch	4
Tonight Alive	3
Three Days Grace	3
The Fray	2
Stone Sour	2
Maneskin	2
System Of A Down	2
Achille Lauro	2

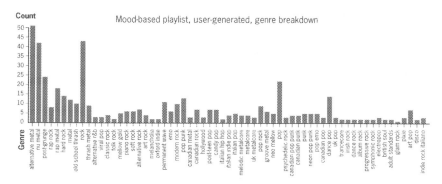

Fig. 3.15. This image shows the breakdown of genres within the user-created, mood-based playlist examined, elaborated by SpotiGem.

Overall, these elaborations show that users' playlist vernaculars seem to be, in general, more diversified than Spotify's grammars of playlist curation. In coherence with the role that genre taxonomies seem to have in relation to the processes of datafication on the Spotify platform, genre emerges from this investigation as an important, albeit not exclusive or absolute criterion for playlist composition by users. A greater degree of heterogeneity can be observed in the playlists created by users when compared to those created by the platform. This suggests that platforms cater to user heterogeneity in music listening by offering similar playlists with a slightly different genre focus, as exemplified by the Workout example, or according to a given context of use, social setting, or mood, rather than playlists with significant internal heterogeneity.

Conclusions, Limitations, and Possible Expansions

We began this chapter by questioning whether forms of music consumption are moving away from genre as the main dimension of listening in plat-formised music streaming, and asked what role music genre has in relation to the grammars and vernaculars that characterise playlist composition on Spotify. While this remains a qualitative, exploratory endeavour, the data presented here allows us to reasonably sustain that genre remains a signifi-cant element that also drives the composition of playlists based on mood and social situations of listening, both from the side of platforms as well as of users. The internal composition of playlists seems to be more diversified on the user side; yet, genre consistency also remains evident among users in terms of playlist composition despite individual taste differences. We can conclude that, while there are signs of moving away from established genre taxonomies in the ways in which users access and consume music through streaming platforms, these are much less evident than the popular narrations pushed by Spotify seem to suggest, which proclaim the transformation of all music into "background music" (Hamilton, 2021).

With respect to the limitations of this kind of research, it must be underlined that this analysis has focused on platform grammars and vernaculars of playlist composition without considering the role played by Spotify's algorithmic recommender system in the user's search for playlists. Digital methods analyses on Spotify, so far, are limited to the possibility of investigating the "relatedness" among individual artists (which can be done using the Spotify Artist Network[6] tool, which allows us to query the Spotify API, starting from a single artist, and to explore the network of "related" content deriving from it). Nonetheless, the possibility of undertaking the same kind of analysis on playlists is currently hindered by the API restrictions imposed by the Spotify platform, which does not consent to collecting data about their "relatedness." Yet, in coherence with Bucher's (2016) precinct that we should not let the "black boxed" status of platforms' infrastructures and internal workings hinder our work as social scientists, we employed the SpotiGem tool to study playlist composition and cultures, looking at what surrounds the black box and its related cultures and practices. Arguably, playlists allow for a kind of "second-order reverse engineering" of Spotify's editorial and algorithmic-driven logics: their analysis reveals more about the way content is organised for algorithmic optimisation on Spotify – and, on the users' side, about how individual listening and cataloguing practices respond to and engage with the affordances of the platform.

In more general terms, this kind of research offers an important array of innovative tools in the study of music consumption practices from the perspective of consumer culture theory. It does so in two main ways: on the one hand, it extends the investigation into the cultural practices that underpin and surround forms of access-based consumption (Bardhi and Eckhardt, 2012) and their inscription into platformisation processes, stressing the need to focus more in-depth on the role that platform affordances play – in their interaction with cultural processes – in facilitating or hindering consumption habits and practices. On the other hand, it also calls into question the allegedly growing "omnivorousness" (Peterson, 1992) of consumers and calls to further probe the continuing significance of this notion in platform-based consumption processes. It has been noted

6   See: https://labs.polsys.net/playground/spotify/.

that active YouTube users who comment under music videos "are far more omnivorous," i.e., they interact with a larger variety of videos, than less active ones. Still, the overall degree of omnivorousness of YouTube users appears to be quite low," and "(o)nly a minority of commenters have crossed genre boundaries in their interactions with music content" (Airoldi, 2021, p. 8). Evidence from Spotify playlist data points to a corroboration of this insight, which deserves further (and larger) investigation in future works.

References

Airoldi, M. (2021). The techno-social reproduction of taste boundaries on digital platforms: The case of music on YouTube. *Poetics, 89,* https://doi.org/10.1016/j.poetic.2021.101563.

Airoldi, M., Beraldo, D., and Gandini, A. (2016). Follow the algorithm: An exploratory investigation of music on YouTube. *Poetics, 57,* 1–13. https://doi.org/10.1016/j.poetic.2016.05.001.

Arditi, D. (2015). The new distribution oligopoly: Beats, iTunes, and digital music distribution. *Media Fields, 10.* http://mediafieldsjournal.squarespace.com/the-new-distribution-oligopoly/2015/11/14/the-new-distribution-oligopoly-beats-itunes-and-digital-musi.html;jsessionid=8BE275AEDEDF1B7F0A3FB8B9DE000697.v5-web016.

Bardhi, F. and Eckhardt, G. M. (2012). Access-based consumption: The case of car sharing. *Journal of Consumer Research, 39*(4), 881–898. https://doi.org/10.1086/666376.

Bardhi, F. and Eckhardt, G. M. (2017). Liquid consumption. *Journal of Consumer Research, 44*(3), 582–597. https://doi.org/10.1093/jcr/ucx050.

Bonini, T. and Gandini, A. (2019). "First week is editorial, second week is algorithmic": Platform gatekeepers and the platformization of music curation. *Social Media+ Society, 5*(4), https://doi.org/10.1177/2056305119880006.

Bonini, T. and Gandini, A. (2020). The field as a black box: Ethnographic research in the age of platforms. *Social Media+ Society, 6*(4). https://doi.org/10.1177/2056305120984477.

Bruns, A. (2019). *Are filter bubbles real?* John Wiley and Sons.

Bucher, T. (2016). Neither black nor box: Ways of knowing algorithms. In S. Kubitschko and A. Kaun (Eds.), *Innovative methods in media and communication research* (pp. 81–98). Palgrave Macmillan.

Eriksson, M., Fleischer, R., Johansson, A., Snickars, P., and Vonderau, P. (2019). *Spotify teardown: Inside the black box of streaming music.* MIT Press.

Gandini, A. (2021). P2P (Peer-to-peer). *The Blackwell encyclopedia of sociology.* https://doi.org/10.1002/9781405165518.wbeosp204.pub2.

Hamilton, J. (2021, October 6). Spotify has made all music into background music. *The Atlantic*. https://www.theatlantic.com/magazine/archive/2021/11/kelefa-sanneh-major-labels-music/620178/.

Hesmondhalgh, D. and Meier, L. M. (2018). What the digitalisation of music tells us about capitalism, culture and the power of the information technology sector. *Information, Communication and Society, 21*(11), 1555–1570. https://doi.org/10.1080/1369118X.2017.1340498.

Mulligan, M. (2022, January 18). Music subscriber market shares Q2. Midia Research. https://www.midiaresearch.com/blog/music-subscriber-market-shares-q2-2021.

Newsroom Spotify (2021, February 25). How to sort your favorite songs with Spotify's new genre and mood filters. https://newsroom.spotify.com/2021-02-25/how-to-sort-your-favorite-songs-with-spotifys-new-genre-and-mood-filters/.

Pasquale, F. (2015). *The black box society: The secret algorithms that control money and information*. Harvard University Press.

Peterson, R. A. (1992). Understanding audience segmentation: From elite and mass to omnivore and univore. *Poetics, 21*(4), 243–258. ttps://doi.org/10.1016/0304-422X(92)90008-Q.

Prey, R., Esteve Del Valle, M., and Zwerwer, L. (2022). Platform pop: Disentangling Spotify's intermediary role in the music industry. *Information, Communication and Society, 25*(1), 74–92. https://doi.org/10.1080/1369118X.2020.1761859.

Prey, R. (2020). Locating power in platformization: Music streaming playlists and curatorial power. *Social Media+ Society, 6*(2). https://doi.org/10.1177/2056305120933291.

Seaver, N. (2018). What should an anthropology of algorithms do? *Cultural anthropology, 33*(3), 375–385. http://orcid.org/0000-0002-3913-1134.

4. Exploring the Role of Fake News and Bots in Brand Communication on Twitter and Their Impact on Brand Value and Consumer Culture

Abstract

Fake news has a notoriously nefarious impact on online brand reputation, which can be further magnified by the activity of social bots. In this chapter, we investigate the relationship between fake news and bots, as well as their impact on brand value and consumer culture. To do so, we analysed a dataset of 461,303 tweets related to Pepsi, New Balance, and Twitter Inc. This analysis highlights that the activities of fake news and bots seem to be quite disconnected, as if fake news creators and bots have separate "businesses on their own." Fake news creators are mostly human actors that create or exploit brand-related fake news to push their (mostly right-wing) political agendas rather than ruin brands' reputation or value. In turn, bots simply piggyback existing controversies triggered by fake news to boost their visibility and, thus, sell commercial products to Twitter audiences.

Keywords: disinformation, bot detection, brands, politics, imaginary

It is impossible to overstate the tremendous amount of attention that fake news, as a concept, garnered in the late 2010s and early 2020s. Google Ngram reports a 9432% increase in citation of the query "fake news" in the 2010–2019 period; Google Trends reports a stable and spectacular uptrend in citations starting from 2016 and peaking in March 2020. This kind of attention is a mirror of social and political events: more than one US presidential campaign has been fought over claims of fake news (Bessi and Ferrara, 2016), while vaccine misinformation has shown the impact that fake news can exert upon human behaviour (Carrieri et al., 2019) and the dire consequences this can entail.

Caliandro, A., A. Gandini, L. Bainotti, G. Anselmi, *The Platformisation of Consumer Culture: A Digital Methods Guide*. Amsterdam: Amsterdam University Press, 2024
DOI 10.5117/9789463729567_CH04

Marketing literature, obviously, is no exception, and a great deal of effort has been dedicated to producing evidence about the impact of fake news on either consumers' perception of brands or brand values (Mills and Robson, 2019; Di Domenico et al., 2021; Ladeira et al., 2022). However, caveats apply: most of these accounts remain anecdotal or, at best, fully qualitative case studies. Measuring the impact of fake news, especially on social media, remains a difficult endeavour. In this chapter, we seek to demonstrate how digital methods can be leveraged to get: a) a quantitative assessment of the impact of fake news on selected brands through message volume; b) a better grasp on the relation between fake news and bots within online brand communications; c) a sense of the impact of fake news and bots activity on brand value; and d) a deeper understanding of the user culture behind brands targeted by fake news production. We will do so by closely looking at three brands on Twitter during specific events in the near past: Pepsi, New Balance, and Twitter itself.

Defining Fake News, Bots, and Their Role in Consumer Communication Online

Before analysing our cases, however, the concept of fake news warrants some specific discussion. Fake news is usually defined as pieces of information that, simply put, are not real but are pretending to be. Thus, they are usually conceived as an explicit effort to spread misinformation for different reasons (politics, click farming, groupthink, etc.) (Venturini, 2019). Most commonly, fake news is disseminated with a malicious intent, which is to inflict an economic or reputational damage on a specific actor (e.g., a celebrity, a politician, a brand, a company, etc.). Yet, we should not overlook the fact that fake news also falls into the more "neutral" logic of visibility and the broader attention economy that permeates web environments and, in particular, social media platforms (Lala, 2022): that is, users create fake news not necessarily with a (specific) malevolent scope in mind, but because, generally, false information generates more online traffic, and thus more advertising revenues, than real news (Gray et al., 2020).

While the concept of "fake news" is as old as journalism itself, it is undeniable that in recent years it has been strongly associated with digital networks; in other words, fake news should be conceptualised as something that is borne out of a given set of affordances (Rogers and Niederer, 2020), in a specific social networking site, and through that (and others) within a wider attention economy, linking both social and legacy media (Bounegru et al., 2018). In fact, digital networks, and especially social media platforms, allowed fake news to circulate and be produced with a degree of velocity and on a scale never seen before in the history of media (Lazer et al., 2018). In this regard, it is worth mentioning that fake news not only propagates faster within digital environments, but it also tends to propagate faster than real news (Vosoughi et al., 2018). On the one hand, this is because of their symbolic components (i.e., fake news tends to be hyperbolic, accompanied by eye-catching headlines and/or images, and stirring strong emotions in the public) (Tandoc et al., 2018); on the other hand, this is due to a key technical component of fake news: bots. In fact, the fake news phenomenon is difficult to disentangle from that of bots, especially social bots (Graham et al., 2020): artificial actors infesting social media platforms, which are, in turn, the most fertile field for fake news to thrive in.

Simply put, social bots are social media accounts (e.g., on Twitter) that are managed and controlled by ad hoc pieces of software, usually programmed to automate specific "social" tasks (such as posting a tweet during a specific time of the day, following users, sharing a particular message multiple times, etc.) (Wischnewski et al., 2022). Social bots play a key role in the diffusion of disinformation within online spaces, since they are commonly used by fake news outlets and creators to magnify the impact of false information (Ferrara, 2020) – in terms of speed of circulation, size of audiences reached, and overall visibility. Consider also that, nowadays, bots are relatively easy to set up thanks to the many user-friendly tools to automatise social media accounts and internet tutorials available (Bessi and Ferrara, 2016), a condition that makes the diffusion of bots even more pervasive. It has been estimated that 9% to 15% of active Twitter accounts are bots; on Facebook, estimates suggest that about 60 million bots are operating on the platform (Lazer et al., 2018).[1] Yet, as Rauchfleisch and Kaiser (2020) underline, it is not sufficient to simply count the number of bots in a dataset of social media posts to assess their impact on society at large (e.g., the capacity of

---

1   It must be specified that after the Covid-19 emergency and the subsequent "infodemic" outburst (Simon and Camargo, 2023), major social media platforms such as Twitter and Facebook declared "war" on fake news and took strong actions to eradicate it (Rogers, 2020) (for example by perfecting their AI systems for fake news detection (Heilweil, 2022)). Twitter permanently suspended the account of the former president of the United States, Donald Trump (@realDonaldTrump), accused of inciting people to violence, also with the use of misleading information (Twitter, 2021). However, a more thorough discussion on diffusion of fake news during the pandemic and its impact on the social media ecosystem and society at large exceeds the scope of this chapter. For further academic analysis on this phenomenon, we invite the reader to check the vast literature produced in the last two years on the subject (see for example, Rogers, 2020; Bruns et al., 2020; Guarino et al., 2021; Simon and Camargo, 2023, among others).

bots to sabotage a political campaign). To do so, it is necessary to combine computational techniques with qualitative ones (e.g., interviews or manual content analysis) in order to understand how people react to bots and, especially, to the fake news they convey. Rauchfleisch and Kaiser call for the use of a more cultural approach in the study of bots – which is exactly the one we have used in this chapter.

Returning to the concept of fake news per se, we must add another epistemological specification. Arguably, the expression itself has become dangerously close to an umbrella term, as it has been employed to describe anything from malicious cyberwarfare attacks by criminal or state entities (Golovchenko, 2018) to personal beliefs springing from involvement in specific echo chambers (Shao et al., 2017). A variety of research reports have been published about the effect of social media echo chambers on any given phenomenon (Maneri et al., 2022), including studies on how legacy media navigate the issue within the wider context and constraints of the attention economy. In terms of actual content, it is important to distinguish between actual fake news (i.e., pieces of news that describe some facts that never happened) or junk news (Venturini, 2019; Caliandro et al., 2021) (i.e., pieces of news that describe something that has indeed happened but in a way that leads to malicious misunderstandings or to polarising interpretations). In this chapter, we will stick to the first meaning of the concept. In particular, we will draw on the definition proposed by Axel Gelfert (2018, p. 108), which the author specifically devised for consumer research purposes, that is: "the fake news term should be reserved for cases of deliberate presentation of typically false or misleading claims as news, where these are misleading by design ... systemic features of the sources and channels by which fake news propagates and thereby manipulates consumers' decisions." While the definition goes on to mention "pre-existing cognitive biases and heuristics," we preferred to exclude this part for two significant reasons: a) it is not possible to infer people cognitive status by a mere digital analysis of social media metadata and textual data (Venturini et al. 2018); b) this strong focus on consumers "pre-existing cognitive biases and heuristics" represents, in our view, one of the main limitations of marketing and consumer research in this field (more on this below).

Fake News in Marketing and Consumer Research

Compared to the disproportionate literature produced by media and jour-nalism scholars, consumer research on fake news is still in its infancy (Di

Domenico and Visentin, 2020). This is quite odd, considering that fake news represents a concrete threat to important processes of digital consumption, such as consumer reviews (Fong, 2010), word-of-mouth (Pfeffer et al., 2014), brand reputation (Etter et al., 2019), and influencer marketing (De Veirman et al., 2017). Arguably, however, consumer scholars have not neglected the phenomenon; on the contrary, they have made a substantial contribution to its understanding. In particular, marketing literature has thoroughly investigated the impact of fake news on consumption processes, pointing out that the principal scope of fake news is to push consumers to change their perception, opinion, and attitude towards certain products, brands, services, or firms (Gelfert, 2018). Consider, for example, the false rumour about McDonalds preparing hamburgers with worms or Coca-Cola using water with parasites (Cheng and Chen, 2021). Such manipulation of consumers' perceptions has an obvious, negative impact on key business assets, such as brand equity (Berthon and Pitt, 2018), brand trust (Visentin et al., 2019), brand reputation (Obadă, 2019), or programmatic advertising (Mills et al., 2019). Speaking of damages to the brand identity, scholars have identified a peculiar and insidious phenomenon related to disinformation in the domain of consumption: that is, that consumers are more prone to believe in fake news if they are associated with a brand name, e.g., a branded hashtag (Berthon and Pitt, 2018). In their systematic literature review on fake news in marketing research, Di Domenico et al. (2021) stressed that, beyond their localised and momentary effect on consumption, fake news might have a more global and permanent effect on society at large. In fact, consumers who are constantly exposed to fake news could easily become incapable of discerning what is real or not, with a negative backlash, for example, on health-related issues (e.g., vaccines) (Carrieri et al., 2019), finance and stock markets (Brigida and Pratt, 2017).

However, we contend that such literature has some limitations. Most empirical marketing research on fake news and brands relies on qualitative case studies (Obadă, 2019) or abstract modelling of consumer preferences after the exposure to fake news about brands (Talwar et al., 2019). By doing so, this stream of research tends to primarily focus on the cognitive aspects of the fake news phenomenon (e.g., *Why do consumers share and/or believe in fake news? Why are consumers incapable of discerning between fake and real news?* etc.) (Nyilasy, 2019). Furthermore, to our knowledge, there is no marketing and consumer research trying to tackle the topic of fake news and brand communication in digital environments using digital methods. This is a notable gap, since digital methods can be a valid support for researchers in understanding how fake news works in their "native environments." For example, by drawing on digital methods, consumer scholars can observe how fake news circulates within specific digital consumers spaces (i.e., brand communities, brand publics, consumer platforms, etc.) and the impact they have on those environments and their members, as well as the impact they have on brand value in terms of online reputation. Furthermore, digital methods can be useful for tracking, measuring, and analysing the activity of bots – something that is extremely hard to do without taking advantage of computational techniques (Giglietto et al., 2020). For example, due to the lack of research based on digital methods, we know very little about the relation between fake news and bots in online communications around brands: do they cooperate or take different paths of action? As a result, we know little about the kind of consumer culture emerging from online conversations hinged on such complex interaction among brands, fake news, bots, and human users.

Keeping these gaps in mind, in this chapter we will use digital methods to answer the following research questions: *What is the relation between fake news and bots within communications about brands on digital platforms? Does fake news circulate independently from bots or does it necessarily need bots to have some kind of circulation and impact? Do bots and ordinary users use fake news differently? If so, how? For what purposes? What is the impact of fake news and bots on brand value? And what is their impact on consumer culture?*

A Last Caveat on Finance and Brand Value

Before we discuss cases and methods, there is a further assumption to make regarding the kind of damage that fake news may produce in the contemporary financialised environment. Obviously, there are different ways to measure brand value. We will consider stock market values as a proxy for brand value. While we are aware of the complexities of measuring brand value and of the inherent oversimplification of conflating brand value with stock prices, we are also aware that modern brands may never be fully understood without a deeper understanding of financialisation (Langley and Leyshon, 2017) and the ways in which it has affected their operations (Arvidsson, 2016). Control over financial flows and enforcement of copyrights is what keeps, for example, a fashion brand or a tech company from dissolving into a mesh of subcontractors, to which the productive (and, increasingly, the design and aftersales) process has been outsourced (Arvidsson, 2005).

Moreover, focusing on financial values gives us the opportunity to explore a parallelism with how value gets produced in the attention economy: again, without getting too deep into the debate on the nature of value within contemporary capitalism (but see, for example, Arvidsson, 2019), we assume that, in digital networks, value springs from the capacity to provoke users' affection and bind it to a specific object or idea, i.e., the more people keep talking about something, the more valuable that entity will become. There is also an empirical rationale behind this choice: 70–90% of all stocks trading is now done by algorithmic traders (Elder, 2022), which employ predictive modelling to guess stock prices in the very near future (more often than not in the next minutes or seconds in the case of high-frequency trading). All models are aimed at pricing a specific stock containing (beyond market fundamentals and macro-economic indicators) information feeds from social media, that is, sentiment analysis from tweets incorporating keywords connected to the brand.

Obviously, this deep connection between social media, sentiment, and financial values has been thoroughly exploited by malicious actors intent on producing "artificial" inflation or deflation of prices through coordinated action by bot networks or "sock puppet" accounts (i.e., multiple fake accounts operated by the same entity) (Yu et al., 2013). This interconnection may be one of the rationales behind the dissemination of fake news. However, as said, we should not assume malicious intent, as the cascading effect of a piece of fake news may be absolutely incidental.

Cases, Methods, and Data

Compared with other contributions in this book, this chapter has a more "computational" bent; however we maintain that this does not detract from our interpretative focus. While there is plenty of unreflexive adoption of computational techniques (Lazer et al., 2014), we contend that, firstly, computational techniques may be used while being well aware of their methodological blindspots; secondly, their usage may add an additional layer of interpretation while trying to chart how affordances shape user behaviour. In essence, in a domain that is made real by algorithmic power and computational resources, much can be accomplished without using computational tools: sense and meaning may (and, eventually, they should) be assessed by virtue of ethnographic techniques (Caliandro, 2018); however, there are some operations that cannot be accomplished without relying on algorithmic power (Lewis et al., 2013). While this makes for less transparent research (for example, we are not fully aware of what training biases machine-learning models may have), we believe that the added descriptive power that comes with a "reflective" usage of these techniques makes this a worthwhile addition to our methodological arsenal (Nelson, 2020).

In this chapter, we will focus on three different cases involving mentions of a brand in the context of a fake news wave over Twitter, namely: Pepsi, New Balance Shoes, and Twitter itself. The first two cases are instances of politically motivated fake news: within the context of the extreme polarisation of American presidential elections, the central product of these brands has been entangled in pre-existing political conflict, becoming another front in the ongoing "culture war" between progressives and conservatives. In the case of Pepsi, on 16 November 2016, an unsourced piece of news began circulating on Twitter attributing a set of anti-Trump statements to Indra Nooyi (then CEO of Pepsi). This resulted in a boycott of the company led by some pro-Trump influencers, who, interestingly, also called for a boycott of the company shares. In the case of New Balance Shoes, something similar happened but "in reverse," as the CEO of the company reported that he felt that Trump was a better alternative to Obama, although, in fact, he was only talking about the Trans-Pacific Partnership. Nevertheless, the declaration became an allegiance of sorts, leading to boycotts (this time from democrats) and endorsement of the product by Trump electors, who declared New Balance "the official shoes of white people" (Mettier, 2016). In the case of Twitter, we considered a piece of fake news that is not political but financial in nature: on 14 July 2015 a fabricated story was shared over Twitter regarding Twitter itself receiving a $31 billion takeover offer. The piece of news was created to resemble an actual Bloomberg article, even mimicking the url address. As the piece of news was shared over Twitter, the company shares sharply increased in a matter of minutes; eventually, after a few hours, a Bloomberg spokesperson, Ty Trippet, released (over Twitter) a statement confirming that the news was, indeed, fake. It is worth noting that this last case is not really comparable with the previous two, as we use a different mechanism to the capture data. Nevertheless, analysing this case offers us considerable insight into a specific feature of Twitter (cashtags[2]) that is seldom investigated in digital methods. Moreover, we are striving to perfect a deep description as opposed to full generalisability (Munk et al., 2022), hence fully fledged comparison is not really a goal of this exploration.

Taking advantage of the v2 Twitter API (which, unlike earlier versions, offers full historical access to all tweets produced on the cases), we have gathered a total of 461,303 tweets (written in English), selecting a time

2   Cashtags are a specific entity on Twitter designating stock prices; for example, a tweet including $TWTR is referring to Twitter stocks.

window for each case a time that spans from one week before the peak of the fake news event to one week after it. For the two "political" cases (Pepsi and New Balance) we gathered all tweets mentioning the name of the brand. In the case of Twitter, due to the financial nature of the issue and to avoid gathering confounding tweets, we gathered tweets containing the Twitter cashtag "$twtr," meaning we gathered all tweets making an explicit reference to Twitter stocks. This led to a fairly unequal distribution of tweets, with 351,189 tweets about Pepsi, 101,773 tweets about New Balance, and 8,341 tweets about Twitter. This is connected to the fact that cashtags are utilised much less than hashtags. We decided not to follow the fake news story per se, but to focus on the brand names (or on the cashtag, in the case of Twitter): this decision was taken because it helps us understand the effect that the sharing of fake news had on the discursive ecosystem centred around the brand. If we had just selected tweets reporting a piece of fake news, we would only have observed the reaction of those directly engaging with it, while we wanted to assess the impact on all users instead. Essentially, this was done because we wanted to ascertain the possible existence of a "contagion effect," in which a dedicated group of users (perhaps aided by bots) produce enough negative effect to affect the brand beyond the circumstances in which the fake news had arisen.

After gathering tweets, we operationalised bot activity through the Botometer API (Bessi and Ferrara, 2016): beyond the technical details,[3] suffice it to say that Botometer provides, for each Twitter account, a bot likelihood score ranging from .0 to .99; the higher it is, the more likely it is that the account is a bot. We decided not to have a "breaking point" but to use daily mean scores.

Fake News Circulation and Retweet Concentration

Social media platforms tend to favour polarisation and "dogpiling" on relevant issues. Twitter is especially geared towards this, as content curation algorithms encourage users to interact with content that has become viral and controversial, and the main way of interacting with that content is through retweeting. Thus, the grammar of Twitter favours the emergence of macro-discourses hinged on a logic of mediation and visibility. This means

---

3   Botometer employs a machine-learning approach to estimate the likelihood of any given account being operated by a bot. For further details, see https://botometer.osome.iu.edu/, and Bessi and Ferrara (2016).

Trend in Twitter stock vs release of fake news

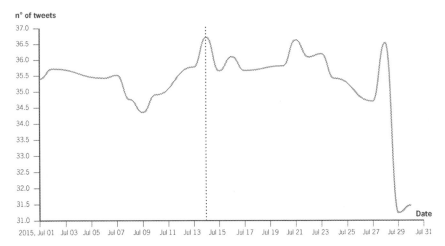

Fig. 4.1. The vertical axis shows the daily number of tweets; the dashed vertical lines indicate the day on which the piece of fake news was released.

Trend in Pepsi stock vs release of fake news

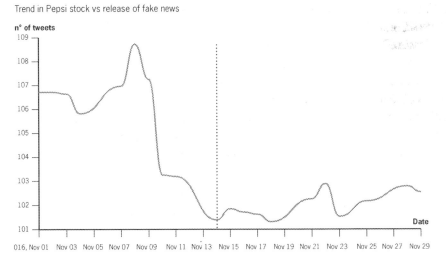

Fig. 4.2. The vertical axis shows the daily number of tweets; the dashed vertical lines indicate the day on which the piece of fake news was released.

that its socio-technical affordances should amplify those voices that produce that kind of content. In this paragraph, we draw on this *grammar* to observe how macro-discourses emerging around pieces of fake news are structured by and propagate around Twitter through the retweet (RT) function.

In terms of tweet distribution, the Twitter and Pepsi cases exhibit a clear peak and valley activity trend, with the day on which the fake news was reported viral as the main peak within a context of lower activity (see Fig. 4.1 and Fig. 4.2). New Balance has two peaks, with the first one corresponding to the day on which the fake news began circulating (12 November 2016), while the second one (14 November 2016) took place when a piece of news about a neo-Nazi website declaring New Balance "the official shoes of white people" (Mettier, 2016) surfaced on legacy media. Regarding stock data, it should be said that New Balance is privately owned, so it will be excluded from this part of the analysis. That said, both in the case of Pepsi and in the case of Twitter, the fake news does not seem to have had an effect on the stock prices: in November 2016, Pepsi stocks were on a downward trend,[4] starting well before the release of the fake news; in July 2015, Twitter[5] stocks are more or less stable with no discernible effect of the fake news release.

Furthermore, we decided to study RT concentration because it can give us a rough proxy on how the imaginary, on any given brand, is controlled by a handful of accounts: we did so by using the Gini coefficient.[6] It is worth noting that we considered all mentions of the brand and not just the number of tweets dealing with the fake news itself. Analysing social media data, we find that the three cases differ for RT concentration as Pepsi and New Balance have a Gini coefficient of, respectively, .77 and .74, while Twitter has a Gini coefficient of .27. This means that, in the first two cases, retweets are rather concentrated (a large number of users retweet few sources) while the third one is fairly deconcentrated (no "superuser cluster" is massively retweeted by others). The stark difference between the three cases has to do with the specific entry point we have selected for gathering data: cashtags (especially back in 2015) tend to be used less and by more professional users, and usually do not give rise to sprawling conversations or networks the way standard capturing by hashtag or keyword does. Moreover, cashtags tend to be used by financial bots commenting on the stock market, in the context of a social network that is usually characterised by a rampant "St. Matthew effect" (Merton, 1968). In such circumstances, RTs are allocated to a minority of hyper-connected nodes; thus, we can safely assume that less interaction means less concentration.

4   see https://www.google.com/finance/quote/PEP:NASDAQ?sa=Xandved=2ahUKEwiOve bA_-v4AhVq_bsIHTI6DdsQ3ecFegQIKRAa.

5   see https://www.google.com/finance/quote/TWTR:NYSE?sa=Xandved=2ahUKEwiiyu WR_-v4AhUGhPoHHUBBCu8Q3ecFegQICRAY.

6   The Gini coefficient measures inequality in a given set of data, originally used to chart wealth inequality; it can be applied to chart any distribution of resources (in our case RT). The Gini coefficient varies from 1 (one individual controls all of the resources) to 0 (everyone has an equal share of resources).

RT network for Pepsi

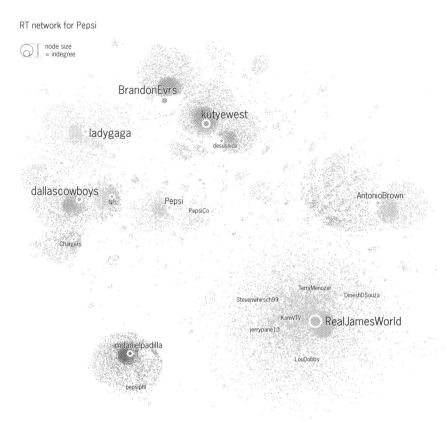

Fig. 4.3. Retweet network; node size is proportional to indegree, colour designates a community that is "denser" than its surroundings.

The network analysis of retweets also draws quite different pictures, with Pepsi and New Balance assuming somewhat polarised structures (Fig. 4.3 and 4.4) while Twitter has a more dispersed one (Fig. 4.5). In the first two cases, retweets tend to gather around high-profile users in a hub and spoke structure. Central accounts in the Pepsi and New Balance networks are digital political entrepreneurs (in either the pro-Trump or anti-Trump fields) or celebrities who, in some cases, appear to be totally unconnected to the fake news itself. A relevant difference between the two is that, in the case of Pepsi, the most prominent account belongs to a Trumpist activist with almost no opposition. Other clusters seem to be apolitical or entirely disconnected from the controversy (e.g., see the cluster around Lady Gaga). Conversely, in the case of New Balance, the RT network is composed of a "main hub" wrapped around the accounts of progressive newspapers commenting on the issue, while a secondary hub is wrapped around the accounts of prominent Trump activists. In

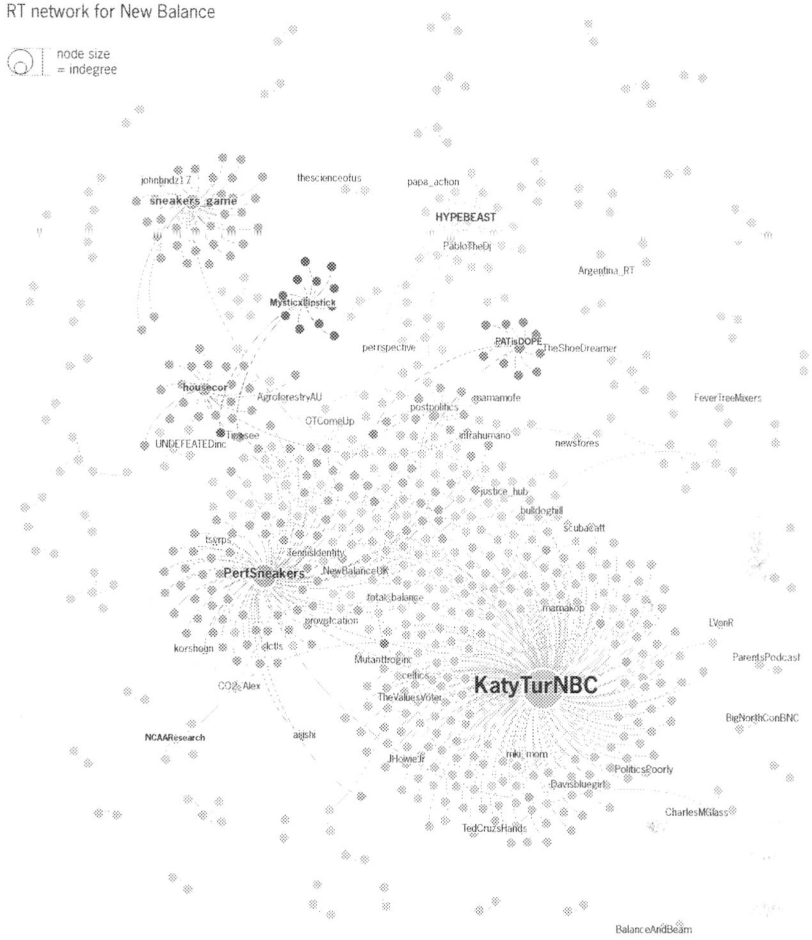

Fig. 4.4. Retweet network; node size is proportional to indegree, colour designates a community that is "denser" than its surroundings.

essence, Pepsi seems to be constituted of a rather isolated echo chamber while New Balance assumes the form of a controversy/flame war. Regarding Twitter, the RT "network" seems to be fairly disconnected, being constituted of retweets of single, specialised accounts relating to financial news.

So far, we can infer two main trends regarding the effect of fake news on brand perception. In all cases, if we consider the whole narrative ecosystem of the brand, fake news neither affects stock prices nor is it being commented on outside very special niches, in this case people who feel strongly about incoming (2016) elections.

RT network for Twitter

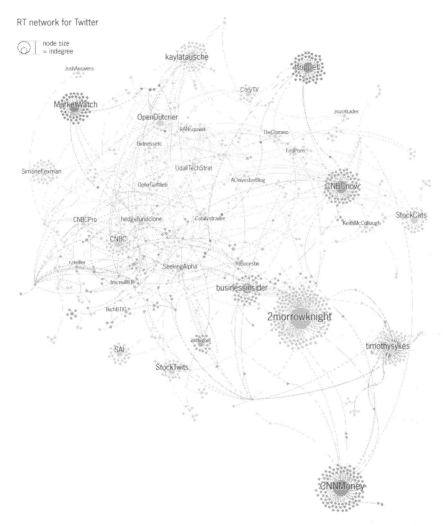

Fig. 4.5. Retweet network; node size is proportional to indegree, colour designates a community that is "denser" than its surroundings.

Bot Analysis

Switching to bot analysis, we will now chart the average botscore value in the time frame knowing that, essentially, a higher daily average means that we will have more bots. The rationale for studying bots sits in the specific role that bots play in the Twitter ecosystem. It is particularly easy to create and operate bots over Twitter and, because Twitter is particularly eager to push controversial content, bots have become a somewhat mythical component of Twitter's socio-technical setup, delivering a constant stream

Bot activity scores vs number of tweets Pepsi

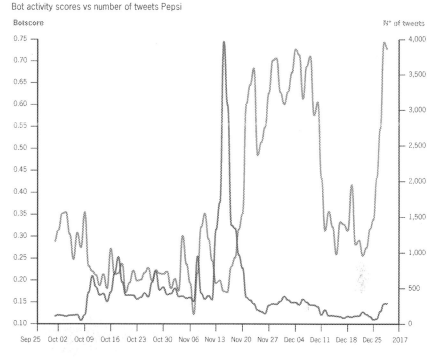

Fig. 4.6. The left vertical axis is the daily average botscore; the right vertical axis is the number of tweets. The dashed line describes the trend in botscores; the full line is the number of tweets.

Bot activity scores vs number of tweets New Balance

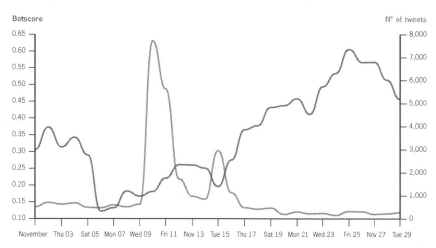

Fig. 4.7. The left vertical axis is the daily average botscore (the higher it is, the more bots we have); the right vertical axis is the number of tweets. The dashed line describes the trend in botscores; the full line is the number of tweets.

Bot activity scores vs number of tweets Twitter

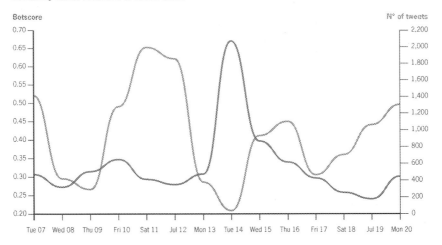

Fig. 4.8. The left vertical axis is the daily average botscore; the right vertical axis is the number of tweets. The dashed line describes the trend in botscores; the full line is the number of tweets.

of polarising content. However, in our case, we seem to find no correlation between daily average bot activity score (see the methods section) and the release of the piece of fake news, or at least no direct correlation. In both the Pepsi and New Balance cases (Fig. 4.6 and 4.7), the days of peak activity also sport lower daily averages in bot scores, while days immediately after the controversy sport higher average bot scores. Twitter, in comparison, has higher values for bot scores but, again, there seems to be no direct correlation between the trend in bot scores and the release of the piece of fake news, as bot scores peak to an impressive .6 average before the release of the piece of fake news (Fig. 4.8) – but remember that we are analysing a cashtag, a feature of Twitter that is predominantly utilised by bots.

While the explanation for Twitter might be just random fluctuation in activity, we may attempt an interpretation of these scores for the two other cases. This can be done by focusing on the nature of bots: while academic literature offers extensive examples of "malicious bots", for example, bots that attempt to achieve political objectives through astroturfing,[7] in fact, "commercial" bots greatly outnumber astroturfers. Commercial bots do not attempt to bring political or social change through digital fraud, but rather they aim to boost the visibility of a given subject, by (among other means) amplifying pre-existing tendencies, piggybacking on other trends,

7   This is the use of multiple bots to stimulate mass participation in something, maybe a protest or an attempt to start financial market manipulation.

so to speak (Lala, 2022). This may explain bots activity in the period after peak days. More specifically (and simply), bots try to hijack peaks in Twitter conversations and attention to push products they wish to sell, as in the two emblematic examples below:

> Kid's New Balance KJ880v2 Running Shoes – White/Pink – NIB! Kid's New Balance KJ880v2 Running Shoes – White/Pink – NIB! http://buy-clothingshoes.com

> Pepsi 12-Packs Just $0.99 At Target! https://www.groceryshopforfree.com/

A further confirmation of this aspect may be found in the distribution of mean bot scores per retweet cluster (clusters identified in Fig. 4.3, 4.4, and 4.5): in the case of Pepsi, all clusters have somewhat normal bot activity scores (between .10 to .30). The one exception is the cluster centred around Lady Gaga, which is totally disconnected from the piece of fake news at the core of the case, as the artist was trying to promote her show (sponsored by Pepsi) at the Superbowl. In the case of New Balance, no cluster seems to be influenced by bots (all mean scores are under .20). In the case of Twitter, the RT network is very small (it consists of 68 nodes), so we decided not to investigate it further.

Therefore, to conclude, we can argue that bots (as well as the agents manoeuvring them) do not seem interested in spreading fake news, but rather in exploiting peaks of conversations brought about by fake news for their own purpose, i.e., visibility. Specifically, they exploit Twitter grammar visibility to sell determinate products to the public.

How Human Users Use and Interact with Fake News

We can now build on the previous results to understand how users articulate different narrations, and thus bring to life shared imaginaries around content related to brand-based fake news, namely, a specific *vernacular*. To do so, we have selected and qualitatively analysed some of the most top shared content. In the case of Pepsi and New Balance, the beef of the controversy (albeit one-sided in the case of Pepsi) is openly political, and mainly driven by right-wing activist accounts. In the specific case of Pepsi, there seems to be an outright attempt to crash stock prices as a form of political protest. This is evident in this tweet by James Woods, which is the top shared tweet for the case:

> #BoycottPepsi And if you really want to be heard, sell any #Pepsi stock you have. We beat #Hillary and #Soros. We can break #Pepsi, too. https://t.co/1ZJxWlDizR

Others follow in the same vein, misunderstanding intraday micro-fluctuation with a long-lasting impact upon stock prices:

> Pepsi stock after CEO tells Trump supporters to "take your business elsewhere" is plummeting. Great job guys. #BoycottPepsi #MAGA

> Pepsi Co. CEO to Trump supporters: "We don't want your business" #BoycottPepsi 💰 👍 Let's watch stock go down some more 😀

> Pepsi has lost $800m in market cap today. And it the boycott just started

This specific narration is hardly contested but somewhat insular, meaning that the vast majority of conversations do not tackle the fake piece of news, focusing on commercials, and on general conversation regarding Pepsi as a product. For example, the cluster built around Lady Gaga mainly consists of retweets of this tweet from the artist:

> It's not an illusion. The rumors are true. This year the SUPER BOWL goes GAGA! @nfl @FOXTV @pepsi #PERFECTILLUSION #GAGASUPERBOWL

While a small "anti Trump" cluster exists, on the one hand it does not challenge the Trumpist cluster; on the other hand, it does not contest the narration backing the piece of fake news: all prominent tweets are, more or less, commentaries on the activity of Trumpists. In general, reactions consist of pairing mocking or humorous images to things said or done by Trumpists:

> because the CEO of pepsi called trump a "terrifying man" trump supporters are now boycotting dozens of brands ... who's triggered now?

> The time they outlined every Pepsi subsidiary so people who dislike Trump know where to shop

In the case of New Balance, as previously said, we have a more polarised exchange; the most populous cluster is, again, the Trumpist one, which here seems to take a jingoistic bent. Again, the attempt to influence a commercial performance is explicit (but in this case with a positive spin).

BUY NEW BALANCE!! NEW BALANCE WANTS TO MANUFACTURE THEIR PRODUCTS IN THE U.S. THANK YOU NEW BALANCE FOR SHOWING YOUR PATRIOTISM!!

Time for me to buy New Balance shoes: The only major company that still makes athletic shoes in the US praised Trump

Interestingly, the original fake piece of information (New Balance CEO praising Trump, as opposed to a specific policy choice) seems to have spawned a secondary narration, which spreads with ease within the Trumpist cluster, namely, that "leftists" are burning New Balance shoes as a form of reaction against the CEO's statements.

Last week, lefties burned New Balance shoes to protest Trump. Now, they're burning Yeezys cuz Kanye supported Trump. Stop global warming!

Instead of burning your New Balance shoes because they supported Trump, donate them to Goodwill, Salvation Army or a homeless shelter.

Other clusters neither challenge nor debunk the fake piece of news but merely report a human and political commentary on the action of Trumpists. More precisely, there are many reactions around the piece of news that has constituted the second activity peak, namely, a white power organisation "endorsing" New Balance.

Neo-Nazis have declared New Balance the "Official Shoes of White People"

Dammit! My New Balance shoes are neo nazi endorsed

Links to legacy media feature prominently in clusters other than the Trumpist one; in essence, the whole discussion is a commentary upon a piece of news that, while not fake in itself, has all of the characteristics of junk news. Interestingly, there is no relevant proof (i.e., nothing in the top retweets) of Trumpists expressing approval of the endorsement done by the white power organisation. In the case of Twitter, instead, all the most relevant tweets are explicitly concerned with the effects of the story on the stock market.

A fake Bloomberg News story sent @twitter's stock soaring http://t.co/4vCOOnFilP $TWTR http://t.co/bUokTpSiZU

Pls note – that $TWTR story everyone talking about is fake

A fake news story that Twitter received a $31 billion takeover bid sent $TWTR briefly surging

It is also worth pointing out that the Twitter case is the only one in which top-level accounts actively promote debunking the fake narration. This is probably connected with the lack of political angle and the fact that users using a cashtag might be more inclined to comprehend how price manipulation through social media works (and the costs that might entail for them). User activity, in these specific cases, seems to stem from a conscious use of Twitter's own grammar, as users explicitly try to produce vernacular content with the clear intent of achieving virality and thus engage with a political debate that is embedded in the larger hybrid media system. Words and stances are chosen for their activation potential, pushing other (potentially interested) users to join a boycott or, in the case of Twitter, to resist an alleged market manipulation.

Conclusion, Implications, and Methodological Limits

The first crucial thing we have learned from the analysis presented in this chapter is that, unlike the political domain, in the context of online consumer communication, the activities of fake news and bots seem to be quite disconnected: it is like fake news creators and bots had separate "businesses on their own." What seems evident from our cases is that: a) fake news has a limited impact upon brand value, if we conflate brand value with stock market prices; b) bots are scarcely relevant as they do not boost (at least on Twitter) the piece of fake news, but tend to piggyback existing controversies to boost visibility of related topics or commercial products. Nevertheless, the perspective of weaponising stock prices or brand value for a political purpose seems to be a powerful motivator for both the pro- and anti-Trump camps. These cases also allow us to gather insights into the relation between militant users and bots: it is widely accepted that bots contribute to the process of polarisation by having some users consume "extreme" information. While we cannot derive general conclusions due to the specificity of our cases, it seems that, at least in this context, this does not happen. The retweeting of fake/junk news is done by humans (or, at the very least, by bots so cleverly disguised to be seen as humans by Botometer) with no intervention from bots either in the circulation of fake news or in the production of polarising content.

For clarity, it should be said that our results are highly dependent upon the assumptions that we have departed from: different assumptions may lead to different results. Firstly, if we had operationalised brand value as something else, namely, sentiment towards the brand, we might have found a different scenario, as the repeated mention of the brand with negative tones would definitely have an effect on sentiment. Nevertheless, all of our cases seem to be rather short-lived, meaning that, even if we had measured brand value as sentiment, any alteration would be very temporary. Second, the lack of effect upon stock prices probably depends on our choice of data for stock prices, namely, we use standard daily prices. Because of this, we may have overlooked micro-variations that could be detected if we had used intra-day trading data. While this does not change the overall conclusions (effects on prices are still negligible), discovering micro-crashes might provide additional insights on the social dynamics of boycotts in a financialised environment. In essence, Twitter-empowered brand boycotts may come with added interests that get fulfilled on the stock market, namely, the price crash might not be significant enough to be seen at the "macro" level but may still be sizable enough to allow price speculation from a group of actors. While tweets about the effect of consumers' narrations on the stock market are also featured in the case of Pepsi, this could be more of a call to action in order to finalise the boycott, rather than a statement of fact. However, the intention to affect stock prices is evident from the concern of top users in the Twitter case.

Lastly, we observed an interesting cultural phenomenon emerging around the interactions between fake news and human users. Different from politics, fake news in the context of digital consumption seems to carry a "subversive" function, rather than a "toxic" one. Meaning that, instead of being a weapon used to crash the reputation of a politician or compromise a political campaign, consumer fake news is used by (human) users as a "platform" (Arvidsson and Caliandro, 2016) to stage and circulate specific "political agendas," through which they re-imagine their social world. This subversive function is evident in fake news appropriated by Trump supporters, through which they imagine to "Make America Great Again" by fighting united against elite tyrants (namely, Clinton, Soros, and Pepsi) as well as supporting New Balance in bringing back factories (and jobs) to US soil. Although such political imaginaries might sound extremist, in fact they are neither monolithic nor have the power to spread virally and "intoxicate" the whole "Twitter community." On the contrary, since Twitter is an open, interactive, and public ecosystem, they are re-appropriated by other groups, who subvert the original political message, as in the case of the anti-Trump users, who, using humour and mockery contest pro-Trump narrations and try to expose their inconsistency. Being a little provocative, we could conclude by saying that consumer fake news opens new possibilities and venues for political debate and discussion on digital platforms.

References

Anselmi G., Maneri M., and Quassoli F. (2020). "Un attentato quasiterroristico". Macerata, Twitter e le opportunità politiche dell'arena pubblica. *Comunicazione punto doc. 23*, 17–36. https://hdl.handle.net/10281/295220.

Arvidsson, A. (2005). Brands: A critical perspective. *Journal of Consumer Culture*, 5(2), 235–258. https://doi.org/10.1177/1469540505053093.

Arvidsson, A. (2016). Facebook and finance: On the social logic of the derivative. *Theory, Culture and Society, 33*(6), 3–23. https://doi.org/10.1177/0263276416658104.

Arvidsson, A (2019). *Changemakers: The Industrious Future of the Digital Economy*. Polity Press.

Arvidsson, A. and Caliandro, A. (2016). Brand public. *Journal of Consumer Research*, 42(5), 727–748. https://doi.org/10.1093/jcr/ucv053.

Berthon, P. R. and Pitt, L. F. (2018). Brands, truthiness and post-fact: Managing brands in a post-rational world. *Journal of Macromarketing, 38*, 218–227. https://doi.org/10.1177/0276146718755869.

Bessi, A. and Ferrara, E. (2016). Social bots distort the 2016 US Presidential election online discussion. *First Monday, 21*, 11(7). https://firstmonday.org/article/view/7090/5653.

Bounegru L., Gray J., Venturini T., and Mauri, M. (2018). *A field guide to "fake news" and other information disorders*. Public Data Lab.

Brigida, M. and Pratt, W. R. (2017). Fake news. *North American Journal of Economics and Finance, 42*, 564–573. 10.1016/j.najef.2017.08.012.

Bruns, A., Harrington, S., and Hurcombe, E. (2020). <? covid19?>'Corona? 5G? or both?': The dynamics of COVID-19/5G conspiracy theories on Facebook. *Media International Australia, 177*(1), 12–29. https://doi.org/10.1177/1329878X20946113.

Caliandro, A. (2018). Digital methods for ethnography: Analytical concepts for ethnographers exploring social media environments, *Journal of Contemporary Ethnography, 47*(5), 551–578. https://doi.org/10.1177/0891241617702.

Caliandro, A., Garavaglia, E., and Anselmi, G. (2021a). Studying ageism on social media: An exploration of ageing discourses related to Covid-19 in the Italian Twittersphere. *Rassegna Italiana di Sociologia, 62*(2), 343–375. 10.1423/101848.

Carrieri, V., Madio, L., and Principe, F. (2019). Vaccine hesitancy and (fake) news: Quasi-experimental evidence from Italy. *Health economics*, 28(11), 1377-1382. https://doi.org/10.1002/hec.3937.

Cheng, Y. and Chen, Z. F. (2021). The influence of presumed fake news influence: Examining public support for corporate corrective response, media literacy interventions, and governmental regulation. In D. Pompper and L. Hoffman (Eds.) *What IS News?* (pp. 103 127). Routledge.

De Veirman, M., Cauberghe, V., and Hudders, L. (2017). Marketing through Instagram influencers: The impact of number of followers and product divergence on brand attitude. *International Journal of Advertising*, 36(5), 798–828. https://doi.org/10.1080/02650487.2017.1348035.

Di Domenico, G. and Visentin, M. (2020). Fake news or true lies? Reflections about problematic contents in marketing. *International Journal of Market Research*, 62(4), 409–417. https://doi.org/10.1177/1470785320934719.

Di Domenico, G., Sit, J., Ishizaka, A., and Nunan, D. (2021). Fake news, social media and marketing: A systematic review. *Journal of Business Research*, 124, 329–341. https://doi.org/10.1016/j.jbusres.2020.11.037.

Elder, B. (2022, July 7). Rule books alone cannot govern the rise of the robots. *Financial Times*. https://www.ft.com/content/973efb17-6b8b-420e-a89d-dbddee06adf4.

Etter, M., Ravasi, D. and Colleoni, E. (2019). Social media and the formation of organizational reputation. *Academy of Management Review*, 44(1), 28–52. https://doi.org/10.5465/amr.2014.0280.

Ferrara, E. (2020). Bots, Elections, and Social Media: A Brief Overview. In K. Shu, S. Wang, D. Lee, and H. Liu (Eds.), *Disinformation, Misinformation, and Fake News in Social Media: Emerging Research Challenges and Opportunities* (pp. 95–114). Springer.

Fong, A. (2010). The influence of online reviews: Case study of TripAdvisor and the effect of fake reviews. In *Digital Research and Publishing* (pp. 106–113). The University of Sydney.

Gelfert, A. (2018). Fake news: A definition. *Informal Logic*, 38(1), 84–117. 10.22329/il. v38i1.5068.

Giglietto, F., Righetti, N., Rossi, L., and Marino, G. (2020). It takes a village to manipulate the media: Coordinated link sharing behavior during 2018 and 2019 Italian elections. *Information, Communication and Society*, 23(6), 867–891. ttps://doi.org/10.1080/1369118X.2020.1739732.

Golovchenko, Y., Hartmann, M., and Adler-Nissen, R. (2018). State, media and civil society in the information warfare over Ukraine: Citizen curators of digital disinformation. *International Affairs*, 94(5), 975–994. https://doi.org/10.1093/ia/iiy148.

Graham, T., Bruns, A., Zhu, G., and Campbell, R. (2020). *Like a virus: The coordinated spread of coronavirus disinformation*. Centre for Responsible Technology.

Gray, J., Bounegru, L. and Venturini, T. (2020). "Fake news" as infrastructural uncanny. *New Media and Society*, 22(2), 317–341. https://doi.org/10.1177/1461444819856912.

Guarino, S., Pierri, F., Di Giovanni, M., and Celestini, A. (2021). Information disorders during the COVID-19 infodemic: The case of Italian Facebook. *Online Social Networks and Media*, 22. https://doi.org/10.1016/j.osnem.2021.100124.

Heilweil, R. (2022, May 11). Twitter now labels misleading coronavirus tweets with misleading label. Vox. https://www.vox.com/recode/2020/5/11/21254889/twitter-coronavirus-covid-misinformation-warnings-labels.

Ladeira, W. J., Dalmoro, M., Santini, F. D. O., and Jardim, W. C. (2022). Visual cognition of fake news: The effects of consumer brand engagement. *Journal of Marketing Communications*, 28(6), 681–701. https://doi.org/10.1080/13527266.2021.1934083.

Lala, K. (2022, August 11). The Hidden Economy of Spam. https://integrityinstitute.org/our-ideas/hear-from-our-fellows/the-hidden-economy-of-spam.

Langley, P. and Leyshon, A. (2017). Platform capitalism: The intermediation and capitalization of digital economic circulation. *Finance and society.*, 3(1), 11–31. https://doi.org/10.2218/finsoc.v3i1.1936.

Lazer, D., Kennedy, R., King, G., and Vespignani, A. (2014). Google Flu Trends still appears sick: An evaluation of the 2013–2014 flu season. *SSRN.* http://dx.doi.org/10.2139/ssrn.2408560.

Lazer, D. M., Baum, M. A., Benkler, Y., Berinsky, A. J., Greenhill, K. M., Menczer, F., and Zittrain, J. L. (2018). The science of fake news. *Science*, 359(6380), 1094–1096. doi: 10.1126/science.aao2998.

Lewis, S. C., Zamith, R., and Hermida, A. (2013). Content analysis in an era of big data: A hybrid approach to computational and manual methods. *Journal of broadcasting and electronic media*, 57(1), 34–52. https://doi.org/10.1080/08838151.2012.761702.

Maneri, M., Pogliano, A., Anselmi, G., and Piccoli, F. (2022). Migration narratives in traditional and social media: The case of Italy, BRIDGES Working Papers, October 2022.

Merton, R. K. (1968). The Matthew Effect in science: The reward and communication systems of science are considered. *Science*, 159(3810), 56–63. doi: 10.1126/science.159.3810.56.

Mettier, K. (2016, November 15). We live in crazy times: Neo-Nazis have declared New Balance the "Official Shoes of White People". *Washington Post* https://www.washingtonpost.com/news/morning-mix/wp/2016/11/15/the-crazy-reason-neo-nazis-have-declared-new-balance-the-official-shoes-of-white-people/.

Mills, A. J., Pitt, C., and Ferguson, S. L. (2019). The relationship between fake news and advertising: Brand management in the era of programmatic advertising and prolific falsehood. *Journal of Advertising Research*, 59(1), 3–8. https://doi.org/10.2501/JAR-2019-007.

Mills, A.J. and Robson, K. (2020). Brand management in the era of fake news: Narrative response as a strategy to insulate brand value. *Journal of Product and Brand Management*, 29(2), 159–167. https://doi.org/10.1108/JPBM-12-2018-2150.

Munk, A. K., Olesen, A. G., and Jacomy, M. (2022). The Thick Machine: Anthropological AI between explanation and explication. *Big Data and Society*, 9(1), https://doi.org/10.1177/20539517211069891.

Nelson, L. K. (2020). Computational grounded theory: A methodological framework. *Sociological Methods and Research*, 49(1), 3–42. https://doi.org/10.1177/0049124117729703.

Nyilasy, G. (2019). Fake news: When the dark side of persuasion takes over. *International Journal of Advertising*, 38(2), 336–342. https://doi.org/10.1080/02650487.2019.1586210.

Obadă, R. (2019). Sharing fake news about brands on social media: A new conceptual model based on flow theory. *Argumentum: Journal of the Seminar of Discursive Logic, Argumentation Theory and Rhetoric*, 17(2), 144–166. https://philpapers.org/rec/OBASFN.

Pfeffer, J., Zorbach, T., and Carley, K. M. (2014). Understanding online firestorms: Negative word-of-mouth dynamics in social media networks. *Journal of Marketing Communications*, 20(1/2), 117–128. https://doi.org/10.1080/13527266.2013.797778.

Rauchfleisch, A. and Kaiser, J. (2020). The false positive problem of automatic bot detection in social science research. *PloS one*, 15(10), e0241045. https://doi.org/10.1371/journal.pone.0241045.

Rogers, R. (2020). Deplatforming: Following extreme internet celebrities to Telegram and alternative social media. *European Journal of Communication*, 35(3), 213–229. https://doi.org/10.1177/0267323120922066.

Rogers, R., and Niederer, S. (2020). *The politics of social media manipulation*. Amsterdam University Press.

Shao, C., Ciampaglia, G. L., Varol, O., Flammini, A., and Menczer, F. (2017). The spread of fake news by social bots. arXiv preprint arXiv:1707.07592, 96, 104.

Simon, F. M. and Camargo, C. Q. (2023). Autopsy of a metaphor: The origins, use and blind spots of the "infodemic". *New Media and Society*, 25(8), 2219–2240. https://doi.org/10.1177/14614448211031908.

Talwar, S., Dhir, A., Kaur, P., Zafar, N., and Alrasheedy, M. (2019). Why do people share fake news? Associations between the dark side of social media use and fake news sharing behavior. *Journal of Retailing and Consumer Services*, 51, 72–82. https://doi.org/10.1016/j.jretconser.2019.05.026.

Tandoc Jr, E. C., Lim, Z. W., and Ling, R. (2018). Defining "fake news". A typology of scholarly definitions. *Digital journalism*, 6(2), 137–153. https://doi.org/10.1080/21670811.2017.1360143.

Twitter (2021, January 8). Permanent suspension of @realDonaldTrump. https://blog.twitter.com/en_us/topics/company/2020/suspension.

Venturini, T. (2019). From fake to junk news: The data politics of online virality. In D. Bigo, I. Engin, and E. Ruppert (Eds.), *Data politics: Worlds, subjects, rights* (pp. 123–144). Routledge.

Venturini, T., Bounegru, L., Gray, J., and Rogers, R. (2018). A reality check (list) for digital methods. *New Media and Society*, *20*(11), 4195–4217. https://doi. org/10.1177/1461444818769236.

Visentin, M., Pizzi, G., and Pichierri, M. (2019). Fake news, real problems for brands: The impact of content truthfulness and source credibility on consumers' behavioral intentions toward the advertised brands. *Journal of Interactive Marketing*, 45, 99–112. https://doi.org/10.1016/j.intmar.2018.09.001.

Vosoughi, S., Roy, D., and Aral, S. (2018). The spread of true and false news online. *Science*, *359*(6380), 1146–1151. 10.1126/science.aap9559.

Wischnewski, M., Ngo, T., Bernemann, R., Jansen, M., and Krämer, N. (2022). "I agree with you, bot!" How users (dis)engage with social bots on Twitter. *New Media and Society*. https://doi.org/10.1177/14614448211072307.

Yu, Y., Duan, W., and Cao, Q. (2013). The impact of social and conventional media on firm equity value: A sentiment analysis approach. *Decision support systems*, *55*(4), 919–926. https://doi.org/10.1016/j.dss.2012.12.028.

5.   Instagram Influencers at the Crossroads between Publics and Communities

Abstract

In this chapter, we map social formations emerging around influencers' accounts on Instagram. Influencers are key social actors shaping how consumption is organised in the digital society. To fully unpack their role, it is relevant to consider their practices at the crossroads between brand publics and communities. In light of this complexity, we ask: In which ways do brand publics and influencer communities coexist on Instagram? What is the relationship between these hybrid social formations and the platformisation of consumer culture? The chapter shows that the coexistence of features typical of both brand publics and communities around the influencer persona leads to the formation of hybrid influencer publics – social formations characterised by the coexistence of mediation and interaction, the emphasis on affective forms of communication, and the presence of a mediated form of identity.

Keywords: brand publics, online social formations, social media influencers, hybrid influencer publics

Social media influencers are influential figures across various digital platforms, and especially on Instagram, where they play a key role in promoting goods, products, and services along with their online persona. This way, they are able to influence, among other things, individuals' lifestyles and consumption practices. Content creators gain visibility and build their careers by carefully crafting and displaying their branded selves (Duffy and Hund, 2019), as well as by nurturing a group of intimate and engaged followers (Abidin, 2015), which they call their "community." The idea of a community of like-minded people gathering around content creators

Caliandro, A., A. Gandini, L. Bainotti, G. Anselmi, *The Platformisation of Consumer Culture: A Digital Methods Guide*. Amsterdam: Amsterdam University Press, 2024
DOI 10.5117/9789463729567_CH05

often emerges in the open and heartfelt messages they share to thank their followers for support and recognition. Moreover, a vast array of influencer marketing books, blogs, and websites share tips on how to create and grow a community as one of the main pillars to increase engagement rates and, therefore, the possibilities of content monetisation. This chapter starts by acknowledging the relevance of the concept of "community" for Instagram influencers and the content creator industry, and at the same time argues for the necessity of understanding the aggregations surrounding content creators in a more complex way. As will be shown, influencers' social forma-tions can be understood at the crossroads between publics and communities (Arvidsson and Caliandro, 2016) or, in other terms, as "influencer hybrid publics", as they are characterised by the coexistence of mediation and interaction, the relevance of affect, and the presence of a mediated form of identity.

Existing literature about influencers highlights the importance of build-ing a relationship with the audience by sharing personal and intimate information (Abidin, 2015), which has the effect of involving the public and providing a feeling that the content creator is "just like us" (Duffy, 2017). The cultivation of a follower base is a necessary practice for content creators (and cultural producers more broadly) to navigate an increasingly platformised and changeable platform ecology (Van Dijk et al. 2018) and to keep alive their activities and small enterprises (see e.g., Cotter, 2019). The notion of "influencer community," however, is not unproblematic. First, the sense of intimacy created between the influencer and their audience is both genuine *and* instrumental, as it is ultimately aimed at generating profit (Duffy, 2017). Secondly, it can be argued that the relationships created around the content creator's branded self are not always stable and long-lasting. As McQuarrie et al. (2013) pointed out in relation to fashion bloggers, with the increase in popularity and number of followers, influential users online shift from nurturing a community to having an audience. While early in their activities fashion bloggers adopt a community-oriented behaviour towards those who browse their blog (e.g., by sharing personal details about their lifestyle and engaging with users' comments), their attitude changes and becomes more detached when they start accumulating views, comments, and interactions (McQuarrie et al., 2013).

Given the relevance and the complex nature of the concept of community, it is pivotal to analyse more closely what the features of the social formations surrounding content creators on Instagram are, and whether they can be really understood as "communities" from a consumer research perspective. The present chapter, therefore, asks: *In which ways do brand publics and influencer communities coexist on Instagram? What is the relationship between these hybrid social formations and the platformisation of consumer culture?* By building on existing literature about brand publics (Arnould et al., 2021; Arvidsson and Caliandro, 2016; Moufahim et al., 2018), we aim to analyse the social formations created around content creators on Instagram at the crossroads between publics and communities. For a long time, the concept of community has represented a useful framework to understand how consumers create a set of social relationships and shared meanings around brands or consumer practices (see e.g., Muñiz and O'Guinn, 2001). More recently, however, research has emphasised the ongoing transformation of communities (Moufahim et al., 2018) and the switch from brand communities to brand publics, which goes hand in hand with the development of social media (Arvidsson and Caliandro, 2016). If brand communities are social formations based on reciprocal interaction, discussion, and deliberation among members, and the presence of a shared identity, brand publics are more ephemeral social formations characterised by mediation, affect, and the search for publicity (Arvidsson and Caliandro, 2016).

To date, brand communities and brand publics have mostly been considered as two distinct concepts and two separate social formations. In this chapter, we instead contend that the logics of brand communities and publics co-exist, not without contradictions, in the creator economy. The social formations developing around influencers arise at the intersection of platforms' affordances and content creators' practices, and in response to the process of platformisation of cultural production (Poell et al., 2021). As such, the emergence of these hybrid social formations can be considered a form of platform practices (Duffy, 2019), aimed at navigating increasingly complex platform ecosystems. At the same time, these social formations, with their own grammars and vernaculars, contribute to re-configuring the processes of value creation as well as the formation of digital consumer imaginaries around a (self-) brand, with important implications for the platformisation of consumer culture.

The analysis of influencers' social formations in light of the concept of brand publics (Arvidsson and Caliandro, 2016) entails a shift in the object of study, which is not a brand per se, but a *branded persona* – the content creator and their self-brand. Existing research and press coverage have already posited that influencers can be considered new brands (Weinswig, 2016) or human brands (Kim and Kim, 2022). Arguably, content creators are continually involved in constructing an image of themselves, a persuasive packaging and a promotional persona aimed at being noticeable and easy to see (Abidin, 2016). In this chapter, attention is focused on how social media affordances play a major role in fostering the creation of different social formations. In particular, we will focus on the social media platform Instagram and its affordances as, to date, it represents one of the most important venues where influencers thrive. Specifically, we will focus our attention on how the characteristics of the platform, which tend to promote a one-to-many form of communication (Leaver et al., 2020), couple with content creators' practices of building a loyal and engaged following (Abidin, 2015) and users' desires to create communities of practices to share their consumption choices, feelings, and perspectives (see e.g., Gurrieri and Drenten, 2019).

By applying the definition of brand public elaborated by Arvidsson and Caliandro (2016), this chapter focuses on a set of three, patterned contradictions to understand the main features of influencers' social formations at the crossroads between publics and communities:

– *Interaction vs Mediation.* One of the main characteristics of brand communities is the interaction among core members, who share their opinions and ideas and get to know each other. Interaction is, therefore, what really constitutes a community (Canniford, 2011). By contrast, a brand public is primarily a discursive phenomenon, an organised media space kept together by practices of mediation centred around a mediation device (e.g., a hashtag), which lasts as long as the media device operates. In the case of influencers' social formations, interaction and mediation are strongly intertwined: the content creator and their branded selves function as mediators, towards which affective communication is directed. Although forms of interaction are present, they are limited and mostly uni-directional (from users to content creators) and mediated by the influencer persona.

– *Collective values vs Affect.* Secondly, unlike brand communities, participation in brand publics is not structured by discussion or deliberation, but around collective affective intensities (Arvidsson and Caliandro, 2016). In brand publics, participants are kept together by affective drives and imitative practices. They mimic each other's behaviours by sharing their perspectives, yet there is a lack of engagement among them. Similarly, in influencers' social formations, a large number of rather isolated expressions with a common affective focus coalesce around the influencer persona. Collective values can be identified, but they are primarily shaped by the affective drive exerted by the influencer and their branded persona, rather than emerging from discussions and deliberations among participants.

- *Identity vs Visibility.* Brand communities usually provide members with a sense of identity and are based on a coherent set of values and worldviews shared by all the participants (Muñiz and O'Guinn, 2001). By contrast, in brand publics, consumers do not develop a collective identity around a certain brand. Rather, the brand represents a medium that can offer publicity and visibility to a variety of perspectives. Instagram content creators foster a sense of identity that, although mediated by their branded selves, works as a shared background to users and provides a sense of belongingness, from which content creators can benefit in terms of visibility and attention.

Ultimately, the coexistence of features typical of both brand publics and communities around the influencer persona leads to the formation of what can be called *hybrid influencer publics* – social formation characterised by the coexistence of mediation and interaction, the emphasis on affective forms of communication, and the presence of a mediated form of identity.

To study the hybrid social formations emerging around influencers on Instagram, this chapter focuses on a specific category of content creators who identify themselves with the label of "Girlboss." Coined by entrepreneur and Nasty Gal founder Sophia Amoruso in 2014, "Girlboss" represents a catch-all term to identify female entrepreneurs and business leaders, moved by a "having it all" mentality and values of female empowerment (Mukhopadhyay, 2021). From a name used to define female leaders and entrepreneurs, "Girlboss" has been translated into a general ethos and aesthetic, thriving on social media platforms such as Instagram and TikTok. "Girlboss" now includes all those content creators involved in the promotion of personal development, entrepreneurialism, and self-growth on, and through, Instagram. Like other kinds of micro-celebrities, life coaches and micro-entrepreneurs who identify as Girlbosses are often the faces of their brands and enterprises, assemble a large audience on social media, and capitalise on the attention they receive by building an authentic online persona. Therefore, although they might not define themselves as such, these personalities are involved in those practices typical of social media influencers (Khamis et al., 2017). More specifically, the content creators in this category build an audience and create a community not only by publicly consuming goods (such as fashion items, health treatments, etc.) but by displaying their aspirational lifestyle and career, as well as selling (figuratively and not) tips to achieve them – including courses and mentoring services, among other things. By sharing content that promotes personal development, self-growth, and female empowerment as conduits to success and equality, these content creators put the concept of "community" at the very centre of their practices, with all the possible contradictions it can entail. For these reasons, this category of influencers is particularly relevant to study to understand the co-existence of publics and communities. In what follows, we illustrate the grammars and vernaculars that characterise a hybrid influencer public, by looking at one specific "Girlboss" content creator.

Research Question, Data Collection, and Analysis Techniques

The main aim of this chapter is to understand influencers at the crossroads between publics and communities. To do so, two main research questions will guide our analysis: *In which ways do brand publics and influencer communities coexist on Instagram? What is the relationship between these hybrid social formations and the platformisation of consumer culture?*

To answer these questions, an analysis that focuses not on Instagram's visual content but rather on the platform's affordances and their impact on fostering the creation of social formations is needed. Existing research has so far addressed, to some extent, the topic of influencers and their publics, for example by focusing on the network of collaborative connections among "alternative" influencers, who share and propagate content related to the reactionary right on YouTube (Lewis, 2018). However, a focus on the social formations arising around content creators on Instagram is still missing, thus representing an overlooked area of research, theoretically and methodologically.

The analysis of influencer hybrid publics requires blending the two methodological perspectives we introduced before (see, *Methodological Introduction*): "follow the medium" and "follow the natives." The Digital Methods paradigm allows researchers to observe a contested issue (revolving around, for example, a Google query or a set of Twitter hashtags) and represent its articulation, with all its complexities, on digital media (see e.g., Rogers et al., 2015; Venturini and Munk, 2021). On the contrary, the study of influencer hybrid publics requires starting the analysis by following one (or more) specific "native," in this case, an Instagram content creator, to delineate and access the research field. Subsequently, it is possible to follow the medium to understand how it prompts and favours the formation of specific types of hybrid aggregations. In this way, the methodological approach shifts from analysing an issue to analysing an influential personality as the starting point of the research.

In line with these considerations, our analysis focuses on one case study, that is, the profile of an Instagram content creator who identifies with the #Girlboss hashtag, ethos, and lifestyle. Despite the critiques of reproducing hustle culture, toxic work environments, discriminatory behaviours, and co-opting feminism for profit (Abad-Santos, 2021), which go beyond the aims of this chapter, this category of content creators enables us to understand the co-existence between publics and communities. Indeed, common values about female empowerment and entrepreneurship represent both a means to create a noticeable, online self-brand and a common background to foster a sense of shared identity and, hence, community.

Our analysis started with the selection of a case study: the profile of a content creator on Instagram, @alivestardust[1] (she/her), belonging to the #Girlboss "community." The choice of going in-depth with one case study allows us to understand more closely the social formation developing around a content creator and its specificities. After having put together a list of some of the top inspiring girl bosses on Instagram, according to different rankings available online,[2] the account under analysis was selected according to the following criteria:

- **Number of followers:** the account under analysis belongs to a so-called micro-influencer. Micro-influencers are more similar to regular consumers than internet celebrities (Abidin, 2018) because of the size of their audience (usually under 100k followers), the content they post and their perceived relatability (see also, Bainotti, 2023). Moreover, as previously mentioned, the larger the number of followers, the less content creators remain engaged with their audience. Therefore, looking at an influencer with a medium-sized following allows the researcher to analyse both the presence of community practices as well as the features of a public.
- **Self-identification as a Girl Boss:** the account under analysis identifies as a Girl Boss, as the bio and the hashtags used in her posts make clear (e.g., #bossbabe)
- **Level of activity:** the account posts regularly on her profile, at least once a week.

---

1   In order to protect users' privacy, all the usernames in the chapter are fantasy names.
2   See e.g., https://glamobserver.com/girl-bosses-follow-instagram/, and https://ladybossblogger. com/inspiring-female-influencers/.

To provide some context, the chosen profile, @alivestardust, is a woman in her thirties, who, at the time of writing, has amassed roughly 50k followers on Instagram. She defines herself as "Co-Founder" of a company aimed at supporting, inspiring, and training other women entrepreneurs to start and grow their businesses. She primarily uses Instagram to promote the activities and services she offers, occasionally sharing glimpses of her everyday life. It is worth mentioning that this account constitutes a particular example of a wider phenomenon and can therefore present some unique features. At the same time, however, similar influencers' profiles populate Instagram and some of the practices observed in this case study resemble what emerges in the existing literature about influencers' audiences and their affective and ephemeral dimensions (see e.g., McQuarrie et al., 2013).

For the analysis, this research made use of PhantomBuster, an online software for extracting data and automating actions on the web.[3] Despite its limitations, such as the restricted free access limited to a 14-day trial and its primary corporate functions, this tool was chosen for its ability to retrieve various types of data and metadata. Contrary to CrowdTangle, which is another useful resource for collecting Instagram data (see also Chapter 1),[4] PhantomBuster allows researchers interested in Instagram analysis to collect data about hashtags as well as users' profiles. Furthermore, this tool allows for the retrieval of comments associated with selected posts,[5] a crucial and valuable feature for the purpose of this research that is not offered by CrowdTangle.[6]

---

3   https://phantombuster.com/
4   https://www.crowdtangle.com/. Despite the limitation, CrowdTangle is a useful software for the collection of Instagram posts. As an alternative, researchers could also use the Firefox extension Zeeschuimer (available at: https://github.com/digitalmethodsinitiative/zeeschuimer). As will be explained more in-depth in Chapter 8, such an extension offers the possibility to collect Instagram data by scrolling a given page (e.g., a profile or a hashtag). Although it is a free tool for data collection, it also presents some limitations in the possibility of formulating complex research designs, and in the number of data that could be collected (see Chapter 8).
5   PhantomBuster allows for the collection of comments received by Instagram posts; however, it does not provide nested comments, which refer to the reply threads associated with the initial main comment. All the alternatives presented here to collect Instagram data have some flaws and limitations; however, the data collected with PhantomBuster represent a good entry point to the analysis of hybrid social formations on Instagram.
6   It is also possible to find other software that allows for the collection of Instagram comments, such as Apify (https://apify.com/) or Export Comments (www.exportcomments.com). Notably, all these solutions offer a free (but limited) plan to collect data, and then ask for a fee to subscribe to the service.

The data collection proceeded in two steps. Firstly, we collected all the posts shared by the account under analysis, @alivestardust, by using Phantom Buster and its "Instagram Profile Post Extractor" module. Such a module allows researchers to extract posts and their metadata (post url included) from a list of Instagram accounts. In this way, it was possible to collect 242 posts, shared between October 21, 2016 and July 7, 2022. Secondly, we used the "Instagram Post Commenters Export" module to extract user comments from a list of Instagram posts' urls (which can be easily inputted through a Google Sheet document). We collected all the comments for all the posts shared by @alivestardust, for a total of 10,907 comments.

The data analysis consisted of three, iterative steps to understand both the platform grammars and vernaculars of hybrid influencer publics. Firstly, we used data about the number of comments and unique users to map the flow of communication around the influencer profile, by looking at comment trends and users' engagement over time. This step was helpful for grasping the structural features of hybrid influencer publics. Secondly, we took into account two of the main features of the Instagram platform, mentions and comments, to understand the structure of interaction of hybrid social formations. By looking at the intersection of Instagram affordances and users' practices, we were able to identify different grammars of interaction useful for better understanding the object of study. Lastly, a content analysis of the five most commented posts and all their comments (for a total of 1,283 comments) was undertaken. In this way, it was possible to grasp the different nuances in the type of communication among the members of the influencer's audience, as well as the presence of affective relationships and shared values. This last part of the analysis was dedicated to analysing how grammars of interaction and platform vernaculars emerging from comments intersect in the formation of hybrid influencer publics. With a process that blends classification, counting, and interpretation, qualitative content analysis allows the researcher to account for the content of a body of texts (Krippendorff, 2012). In our case, qualitative content analysis is informed by digital methods, as it takes advantage of digital tools for data collection, organisation, and management, and of the metadata embedded in digital texts (Caliandro and Gandini, 2017). The categories for the analysis, summarised in Table 5.1., are informed by the theoretical concerns of the research, with some space for new categories to emerge directly from the data, in a grounded theory spirit (Charmaz, 2000).

Table 5.1.   Comment qualitative content analysis – codebook

Type of Comment	Definition	Examples
Sharing personal experience	Comments where users share their personal experiences and/or perspective on the topic addressed by the content creator's posts.	*Literally going through this rn with my business! It's growing and it is being handled by just one person, ME! I'm such a control freak that I'm finding it difficult to accept that I need to start to delegate … so that the business can continue to grow, and I don't continue to burn myself out.* 🔥
Identification	Comments where users relate and connect to the influencer persona and/or the content of her posts.	*This is totally me* 😅*; You are not alone!; Couldn't agree more* 🖤
Emoji (*)	The comments are exclusively composed of emojis.	🖤🔥😅; 💯
Mention	The comments present a mention (@) to one (or more) Instagram account.	*@inoooo that's me! Lol @AABBCC this!*
Appreciation	The comments express a positive feeling of admiration and gratefulness toward the content creator and/or her content.	*Cannot love this enough!* 😊🖤*; Such a great reminder!!!* 🖤🖤 *this is something I had to work on for myself!*
Spam	The comments are unrelated to the content of the posts and exemplify the activity of a bot or automated response.	*Invest with @XXX, is a perfect choice! I invested $2,500 and got $22,400 within 7 days. Very reliable!; Come visit our account @XYZ and tell us what you think!* 🔥🔥
Disagreement	The comments express an explicit disagreement with what is claimed or expressed by the content creator.	*Nope, I think it's all about the details. Thus, all have to be about the details as well.* 🙄*; Don't agree. And where do these statistics come from btw?*
Other	The comments do not fit in any other previous category.	*Happy Sunday* 🖤

(*) the category emoji was coded but not considered in the analysis. Although the importance of emojis is well acknowledged (see e.g., Highfield and Leaver, 2016), in this study the lack of other textual information makes it difficult to interpret this kind of content fully and neatly.

Before moving to the presentation of the results, one further note about the ethics of the research is needed. To protect users' privacy, all the usernames in the chapter are fantasy names, the results will be presented in an aggregate form, and no screenshots will be added to the text. However, to provide some instances of the tones and content of both posts and comments, the presentation of the results relies on the fabrication method (Markham, 2012). Such a method consists of the re-elaboration of original data into composite accounts and fictional narratives, with specific attention to the maintenance of the original meanings conveyed by the data (Markham 2012).[7]

The Flow of Communication around an Influencer's Profile

In order to understand the features and structure of hybrid influencer publics, we started our study by mapping the flow of communication around the @alivestardust profile. Firstly, we considered the trend of posts and comments over time, in particular by counting the occurrence of comments and linking them to unique user identities. An overview of post and comment trends is available in Fig. 5.1.

Overall, each post of the @alivestardust profile receives an average of 45 comments. As Fig. 5.1 shows, the number of comments increases over the years, with one of the highest spikes in January 2021, yet it continues to fluctuate over time. The increase in the number of comments goes hand in hand with an increase in the activity of the influencer, in terms of the quantity and frequency of posts shared, and, presumably, with the growth of the account's following.

Delving deeper into the analysis, we focused on the number of users who interacted with the content shared on the profile via the comment feature. In total, we found 6,387 unique users who engage with @alivestardust's posts. Interestingly, as illustrated in Fig. 5.2, only a small portion of users demonstrates high engagement with the content shared by the influencer. Specifically, there are 84 users who commented between ten to 19 times, 18 users who commented 20 times or more (the first 15 most engaged users are listed in Table 5.2), and only one user who left 90 comments. On the contrary, the vast majority of users exhibited minimal engagement, posting between one and four comments. This is the case for a significant number of users, with 4,898 individuals having commented only once from 2016 to 2022. These results are in line with the definition of brand public since, similarly to the Louis Vuitton case study (Arvidsson and Caliandro, 2016),

---

7   As Markham (2012) argues, the fabrication method has often been considered research misconduct and a process that falsifies data analysis. However, despite the critiques, and given the personal nature of the content related to singular users, the fabrication method is deemed appropriate for providing accounts of empirical data while assuring users' privacy.

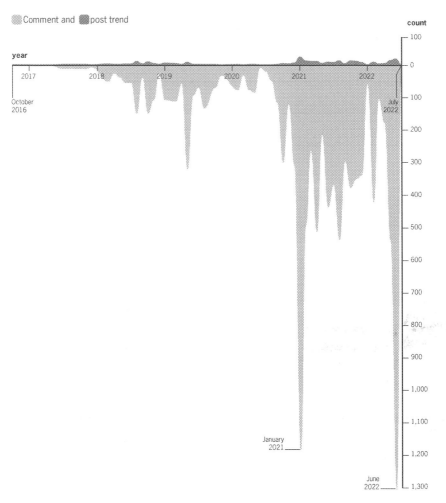

Fig. 5.1. The graph above (light blue) shows the number of posts shared by @alivestardust per month, between October 2016 (the date of the first post published on the account) and July 2022. The graph below (pink) represents the number of comments per post. The two most-commented posts were shared in January 2021 and June 2022.

the vast majority of users who interact with the influencer under analysis only participate once by commenting on her posts. Despite content creators' emphasis on building a community, we can see that, overall, users' participation is rather sporadic and discontinuous, thus aligning with the limited temporality typical of brand publics.

Apart from the large number of loosely engaged users shown in Fig. 5.2, other accounts are more active in commenting regularly and frequently on the influencer's content. The results point to the presence of some core members in the influencer's audience, who are highly engaged (in terms of

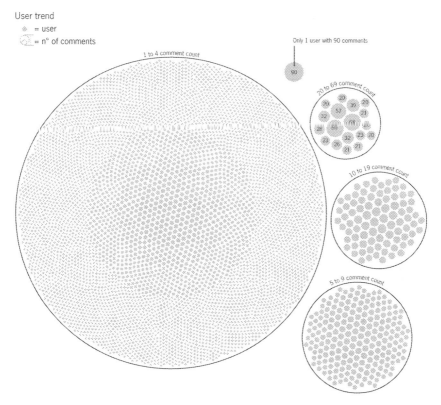

Fig. 5.2. The circle packing graph was made with RAWGraphs. In the graph, users are represented by dots and clustered per number of comments. The graph shows that the vast majority of users only post between one and four comments over the time period investigated, while 18 users comment 20 times or more, and only one user posted 90 comments.

number of comments) and who remain consistently active over the years. As the Beeswarm Chart in Fig. 5.3 shows, the users who comment the most are also the ones whose presence can be registered since the very beginning of the influencer's activity (October 2016) and persists over time, until the data collection (June 2022) (e.g., users @girlpowerdetail, @emmahealth, and @elibar). The results highlight that a hybrid influencer public can be constituted by a core of "aficionados," namely, highly and regularly engaged users, who frequently and habitually interact with the content creator in a community-like fashion. In sum, a periphery of occasional commenters and interactions co-exists with a core of recurrent and prolific users, thus showing the coexistence of both public and community dynamics.

A closer, qualitative look at the core members' profiles reveals that the most engaged users are predominantly fellow influencers, who are often related to the #Girlboss "movement" (Table 5.2). The core members are either

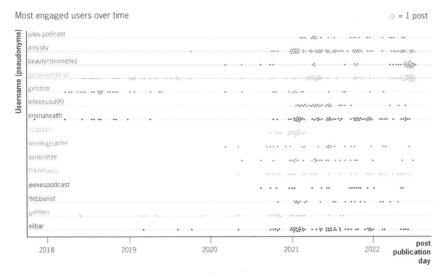

Fig. 5.3. is a Beeswarm chart created with RAWGraphs. Each dot represents a post made by a user and is positioned according to the date of publication (in the time frame 2016–2022). This visualisation is useful for highlighting the core of the influencer's hybrid public, which is composed of 15 highly and regularly engaged users, who have been interacting with the content creators throughout the duration of her Instagram activities.

influential life coaches with an established following (more than 100k), or aspirational ones, who are in the phase of building their audiences (less than 5,000 followers). Moreover, it clearly emerges that the two most engaged users are @girlpowerdetail, which is the official account of the content creator's company and @emmahealth, the influencer's business partner and co-founder. In only a couple of cases are highly engaged accounts regular Instagram users, with less than 1,000 followers.

Table 5.2.   Core members of the hybrid influencer public – type of users

n.	Username	Comment Count	Follower Count	Type of User
1	girlpowerdetail	90	3,6M	Company
2	emmahealth	69	248K	Life Coach
3	amysky	68	40,4K	Life Coach
4	elibar	57	321K	Life Coach
5	girlsbox	39	3,708	Brand
6	fflkindness	32	230K	Life Coach
7	beautycommitted	32	612	Regular User
8	infintesoul99	28	3,699	Expert
9	iamkristze	26	4,039	Life Coach
10	winningjeanne	23	164K	Life Coach

n.	Username	Comment Count	Follower Count	Type of User
11	jules.podcast	23	104K	Life Coach
12	girldam	21	81	Regular User
13	jeevespodcast	21	2,294	Life Coach
14	itsaplum	21	1,045	Expert
15	debbielist	20	49	Regular User

The core of the hybrid public, therefore, is composed of users that share the same background and interests: self-growth, personal development, and female entrepreneurship. These are all "real" accounts, meaning that no bots or spam accounts can be found among the core members. The presence of this group of similar and highly engaged accounts can be interpreted as the presence of some long-lasting and affective bonds between the content creator and fellow influencers. At the same time, it can also represent a way of creating support networks among fellow influencers, with the purpose of increasing the engagement rate of each post by mutually commenting on each other's content in a manner similar to a more or less spontaneous engagement pod (i.e., grassroots communities that agree to mutually like, comment on, and share, each other's Instagram posts, see, O'Meara, 2019).

The Structure of Interaction

The second step of our analysis aims at understanding the structure of interaction of a hybrid influencer public. Given the definitions of public and community previously introduced, interaction plays a pivotal role in understanding how publics and communities coexist on Instagram. By looking at the trends in the use of mentions (@) and comments, we identified three types of grammars of interaction: uni-directional, bi-directional, and multi-directional.

Our data show that the structure of communication is mostly charac-terised by a grammar of *uni-directional interactions*. This observation is directly linked to the platform's architecture and the nature of Instagram as a medium where individuals can express themselves and share their lives with a potentially large audience (Leaver et al., 2020). The main form of interaction afforded by the platform is a top-down one, which goes from the content creator to their users (content creator → users). On the other hand, the comment section enables users to express their opinions, thoughts, and feedback in relation to the content creator's posts, often with the possibility of creating a sense of intimacy and relatedness (Abidin, 2015) (users → content creator). The type of interaction among the members of the hybrid public is mostly uni-directional, meaning that comments are mainly directed to the content creator's profile in a user–influencer type of communication. The same applies when the core members of the social formation are involved: although their participation is higher and more constant, it does not translate into reciprocal forms of communication. The prominence of uni-directional interactions is prompted by Instagram's affordances, which contribute to directing users' attention and affect towards the influencer persona.

In the case of *bi-directional interactions*, there is a form of reciprocity, which consists of the influencer responding to some of the comments from her audience. However, this remains a one-to-one communication (user → ← content creator). From the analysis of the comment sections of the five most commented posts, we can see that @alivestardust responds 34 times out of 1,283 comments. The kind of answers given consists mostly of a short comment or an emoji:

@mim94: Let's do this! *pulls up sleeve*

@alivestardust: @mim94 💯💯💯

Given the limited number of responses and the type of content shared, it can be said that bi-directional forms of communication resemble those practices of perceived interconnectedness (Abidin, 2015) whereby influencers interact with followers to give the impression of intimacy. The data shows that bi-directional interactions seem to be oriented towards giving the impression of a conversation, with the final purpose of increasing the number of comments, the engagement rate, and, in turn, the visibility and value of content (O'Meara, 2019). In other words, by providing the impression of being present and relatable, content creators are able to provide a sense of community and fuel the number of comments below their posts, hence improving the metrics and analytics, which make them competitive in the influencer economy. The data points to the presence of interactions between the influencer as a branded persona and some of the members of the so-called community; yet, such interactions do not go beyond this form of bi-directional communication and, most importantly, do not end up creating an interactive discussion, which is a pivotal feature of a community.

By looking more closely at the use of mentions in the comment section, the lack of multivocal conversations is confirmed. More precisely, despite the presence of a grammar of *multi-directional interactions*, no real dialogue is established among users:

@imdeanna: Thought of you @abstacy 😶😶😅

@abstacy: @imdenanna 😫🙈

Mentions are used to share content with other, like-minded people, or to attract attention on a specific topic addressed by the content creator. The interactions vehiculated by mentions in the comment section are once again ephemeral forms of participation, mediated by the influencer persona. Instagram's comment section, therefore, does not fully serve as a venue for articulated interactions and forms of communication.

The results show that, in the case of a hybrid influencer public, interactions among users are somehow limited. The predominant grammars are those of uni-directional interactions (from content creator to users, and vice versa) and bi-directional interactions (when there is reciprocity between the content creator and users). The predominance of the uni-directional grammar of interaction represents a sign of the co-existence between interaction and mediation. Furthermore, the analysis shows the presence of some forms of dialogue, which, however, are more similar to affective responses directed to the influencer and her persona rather than collective discussions. The influencer's branded self thus functions as a device of mediation towards whom communication is directed and affect is shared, similarly to what happens in a brand public (Arvidsson and Caliandro, 2016). In sum, Instagram affordances play a pivotal role in structuring the interaction of a hybrid social formation, as their material component, together with how individuals use them, contribute to providing the impression of community and reciprocal interaction, while at the same time promoting an ephemeral, unidirectional, and mediated type of communication.

Types of Communication: Comment Analysis

Delving into the qualitative analysis of comments it is possible to integrate the insights about the influencer's structure of communication and the grammars of interaction with reflections on the common values and sense of identity conveyed in an influencer's social formation. The research now focuses on the vernacular expressions emerging from Instagram users and their comments. The analysis of vernaculars is complementary to that of grammars and enables a better understanding of the relationship between the content creator and her audience. The results of the qualitative content analysis of comments are summarised in Table 5.3.

Table 5.3.   Qualitative content analysis of comments – results

Type of Comment	Number	Percentage
Sharing personal experience	457	35.6
Identification	350	27.3
Emoji	248	19.3
Appreciation	83	6.5
Mention	72	5.6
Spam	55	4.3
Disagreement	10	0.8
Other	8	0.6
Total	**1,283**	**100.0**

As the results show, the most recurrent type of comment is "sharing personal experience" (35.5%). In these cases, users share their personal experiences and perspectives on the topic addressed by the content creator in her posts. Some of the comments in this category provide tips and tricks for creating video content, specifically Instagram reels, and discuss how to find a life-work balance based on users' everyday lives and the importance of delegating tasks, as shown by the following examples:

> I don't even worry about looking good half the time! I've promised my audience real life so that's what they get 😂

> I've started making myself take one day off a week and tell myself that I'm not allowed to work, which helps ease the guilt of not working!

> It's so hard for me to loosen my grip on every micro aspect of my business, but so amazing how much time I can free up when I do to focus on what matters!

These comments present themselves as a flow of individual experiences, which is directed towards the content creator. Interestingly, the sharing of personal experiences is, at times, elicited by the content creator herself, for example with captions like: "And you? How would you describe your experiences of working over weekends?" Once again, the influencer assumes the role of a mediator, towards whom interaction is directed and individual experiences are shared. The comments in this category are, in most cases, not aimed at gaining visibility, but at sharing personal experience, affect, and relatedness to the influencer. In line with the results found by Arvidsson and Caliandro (2016) in their research, we can interpret these comments as forms of private sociality, that is, the public sharing of private affects (Papacharissi, 2014).

From the analysis of the experiences shared by users, a set of common values and meanings emerge, which unite the influencer's followers. Such a sense of belongingness becomes apparent in the "identification" type of comments, the second per number of occurrences (n–349, 27.2% of the total comments). In this case, users relate and connect to the content posted by the influencer, as well as to the values surrounding the #Girlboss philosophy more broadly. Users identify, for example, with the challenges of being a female entrepreneur, such as the struggle to keep up with the ever-changing requests of the Instagram algorithm: "Omg this couldn't be more true [sic]!!! All the effort and work, only to have IG deciding whether your content will be seen or not! 😞." These practices can also be interpreted as ways to navigate the ever-changing requests of digital platforms in a platformised environment (Duffy et al., 2019). Furthermore, a large number of comments show followers' identification with the content creator, such as "literally me" or "just happened to me," as well as with a group of like-minded people, when commenting "you are NOT alone" and "Oh thank God it's not just me 😄 You are me ... I am you ... we are we 🙂." Therefore, we can find some collective values that glue an influencer's following together in a community-like social formation, as well as a common background that leads to the impression of a shared sense of identity. These two elements – collective values and identity – are typical of a community and are coexisting here with manifestations of affect, one of the main features of a brand public.

Feelings of identification are often accompanied by "appreciation" comments, which represent the third most common type of reaction, emojis excluded (6,1%). These comments express a positive feeling of admiration and gratefulness towards the content creator and her content. Some appreciation comments are directed specifically towards the ideas and suggestions provided by the content creator: "Someone had to say it! Thank you so much🖤🙏💧🙌"; "Such a wonderful message 🖤 Keep inspiring 😍✨." Others, instead, are addressed to the influencer as a person who shares parts of her life with the audience, such as "Hair looks amazing FYI" or "you 🖤 and that dress 😍." As the content and tone of these comments suggest, appreciation can be considered yet another manifestation of affect directed to the content creator. Such an affective relationship, however, is neither stable nor continuative over time, as seen in the analysis of users' participation and engagement (see Fig. 5.2.).

Another relevant point is the prevalence of positive comments of iden-tification and appreciation over negative expressions or disagreement. As Table 5.3 shows, only 0.8% of comments are users expressing disagreement regarding the content creator. In these cases, users share different opinions or open disagreement with the perspective shared by the influencer, although the ways in which these opinions are expressed remain polite, and neither aggressive nor harassing. This kind of negative content has not been found in the content analysis of comments. The lack of disagreement and, therefore, discussion, confirms that, in the hybrid influencer public, there is mostly a manifestation of affect, rather than a joint discussion and deliberation around the common values of an apparent community.

Overall, the results of the qualitative content analysis of comments highlight that collective values and a shared sense of identity represent an important component of an influencer hybrid public. The data point to the presence of some collective values that keep an influencer's following together in a community-like social formation, as well as a shared sense of identity. What is missing, however, is the element of discussion and delibera-tion among participants, a pivotal feature of a community. The coexistence of community and public features leads to a *mediated sense of identity*, which is nurtured by the content creator to gain visibility and acquire engagement, and embraced by users as means to find recognition in a hybrid social formation centred around the influencer persona. Therefore, in contrast to brand publics, in hybrid influencer publics a dimension of identity is not completely replaced by quests for publicity (Arvidsson and Caliandro, 2016), but rather persists in the form of a mediated identity. Such a mediated sense of identity is purposefully and carefully constructed by content creators as a means to achieve visibility in an increasingly platformised ecosystem. Although we cannot deny the presence of some users' attempts at gaining publicity through the influencer persona, the quest for visibility is first and foremost the influencer's priority. Put differently, visibility is built exactly by fostering a sense of identity, which, although mediated, works as a shared background among users and provides a sense of identification and belongingness.

Conclusion

The focus of this chapter was shedding light on the features of influencers' social formations at the crossroads between publics and communities. The results show that brand publics and communities coexist in complex ways on Instagram, giving birth to what we called hybrid influencer publics. To answer our first research question (*In which ways do brand publics and influencer communities coexist on Instagram?*), it is possible to identify three main elements that characterise the coexistence between publics and communities on Instagram. First, the flow of communication has a limited temporality, which shows the ephemerality of mediation and affect. Moreover, the hybrid public is composed of a periphery of occasionally engaged users and a core of very involved members – a coexistence that shows the entanglement of public and community. Secondly, grammars of uni-directional and bi-directional interactions prevail. The structure of interaction is mostly linear and mediated by the influencer persona. Despite the appearance of a sense of community through the presence of multi-directional forms of interaction, as well as evidence of appreciation and identification, there is a lack of discussion and deliberation around the collective values shared by the so-called community. Lastly, the type of communication in hybrid influencer publics is driven by sharing affective relationships directed towards the content creator and is characterised by a mediated sense of identity. Although existing research shows that social media support a publicity oriented consumer culture based on appearance and visibility rather than identity and belongingness (see e.g., Marwick, 2015), the contemporary logic of platformisation contributes to changing and complexifying this relationship. As we can see in the analysis of hybrid influencer publics, publicity oriented consumer culture persists but becomes increasingly based on the creation of a mediated sense of identity – that is, a specific sense of identity and belongingness, which is vehiculated by, and directed to, the influencer persona, and used by influencers themselves to attain visibility and maximise profit.

More generally, the analysis of hybrid influencer publics allows us to point out the relationships between hybrid social formations and the platformisation of consumer culture. As explained in the Introduction, with the platformisation of consumer culture, the systems of meanings and practices consumers articulate around products, brands, or services, including a self-brand, are increasingly shaped by the socio-technical architecture of digital environments. In this chapter, we showed exactly the role played by the Instagram platform and its affordances in orienting the flow of communication and the grammars of interaction characterising content creators' social formations. Furthermore, hybrid influencer publics represent a response to the increasing penetration of platforms and their logic in the field of cultural production (Poell et al., 2022), and are used to maintain a position in an increasingly saturated influencer economy. As such, hybrid social formations can be interpreted at the intersection of affordances and platform practices, understood as the "strategies, routines, experiences, and expressions of creativity, labour, and citizenship that shape cultural production through platforms" (Duffy et al., 2019, p. 2). In light of the results presented here, we can add to the work of Duffy et al. (2019), which shows that platform practices contribute to shaping not only cultural production, but also to consumer culture. We could suggest that the platformisation of cultural production and consumer culture are closely linked in the case of Instagram influencers, in that they share similar logics, but differ from the different domains of "culture" that they insist on. Such a relationship would be an interesting topic to address in future research about content creators from an interdisciplinary perspective.

Hybrid influencer publics, therefore, emerge as a response to increasingly platformised ecosystems. At the same time, they contribute to fuelling forms of platformisation of consumer culture. These social formations play an important role in the processes of value co-creation (Zwick, 2008), which rely on temporary affective relationships and a mediated sense of identity. The value that both influencers and users co-create in the context of hybrid influencer publics benefits content creators to some extent (as they can hopefully be rewarded in visibility), but it predominantly benefits social media platforms, which capitalise on the production of user-generated content. In these processes, the formation of digital consumer imaginaries around a (self-) brand also change, as they become increasingly oriented by the requirements of platforms in terms of visibility and profit-making (Nieborg and Poell, 2018).

Limitations and Future Research

It is worth noting that this chapter focuses on one case study, which was chosen for its peculiar characteristics. Despite this being only one example of a hybrid influencer public, it is useful for highlighting some general features of the social formations around Instagram influencers and their hybrid nature. However, it is also true that other types of content creators, who address more divisive topics, might also use the platform for other aims, and be surrounded by other types of social formations – for example, with a larger number of users engaged in interacting among each other. The main aim of this chapter is, therefore, to provide some general guidelines for the analysis of hybrid influencer publics. The different dimensions constituting these social formations can then appear in different combinations and intensities, depending on the type of content creators analysed and the platforms in which they operate. The architecture of other platforms and apps (e.g., Telegram) can, indeed, have different effects on how communities and publics coexist. Ultimately, the main contribution of this chapter is to highlight the ways in which brand publics and influencer communities coexist, a phenomenon that complexifies the general discourse about content creators' "communities" and provides relevant insights into the understanding of the platformisation of cultural production.

References

Abidin, C. (2018). *Internet celebrity: Understanding fame online*. Emerald Publishing.

Abidin. C. (2016). Aren't these just young, rich women doing vain things online?: Influencer selfies as subversive frivolity. *Social Media + Society*, 2(2), 1–17. https://doi.org/10.1177/2056305116641342.

Abidin, C. (2015). Communicative ♥ intimacies: Influencers and perceived interconnectedness. *Ada: A Journal of Gender, New Media, and Technology*, 8. https://adanewmedia.org/2015/11/issue8-abidin/.

Arnould, E. J., Arvidsson, A., and Eckhardt, G. M. (2021). Consumer collectives: A history and reflections on their future. *Journal of the Association for Consumer Research*, 6(4), 415–428. https://doi.org/10.1086/716513.

Arvidsson, A. and Caliandro, A. (2016). Brand public. *Journal of Consumer Research*, 42(5), 727–748. https://doi.org/10.1093/jcr/ucv053.

Bainotti, L. (2023). How conspicuousness becomes productive on social media. *Marketing Theory*. https://doi.org/10.1177/14705931231202435.

Caliandro, A. and Gandini, A. (2017). *Qualitative research in digital environments: A research toolkit*. Routledge.

Canniford, R. (2011). A typology of consumption communities. In R. W. Belk, K. Grayson, A. M. Muñiz, and J. H. Schau (Eds.), *Research in consumer behavior* (pp. 57–75). Emerald Group Publishing Limited.

Charmaz, K. (2000). Grounded theory: Objectivist and constructivist methods. In N. Denzin and Y. Lincoln, Y. (Eds.), *Handbook of qualitative research* (pp. 509–535). Sage.

Cotter, K. (2019). Playing the visibility game: How digital influencers and algorithms negotiate influence on Instagram. *New Media and Society*, 21(4), 895–913. https://doi.org/10.1177/1461444818815684.

Duffy, B. E. (2017). *(Not) getting paid to do what you love: Gender, social media, and aspirational work*. Yale University Press.

Duffy, B. E. and Hund, E. (2019). Gendered visibility on social media: Navigating Instagram's authenticity bind. *International Journal of Communication, 13*, 4983–5002. https://ijoc.org/index.php/ijoc/article/view/11729.

Gurrieri, L. and Drenten, J. (2019), Visual storytelling and vulnerable health care consumers: Normalising practices and social support through Instagram. *Journal of Services Marketing. 33*(6), 702–720. https://doi.org/10.1108/JSM-09-2018-0262.

Khamis, S., Ang, L., and Welling, R. (2017). Self-branding, "micro-celebrity" and the rise of

social media influencers. *Celebrity Studies, 8*(2), 191–208. https://doi.org/10.1080/1 9392397.2016.1218292.

Kim, D.Y. and Kim, H.-Y. (2022). Social media influencers as human brands: An interactive marketing perspective. *Journal of Research in Interactive Marketing, 17*(1), 94–109. https://doi.org/10.1108/JRIM-08-2021-0200.

Krippendorff, K. 2012. *Content analysis: An introduction to its methodology.* Sage.

Leaver, T., Highfield, T., and Abidin, C. (2020). Instagram: Visual social media cultures. Polity Press.

Lewis, B. (2018). Alternative influence: Broadcasting the reactionary right on YouTube. Data and Society Research Institute. https://datasociety.net/wp-content/uploads/2018/09/DS_Alternative_Influence.pdf.

Markham, A. (2012). Fabrication as ethical practice. *Information, Communication and Society, 15*(3), 334–353. https://doi.org/10.1080/1369118X.2011.641993.

Marwick, A. E. (2015). Instafame: Luxury selfies in the attention economy. *Public Culture, 27*(1/75), 137–160. https://doi.org/10.1215/08992363-2798379.

Maheshwari, S. (2018, November 11) Are you ready for the nanoinfluencers? *The New York Times.* https://www.nytimes.com/2018/11/11/business/media/nanoinfluencers-instagram-influencers.html?smtyp=curandsmid=tw-nytimes.

McQuarrie, E. F., Miller, J., and Phillips, B. J. (2013). The megaphone effect: Taste and audience in fashion blogging. *Journal of Consumer Research, 40*(1), 136–158. https://doi.org/10.1086/669042.

Moufahim, M., Wells, V., and Canniford, R. (2018). The consumption, politics and transformation of community. *Journal of Marketing Management, 34*(7/8), 557–568. https://doi.org/10.1080/0267257X.2018.1479506.

Mukhopadhyay, S. (2021, August 31). The girlboss is dead. Long live the girlboss. *The Cut.* https://www.thecut.com/2021/08/demise-of-the-girlboss.html.

Muñiz, A. M. and O'Guinn, T. (2001). Brand community, *Journal of Consumer Research, 27*(4), 412–432. https://doi.org/10.1086/319618.

Nieborg, D.B. and Poell, T. (2018). The platformization of cultural production: Theorizing the contingent cultural commodity. *New Media and Society, 20*, 4275–4292. https://doi.org/10.1177/1461444818769694.

O'Meara, V. (2019). Weapons of the chic: Instagram influencer engagement pods as practices of resistance to Instagram platform labor. *Social Media+ Society, 5*(4), https://doi.org/10.1177/2056305119879671.

Papacharissi, Z. (2014). *Affective publics: Sentiment, technology, politics.* Oxford University Press.

Poell, T., Nieborg, D. B., and Duffy, B. E. (2021). *Platforms and cultural production.* Polity Press.

Rogers, R., Sánchez-Querubín, N., and Kil, A. (2015). *Issue mapping for an ageing Europe.* Amsterdam University Press.

Van Dijck, J., De Waal, M., and Poell, T. (2018). *The platform society: Public values in a connective world.* Oxford University Press.

Venturini, T. and Munk, A. K. (2021). *Controversy mapping: A field guide.* John Wiley and Sons.

Weinswig, D. (2016, October 5). Influencers are the new brands. *Forbes.* https://www.forbes.com/sites/deborahweinswig/2016/10/05/influencers-are-the-new-brands/?sh=20e0345b7919.

Zwick, D., Bonsu, S. K., and Darmody, A. (2008). Putting consumers to work: "Co-creation" and new marketing govern-mentality. *Journal of Consumer Culture, 8*(2), 163–196. https://doi.org/10.1177/1469540508090089.

6. Assessing the Impact of *Kitchen Nightmares* through TripAdvisor

Abstract

Drawing on 5,608 customer ratings and reviews scraped from TripAdvisor, the chapter assesses how the restaurants appearing on *Kitchen Nightmares* Italy are doing after the airing of the show. Based on ad hoc statistical analysis of reviews and rating scores, we observe that the show has a very limited impact on the restaurants' visibility, reputation, and quality on TripAdvisor; reviews do have a boost thanks to *Kitchen Nightmares*, but only in conjunction with the airing of the show. However, scores are disconnected from the programme airing date, and display a paradoxical relationship with reviews: the more the reviews, the lesser the score. Finally, through a qualitative analysis of customers' reviews, we highlight a particular tension, namely, that, on the one hand, the show enhances the restaurant's conditions while, on the other hand, it sets high expectations for both customers and restaurant owners.

Keywords: reality, cooking show, scraping, ratings, customer review, audience.

Admittedly, this chapter stems from a combination of the authors' passion for reality television shows, and for the show *Kitchen Nightmares* in particular, and a scientific curiosity about the possible social impact this and similar programmes might have. This is not odd in consumer culture research; consider, for example, Schouten and McAlexander's seminal article *Subcultures of consumption* (1995), which consists in an ethnographic study of a Harley Davidson community of which the authors were active members. For those who might not know it, *Kitchen Nightmares* is a food reality show hosted by the famous chef and TV star Gordon Ramsay. In this show, chef Ramsey visits real restaurants that go through serious business troubles (due to, for example, bad management, poor quality of food, or simply bad

Caliandro, A., A. Gandini, L. Bainotti, G. Anselmi, *The Platformisation of Consumer Culture: A Digital Methods Guide*. Amsterdam: Amsterdam University Press, 2024
DOI 10.5117/9789463729567_CH06

luck) and offers his help to revitalise them. Initially, the show was set in UK (the first episode was aired in 2004 on Channel 4), then it landed in the US (first season 2007), and subsequently became a global franchise with local editions (see for instance *Pesadilla en la cocina* (first season 2012), the Spanish version of the programme hosted by chef Alberto Chicote).

Our personal fascination for the show grew from watching the Italian version of the programme: *Cucine da Incubo* (first season 2013), hosted by the five- Michelin-starred chef and co-host of *MasterChef* Italia Antonino Cannavacciuolo. At the end of each episode, the very same questions haunted us: *How about the restaurant now? Did chef Cannavacciuolo (and the show in general) really help the restaurants' owners to sort out their business troubles? Has the owner been able to maintain the high quality standards set by chef Cannavacciuolo?* By randomly checking some comments on YouTube or TripAdvisor it is possible to get some answers, albeit very scattered and contradictory ones (for instance, some claim that the restaurant is better now while others state exactly the opposite). We started wondering, therefore, whether digital methods could help us to answer more systematically the aforementioned questions and, in turn, answer a broader and interesting scientific question: *What is the social impact of Kitchen Nightmares? More generally, what is the social impact of a reality show that aims at having a positive impact on society? Does it redistribute value within the social or simply extract value from it?*[1]

The topic of reality television has been long covered by consumer culture and sociological literature (Rose and Wood, 2005; Parmentier and Fischer, 2015; Canavan, 2021), which, among other things, has reflected extensively on its social impact. Contributions span from analysis on how reality shows reconfigured TV audiences (introducing new ways of consuming TV contents, like co-viewing (Doughty et al., 2011)) or second-screen (Stewart, 2020) to discursive representations of key social issues like authenticity (Rose and Wood, 2005), gender (Negra et al., 2013; Herkes and Redden, 2017), and social class (Allen and Mendick, 2013). Some scholars focused on healthy nutrition (Phillipov 2013) and the identitarian (Rimoldi, 2015) and even therapeutic (Grosglik and Lerner, 2020) function of reality programmes; others critically reflected on the exploitation of

1   This question is not trivial; in fact, a show like *Kitchen Nightmares* would be impossible to air without the active collaboration of the restaurant owner as well as her family and staff, not to mention the significant amount of emotional labour (Hochshild, 1983) required (and sometimes explicitly demanded) from those people. Consider, for example, how the host – and the show script – constantly exhorts participants to explore and express their deep emotions or psychological status (e.g., anger, frustration, aggressivity, depression, anxiety, etc.).

"emotional labour" (Hesmondhalgh and Baker, 2008) or "amateur labour" (Seale, 2012) in these kinds of shows. Regarding *Kitchen Nightmares* in particular, the literature focused more on its cultural impact, studying, for example, the representation of food waste (Thompson and Haigh, 2017) or the emergence of a new "culture of incivility" (Higgins et al., 2012), rather than its social one (Dajem and Alyousef, 2020). Moreover, to our knowledge, no research, to date, has tried to assess the social impact of *Kitchen Nightmares* by taking advantage of digital and computational methods. It should be noted, however, that several past contributions have focused on analysing Tripadvisor data with computational techniques (Van Laer et al., 2019; Alexander et al., 2019) or, more specifically, on the effect of extra digital reputation events on Tripadvisor reviews (Li et al., 2022; Wang et al., 2015).

Methodology and Ethical Considerations

To answer the aforementioned research question, we took advantage of TripAdvisor, by far one of the most popular platforms in the hospitality industry, which, among other things, gathers a lot of useful information on restaurants worldwide, along with consumers' ratings and reviews (Galov, 2023). In order to get data from TripAdvisor we built an ad hoc web scraper. Different from API calling, scraping consists in developing an ad hoc script – in our case we used the software Python –programmed to "grab" specific digital entities (e.g., the title of a blog post, the comments below a blog post, etc.) directly from the HTML code of a target webpage (Weltevrede, 2016). Although scraping is not a "prohibited technique" in social research, it is still a controversial one, which needs to be managed conscientiously and ethically (Landers et al., 2016; Bainotti et al., 2021). To do that, it is important not to break three "golden" rules, that is, the researcher must not use a scraper to: 1) bypass platforms' restrictions or blocks; 2) disguise the non-human identity of the collector of data; 3) access content protected by privacy settings or passwords (Caliandro 2021; see also Fiesler et al., 2016). In our research, we followed all these rules, since we collected only publicly available data using a full-fledged automated scraper. Moreover, in our analysis, we presented our results in numerical and aggregated form – thus respecting the privacy of the single users (Markham and Buchanan, 2012, see also Chapter 5). Furthermore, although public, we omitted the names of the restaurants and TripAdvisor's posters in the presentation of results. Lastly, all the comments displayed are part of customer reviews that have been translated into English from Italian – something that makes it more difficult to trace back the actual users posting them.

Data Collection and Techniques of Analysis

Firstly, we downloaded all the available Italian language reviews for all those venues (41) that featured in the last six editions of the Italian edition of *Kitchen Nightmares*; that is, from Season 2 (2014) to 7 (2019). We excluded the first and the current seasons (Season 8) because the former was aired too early (2013) and the associated reviews were very sporadic, whereas the latter was ongoing at the time of the data collection, and this could have led to incomplete data. We obtained the list of the restaurants, segmented by season, through Wikipedia (*Cucine da incubo (Italia)*[2]). Out of 41 venues, only 28 have TripAdvisor pages (although some of those appear to be inactive, or have very low activity). Ten of these restaurants are now out of business. Out of those 28 TripAdvisor pages, we gathered 5,608 reviews, which span a time frame of 11 years, from March 2011 to March 2022. As we shall see, these reviews are not evenly distributed in time and space: some venues have hundreds of reviews while others have just a few. Moreover, reviews tend to have a somewhat bell-shaped distribution, with the central years of the show (roughly from 2015 to 2018) having the lion's share of reviews, while other years have much less. While we cannot claim any strong empirical evidence for our specific data, we suspect that this distribution is pretty common across TripAdvisor: reviews are unevenly distributed across venues and have been in a slow but steady decline since the late 2010s (Singh, 2019).

To analyse our data, and thus assess the impact of the TV show, we have plotted the time series of reviews and controlled for any effect of *Kitchen Nightmares* on: a) the distribution of reviews (which has been useful to evaluate the impact of the show on the restaurants' visibility and reputation); and b) the review scores (which have been useful to determine the impact of the show on the quality of food and service of the restaurants – as perceived by clients). Furthermore, we separated reviews that mention the show *Cucine da incubo* (*Kitchen Nightmares*) or the show's host "Cannavacciuolo" from those that do not. We assumed, as

2   https://it.wikipedia.org/wiki/Cucine_da_incubo_(Italia)#Stagione_1.

a starting hypothesis, that users posting reviews that explicitly mention the show got to the venue because of the show, and so that they will behave in a different way from users that, in their reviews, mention neither the show nor the host. Eventually, to estimate the effect of the TV show, we tracked whether reviews mentioning keywords connected to the show produce a higher (or lower) evaluation of the venue. Furthermore, to assess whether reviews mentioning the show produced different narrations in respect to others, we investigated the content of reviews using both quantitative text analysis and qualitative content analysis, by focusing on the sentiment, topic, and narration style of the comments taken into account. The qualitative analysis of comments gave us further clues to the motives behind specific increases or decreases in the number of reviews and review scores.

Before proceeding with the presentation of the results, a word of caution is needed: as we have previously claimed, venues are highly unequal in terms of reviews; so, while we are not striving for statistical significance, as our goals are purely descriptive, it should be said that some venues have contributed much more than others to the final results. In addition, for some analysis (i.e., analysis of reviews' scores) only those venues (13) with more than 200 reviews have been considered.

The Distribution of the Reviews

The analysis of the number of reviews obtained by each restaurant participating in the show is a simple but nonetheless important one. In fact, it gave us an insight into whether the programme really helped the restaurants to increase their visibility and reputation (either good or bad). In fact, one can consider the number of reviews as a proxy of both the attention of users towards the restaurants and the flow of clients.

As we can see from Fig. 6.1, reviews are unevenly distributed in time, with the "central" years of our time frame sorting far more reviews than years before or after. The monthly average of review scores (Fig. 6.2) seems to have an inverse shape, compared to review distribution (Fig. 6.1), meaning the more reviews all venues have, the lower the average monthly reviews are. As we can see from looking at the y-axis of Fig. 6.3 – and as we previously anticipated – the distribution of reviews is strongly unequal, as the top four venues account for one third (36%) of reviews.

Review distribution for 28 venues in 11 years

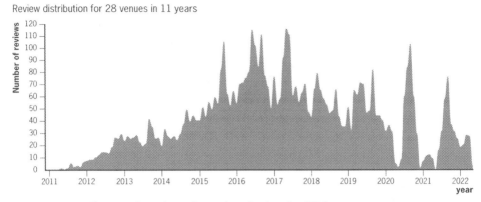

Fig. 6.1. The vertical axis shows the number of reviews for all (28) venues.

Monthly average score for 28 venues

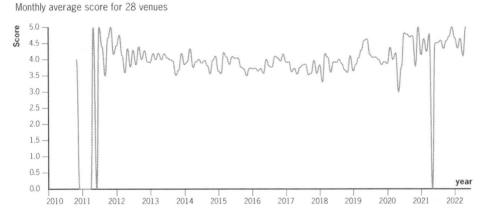

Fig. 6.2. The vertical axis shows the monthly average score for all (28) venues

Looking at the distribution of reviews, it seems that the effect of the TV show is, at best, ambivalent. On the one hand, if we consider the two months following the venue being featured in *Cucine da Incubo*, there seems to be a boost in reviews: being featured on the TV show led to an increase of reviews by, on average, 13%, as compared to the average of all other two months periods. On the other hand, the boost appears to be short-lived, as all venues do not experience a sizable increase for a longer period. They may have other "spikes" (perhaps connected to reruns) but, in general, reviews seem to follow their own, descending, trend. We can therefore conclude that the show does help restaurants to increase their visibility and reputation, but only for a very limited span of time.

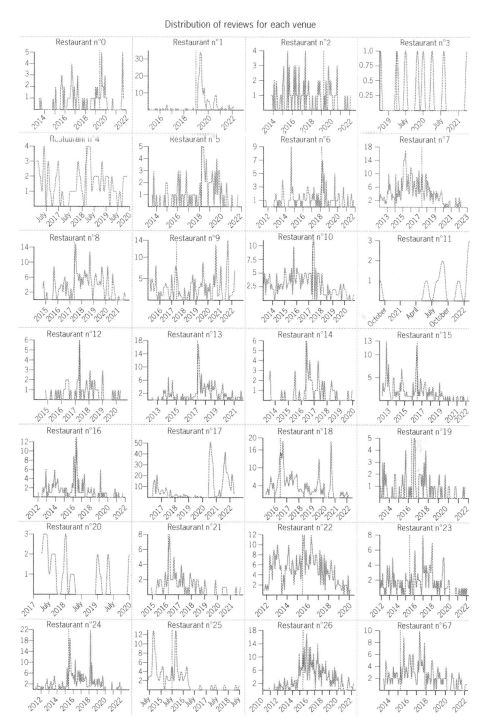

Fig. 6.3. These graphs report the number of reviews for each month. The dashed line marks the day on which the restaurant featured on the TV show (venue names have been anonymised).

The Distribution of Review Scores

The analysis of the review scores adds further useful insights: a) it says something more about the reputation of the restaurants (is it good or bad?); and b) review scores can be considered as a proxy of the quality of food and service provided by the restaurants. If we consider the top 13 venues, looking at the trends of scores in the two months following the original airdate, there seems to be little appreciable difference between that period and the average of other two months periods. The difference in scores is always in the realm of zero point something (0.01 on average), with only two cases having a difference that is larger than one point. In general, review scores seem to be disconnected from the airdate, as can be seen in Fig. 6.4. If a venue was performing in a given direction, meaning that its scores were increasing or decreasing, it seems as though its appearance on the show did not alter in any significant way the trend of the reviews. This can be explained if we look at Fig. 6.3 and Fig. 6.4, where we see a paradoxical relation between the number of reviews and review scores, as they seem to be in counterphase to each other, meaning: the more reviews a restaurant has, the lesser the score. This may be due to an effect at the platform level: essentially, we need to account for the fact that TripAdvisor is losing traction. This is because, in 2022, the market niche became oversaturated with competitors, as opposed to the 2010s when TripAdvisor had a virtual monopoly (Anselmi et al., 2021). Furthermore, we may also need to account for an "exposition" effect, due to the fact that the airdate seems to increase the number of reviews but not the average score. Essentially, what seems to happen is that small venues (just like those selected for the TV show) experience a small(ish) number of reviews, which are, probably for the most part, from regular customers. As the attention on the restaurant increases, reviews increasingly come in from casual customers who may have less of an emotional connection with the venue and hence be more inclined to assign lower scores. Assuming that reviews are declining (and scores are going up, as per Fig. 6.4) this may be due to the same effect: aficionados (i.e., those who have an emotional investment in the venue) crowding out casuals. This is partly confirmed if we zoom in and consider only those reviews featuring keywords connected to the TV show: there seems to be no sizable effect on scores for both reviews featuring the keywords, which, on average, feature a score of 3.7 points, and those without the keywords, which feature a score of 3.9 points.

   In conclusion, it may be argued that the overall impact of the show on the restaurants' scores is modest. In fact, we discovered that review scores

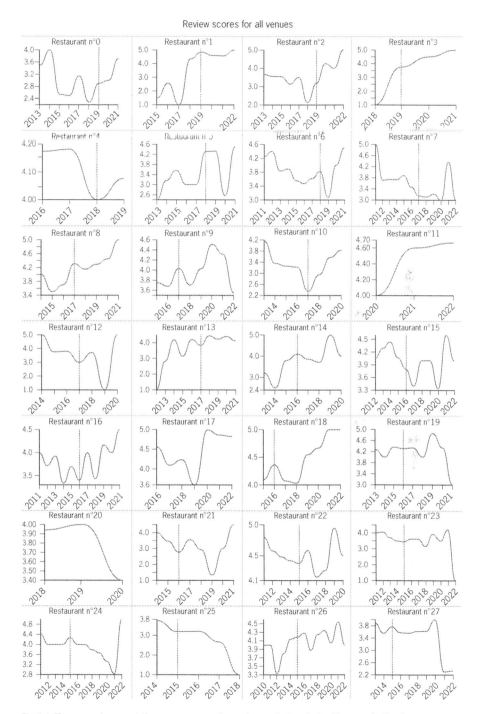

Fig.6.4. These graphs report the average score for each month; the dashed line marks the day on which the restaurant featured on the TV show (venue names have been anonymised).

seem to be rather disconnected from the airdate of the show. Moreover, our analysis points to a somewhat paradoxical result: the more reviews a restaurant has, the lower the score it gets. Arguably, this is due to a mediatic overexposure of the restaurant – something that is not necessarily good for small businesses. In conclusion, we can say that there is no appreciable effect of *Kitchen Nightmares* on restaurants' scores.

Qualitative Analysis of Comments: Sentiment, Topics, and Storytelling

In this last section, we present a qualitative analysis of customers' reviews. This was carried out on a small sample of 200 comments (over 5,608), a number we reached through saturation (Weber 2005). All the comments taken into consideration were posted on TripAdvisor after the airing of the show. The manual and qualitative analysis of users' comments has been very useful for giving context to the quantitative results presented above. Customer reviews helped us better understand "what went wrong"; that is, why restaurants are still in dire straits notwithstanding the intervention of chef Cannavacciuolo. Before showing the results, a further specification is due: although the exploration of comments took advantage of quantitative techniques (namely, quantification of coding categories and automated text analysis), the analysis itself is eminently interpretative, since it focuses specifically on the narrative aspects of customers reviews (e.g., narrative structures, recurrent patterns of storytelling, etc.) (Georgakopoulou, 2021).

Firstly, let us give a general overview of our dataset. As the sentiment distribution shows (Fig. 6.5), customers' evaluations of restaurants are very polarised: 53% are negative and 47% are positive, and there is no neutral sentiment. We also see that most of these evaluations focus primarily on the quality of the food (64%) offered by restaurants, and, secondarily, on management (29%).

The fact that we have a large share of positive reviews does not contradict the quantitative analysis demonstrated in the previous paragraphs. In fact: a) the present analysis was carried out on a small sample of comments, extracted without probabilistic techniques and purposes; and b) the statistical analysis of scores shows the existence of a peak of positive reviews, which nonetheless are disconnected from the programme airdate. Reading the comments, it is possible to confirm some of the previously articulated hypotheses. Most of the positive comments seem

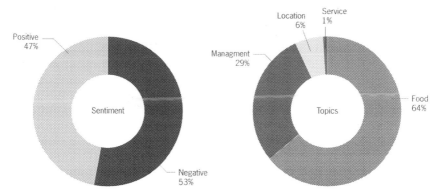

Fig. 6.5. The figures show the results of the manual sentiment and content analysis made on our sample of customer reviews (n= 200).

to be written by regular customers, while negative ones appear to be posted by new customers brought to the restaurant by the TV show. In particular, this result seems to confirm the existence of what we have called the "exposition effect": something that is well exemplified by the following comments:

> [Positive Comment]. To be honest we were afraid about the fact that Cannavacciuolo dropped by the Restaurant. We were so in love with that restaurant and its owners, that we feared that Cannavacciuolo might revolutionise the place, that we wouldn't recognise it anymore. Last Saturday, driven by the desire to eat a delicious paella, we finally took the courage to step into the restaurant. The restaurant has been renovated, but not that much: the good old paella, delicious and abundant as always. The Catalan cream: delicious as always

> [Negative Comment]. I went to this restaurant after watching the episode of *Kitchen Nightmares* on TV. Such a delusion: no trace of the menu devised by Chef Cannavacciuolo. Everything was bad: food, service, cleanliness

Nonetheless, the main question remains: *what went wrong after the departure of chef Cannavacciuolo?* To answer this question, we explored more thoroughly the grammar, vernacular, and storytelling of customer reviews (i.e., narrative structures and plots) (Van Laer et al., 2019), with a particular focus on negative ones.

The Grammar and Vernacular of Reviews

Shifting the focus from topics to narrations, it is interesting to notice how consumers' comments are articulated through common patterns of storytelling. This, in turn, seems to be shaped by the platform's grammars and vernaculars – and this occurs independently from the sentiment. First, the comments exhibit a structure that seems driven by the grammar of TripAdvisor. In the comments section, TripAdvisor invites users to rate, through an ad hoc rating interface, the "food," "service," "value,"[3] and "atmosphere" of the restaurant the user wishes to review. For each of these variables, the user can assign a specific score on a scale from 1 to 5. Similarly, TripAdvisor offers an interface in which the reviewer can specify the reason why she was at the restaurant, by ticking one of the following boxes: "families," "couples," "solo," "business," "friends" (see Fig. 6.6). Curiously, although reviewers rarely fill out such digital forms, they do provide the information required in written form within their comments. Indeed, most of the reviews we analysed do specify the reason why the reviewer was at the restaurant and with whom, and they also provide ample feedback on the "food," "service," "value," and "atmosphere" of the restaurant.[4]

In addition to this grammar, it is possible to observe a very distinctive vernacular. Most of the comments do not sound like generic customer complaints or expressions of satisfaction; rather, the reviewers tend to assume the tone and stance of the food critic. Specifically, when expressing their evaluations of the restaurant (even very negative ones), users make an effort to keep a polite, detached, and neutral tone of voice. Moreover, they try to offer "technical" comments about the whole experience at the restaurant (e.g., "the meat wasn't cooked properly"; "the premises were not clean enough; the owner didn't valorise the location"; etc). The presence of this review vernacular can be seen more extensively in the following comment:

> Nice place in a good location. It is a pity that the owners didn't learn anything from Chef Cannavacciuolo. The staff was quite rude and unprofessional. We ordered ravioli, risotto, and octopus: not very good. The fish-fry contained too big chunks of squid, very difficult to eat. Also the shrimps were not good and too salty, plus, they seemed frozen. The cost was average. We booked a table at 8:30 pm and the restaurant was empty.

3   That is the balance between the cost of the meal and the quality of the food.
4   See how our grounded categories in Fig. 6.5 resonate with the standard categories provided by TripAdvisor.

Fig. 6.6. This figure shows the form provided by TripAdvisor to evaluate a venue as well as a customer review. It was randomly extracted from our dataset and carefully anonymised. It is a good example of how the grammar of TripAdvisor shapes customers' writing style: *When advice is wasted. I saw the restaurant on TV (on Kitchen Nightmares) as well as Chef Cannavacciuolo renewing it. I was nearby for business reasons and I decided to try the menu that Channavacciuolo proposed in the programme … that menu wasn't there anymore … epic fail: courses, service, cleanliness. Such a delusion, you have been pretentious to go back to your pre-Cannavacciuolo state.*

> Customers started arriving around 10:00 pm. We ate outside: unfortunately the many scooters passing by were very annoying and unhealthy

Probably, TripAdvisor's users "learn" this vernacular through a *memetic process* (Caliandro and Anselmi, 2021), in which they copy each other's writing style (Nicoll and Nansen 2018). It is also likely that such vernacular is borrowed from *Kitchen Nightmares* itself and other popular food shows (e.g., *MasterChef*). Of course, however interesting this question might be, to establish the exact source of this vernacular exceeds the scope of this chapter – most likely, it is a combination of the two.

The Storytelling of Negative Reviews

Let us focus more specifically on the storytelling of the negative reviews, since these are more helpful in revealing what went wrong after Cannavacciuolo's departure. All the reviews present the same narrative structure comprising an "introduction," "discussion," and "conclusion." In the introduction, users clarify why they decided to visit the restaurant. The main motive is curiosity: users decide to visit after seeing the restaurant on TV. The most recurrent phrases, which we automatically extracted from the dataset, are explicit: "after watching an episode of *Kitchen Nightmares*" (freq. 10); "an episode of *Kitchen Nightmares* with chef" (freq. 9); "after watching the episode with Cannavacciuolo" (freq. 8); "we were curious after watching an episode of *Kitchen Nightmares*" (freq. 8). In the discussion, customers review the "food," "service," "value," and "atmosphere" of the restaurant. As mentioned earlier, users tend to focus more on the quality of the food, which they commonly find very low and/or mediocre – something that they did not expect after watching the TV show. In the conclusion part, users usually discourage other customers from visiting the restaurant and/or blame the owners for not having taken advantage of chef Cannavacciuolo's good advice. The following excerpt exemplifies a typical comment:

> We ate at the restaurant with some friends, after watching the show of chef Cannavacciuolo. After an endless wait the menus came. The menu was disappointing, the choice was limited. There were very few vegetarian dishes. We asked the staff for clarifications but they replied very rudely: "all we got is on the menu!". The food, in general, was not good. Small plates and super high prices. In particular the prices of beverages were very high. What can I say? The restaurant is deeply disappointing in all aspects, I do not recommend it.

Another interesting narration consists of customers reflecting on what some of them explicitly refer to as "the Cannavacciuolo cure" (*la cura Cannavacciuolo*). More specifically, users try to reckon what actually changed in the restaurant after chef Cannavacciuolo improved the menu, refurbished the venue, and gave the owner an injection of self-esteem. In this regard, two main sub-narrations emerge: a) "nothing changed": the restaurant went back to its pre-Cannavacciuolo status; b) "a missed opportunity": the owner tried to follow Cannavacciuolo's suggestions, perhaps for a while s/he stuck to them, but ultimately s/he did not manage to keep to the right path for long. But why do reviewers have the impression that "nothing changed" or the "owner missed" a good opportunity? It is possible to find some clues by delving further into consumers' storytelling. Both explicitly and implicitly, users direct their attention to a particular tension between the "Cannavacciuolo cure" and the "*Kitchen Nightmares* effect" (something similar to the previously discussed "exposition effect"). In fact, although "the cure" had the positive effect of enhancing the restaurant's conditions, the

TV show had the negative effect of setting too high expectations, for both customers and owners, as emerges from the following comment:

> After watching the episode of *Kitchen Nightmares*, out of curiosity, we decided to dine in this restaurant. We went there with high expectations, after the intervention of the great chef Cannavacciuolo. The location is not bad, but they didn't do an excellent job with the refurbishment. The menu is pretty long, but we focus on the daily specials, believing that they are made out of fresh products. We get orecchiette with cream of eggplants, octopus with potatoes, and sea bass. The plates come early but they do not look like the plates we saw on TV. The orecchiette are not super tasty, but the octopus is fresh. The sea bass is fresh as well, but it comes along with a plate of flavourless peas and green beans – they remind me of those served in school canteens. Overall the restaurant is not so bad, but for sure is not anymore the one that appeared on TV. Maybe it has been so in the past, but not now, and you can see that from the dish presentation, the menu, and the division of labour among the staff.

On the one hand, customers go to the restaurant thinking of having a "Cannavacciuolo-like" food experience – something they will never get, even if the restaurant performs well ("Overall the restaurant is not so bad, but please do not expect any wow effect due to Cannavacciuolo's intervention"). On the other hand, the show "pushes" the owners to set very high culinary standards, which they struggle to maintain in the long run ("now they just make pretentious small plates at high prices"). In fact, these comments led us to think about something that is also evident when one watches the show: most of the owners, at the moment they ask for Cannavacciuolo's help, have serious financial issues (e.g., endemic lack of clientele, debts, etc.). These kinds of issues are usually very difficult to sort out, and certainly cannot be solved by simply revising the menu or refurbishing the premises of the restaurant. Moreover, frequently, the owners seem to lack basic cooking and/or management skills – fundamental issues that cannot be magically solved by simply participating in an episode of *Kitchen Nightmares*. As another user points out:

> For sure, the Cannavacciuolo "cure" had a positive impact on the menu, which is rich, varied and oriented towards cold dishes: the dishes we had were good but not exciting. The premises have been nicely refurbished; although one can see here and there some bags, boxes, and a vacuum cleaner. What is totally missing is the hospitality and the attention for the

client. In general the service can be deemed indecent. The only working-hard person was a very young waitress. Instead, the young owners loiter around, doing nothing: they just sit there playing with their smartphones, unconcerned of what is going on in the restaurant (we waited 20 minutes for the beverages); plus they always seem super annoyed. It is a real shame, they have a place with a very good potential, plus they could exploit the media coverage the restaurant had. Rather than incompetent, it seems to me that they are lazy and unconcerned. They seem masochistic, as if someone obliged them to be there. Beware guys, the food business is not a game.

Conclusion and Implications

We started this chapter asking the following question: *What is the social impact of Kitchen Nightmares? More generally, what is the social impact of a reality show that aims at having a positive impact on society? Does it redistribute value within the social or simply extract value from it?* To answer this question, we turned to TripAdvisor, and analysed the reviews and rating scores of the restaurants that participated in the Italian edition of *Kitchen Nightmares*. To answer our main questions we used the number of reviews received by each restaurant as a proxy of visibility and reputation, while the rating score was a proxy of quality (globally intended: "food," "service," "value," and "atmosphere"). Based on our statistical analysis of reviews and rating scores, we can conclude that the show has a very limited impact on the restaurants' visibility, reputation, and quality. On the one hand, reviews do have a boost thanks to *Kitchen Nightmares*, but only in conjunction with the airdate of the show – soon after, they follow a descending trend. On the other hand, scores are disconnected to the programme airdate; moreover, they reveal a paradoxical relation with reviews: the more the reviews, the lower the score. Finally, we conducted a qualitative analysis of customer reviews, focusing on their grammar, vernacular, and storytelling structure. This analysis was very useful for contextualising the results of the statistical analysis, in so far as users' accounts helped us to understand what went wrong after the departure of chef Cannavacciuolo. Following the users' storytelling, we discovered a particular tension between the *Cannavacciuolo cure* and the *Kitchen Nightmares effect*: on the one hand, "the Cannavacciuolo cure" has a positive effect, enhancing the restaurant's conditions; on the other hand, the TV show has a negative effect, setting too high expectations for both customers and restaurant owners – expectations that are always frustrated on the side of customers, and never fully met on the side of owners. Furthermore, one should also consider that the serious financial, cooking, and management issues that the restaurant owners find themselves in not easily solved by simply participating in one episode of a reality show.

Therefore, to give a more straightforward answer to the research questions, we can argue that, despite its noble intent and its (temporary) effectiveness, *Kitchen Nightmares* has scant impact on society. It seems that *Kitchen Nightmares* extracts more value from the restaurants than the value the restaurants gains from the programme; and the same goes for society at large. In fact, these are not just "single" restaurants participating in the show, but rather a complex network of social actors comprising owners, family members, friends, restaurant staff, customers, platforms, and platform users. All these social actors seem to work hard to increase the visibility, reputation, and quality of the programme, and not vice versa.

Of course, the empirical research we presented in this chapter is not without limitations. First, we focused exclusively on the Italian edition of *Kitchen Nightmares*; future studies might try to concentrate instead on the UK or US editions of the show, which are older and so offer the opportunity to obtain more data. Second, we relied on a single digital source, TripAdvisor. In our case, this source turned out to be incomplete: only some of the restaurants featured by *Kitchen Nightmares* had a TripAdvisor page. To overcome this problem, future research should try to conduct a cross-platform analysis, taking into consideration, for instance, Google Reviews and Yelp. Finally, in the future, a cross-national analysis could be useful for understanding whether the limited impact of *Kitchen Nightmares* on a restaurant's destiny is only an Italian phenomenon or a more global one.

References

Alexander, V. D., Blank, G., and Hale, S. A. (2018). TripAdvisor reviews of London museums: A new approach to understanding visitors. *Museum International*, *70*(1/2), 154–165. https://doi.org/10.1111/muse.12200.

Anselmi, G., Chiappini, L., and Prestileo, F. (2021). The greedy unicorn: Airbnb and capital concentration in 12 European cities. *City, Culture and Society*, *27*. https://doi.org/10.1016/j.ccs.2021.100412.

Allen, K. and Mendick, H. (2013). Keeping it real? Social class, young people and "authenticity" in reality TV. *Sociology*, *47*(3), 460–476. https://doi.org/10.1177/0038038512448563.

Bainotti, L., Caliandro, A., and Gandini, A. (2021). From archive cultures to ephemeral content, and back: Studying Instagram Stories with digital methods. *New Media and Society*, *23*(12), 3656–3676. https://doi.org/10.1177/1461444820960071.

Caliandro, A. (2021). Repurposing digital methods in a post-API research environment: Methodological and ethical implications. *Italian Sociological Review*, *11*(4S), 225–242. https://doi.org/10.13136/isr.v11i4S.433.

Caliandro, A. and Anselmi, G. (2021). Affordances-based brand relations: An inquiry on memetic brands on Instagram. *Social Media+ Society*, *7*(2). https://doi.org/10.1177/20563051211021367.

Canavan, B. (2021). Post-postmodern consumer authenticity, shantay you stay or sashay away? A netnography of RuPaul's Drag Race fans. *Marketing Theory*, *21*(2), 251–276. https://doi.org/10.1177/1470593120985144.

Dajem, Z. A. S. and Alyousef, H. S. (2020). An analysis of mood and modality in workplace discourse and the impact of power differentials: Ramsay's Kitchen Nightmares. *Advances in Language and Literary Studies*, *11*(4), 48–61. https://doi.org/10.7575/aiac.alls.v.11n.4p.48.

Doughty, M., Rowland, D., and Lawson, S. (2011). Co-viewing live TV with digital backchannel streams. In *Proceedings of the 9th European Conference on Interactive TV and Video* (pp. 141–144). https://doi.org/10.1145/2000119.2000147.

Fiesler, C., Beard, N., and Keegan, B. C. (2020). No robots, spiders, or scrapers: Legal and ethical regulation of data collection methods in social media terms of service. In *Proceedings of the international AAAI conference on web and social media* (vol. 14, pp. 187–196). https://doi.org/10.1609/icwsm.v14i1.7290.

Galov, N. (2023, May 20). Where is TripAdvisor going? 39+ signpost statistics. https://review42.com/resources/tripadvisor-statistics/.

Georgakopoulou, A. (2021). Small stories as curated formats on social media: The intersection of affordances, values and practices. *System*, *102*. https://doi.org/10.1016/j.system.2021.102620.

Grosglik, R. and Lerner, J. (2020). Gastro-emotivism: How MasterChef Israel produces therapeutic collective belongings. *European Journal of Cultural Studies*, *24*(5), 1053–1070. https://doi.org/10.1177/1367549420902801.

Herkes, E. and Redden, G. (2017). Misterchef? Cooks, chefs and gender in MasterChef Australia. *Open Cultural Studies*, *1*(1), 125–139. https://doi.org/10.1515/culture-2017-0012.

Hesmondhalgh, D. and Baker, S. (2008). Creative work and emotional labour in the television industry. *Theory, Culture and Society*, *25*(7/8), 97–118. https://doi.org/10.1177/0263276408097798.

Higgins, M., Montgomery, M., Smith, A., and Tolson, A. (2012). Belligerent broadcasting and makeover television: Professional incivility in Ramsay's Kitchen

Nightmares. *International Journal of Cultural Studies*, *15*(5), 501–518. https://doi. org/10.1177/1367877911422864.

Hochschild, A. R. (1983). *The managed heart: Commercialization of human feeling.* University of California Press.

Landers, R. N., Brusso, R. C., Cavanaugh, K. J., and Collmus, A. B. (2016). A primer on theory-driven web scraping: Automatic extraction of big data from the internet for use in psychological research. *Psychological Methods*, *21*(4), 475. https://doi. org/10.1037/met0000081.

Li, B., Forgues, B. and Jourdan, J. (2022). The consequences of status loss on the evaluation of market actors. *Academy of Management Proceedings*, *2022*(1). https://doi.org/10.5465/AMBPP.2022.15910abstract.

Markham, A. and Buchanan, E. (2012). Ethical decision-making and internet research: Recommendations from the AoIR Ethics Working Committee (Version 2.0). *Association of Internet Researchers*, 1–19. https://aoir.org/reports/ethics2.pdf.

Negra, D., Pike, K., and Radley, E. (2013). Gender, nation, and reality TV. *Television and New Media*, *14*(3), 187–193. https://doi.org/10.1177/1527476412458163.

Nicoll, B. and Nansen, B. (2018). Mimetic production in YouTube toy unboxing videos. *Social Media + Society*, *4*(3). https://doi.org/10.1177/2056305118790761.

Parmentier, M. A. and Fischer, E. (2015). Things fall apart: The dynamics of brand audience dissipation. *Journal of Consumer Research*, *41*(5), 1228–1251. https:// doi.org/10.1086/678907.

Phillipov, M. (2013). Mastering obesity: MasterChef Australia and the resistance to public health nutrition. *Media, Culture and Society*, *35*(4), 506–515. https:// doi.org/10.1177/0163443712474615.

Rimoldi, L. (2015). How to show a national cuisine: Food and national identities in the MasterChef Kitchen. *Academic Journal of Interdisciplinary Studies*, *4*(2), 257–262. https://dx.doi.org/10.5901/ajis.2015.v4n2p257.

Schouten, J. W. and McAlexander, J. H. (1995). Subcultures of consumption: An ethnography of the new bikers. *Journal of Consumer Research*, *22*(1), 43–61. https://doi.org/10.1086/209434.

Seale, K. (2012). MasterChef's Amateur Makeovers. *Media International Australia*, *143*(1), 28–35. https://doi.org/10.1177/1329878X1214300105.

Singh, V. (2019, April 10). How Google reviews is crushing TripAdvisor. https://www. hospitalitynet.org/opinion/4092845.html.

Rose, R. L. and Wood, S. L. (2005). Paradox and the consumption of authenticity through reality television. *Journal of Consumer Research*, *32*(2), 284–296. https:// doi.org/10.1086/432238.

Stewart, M. (2020). Live tweeting, reality TV and the nation. *International Journal of Cultural Studies*, *23*(3), 352–367. https://doi.org/10.1177/1367877919887757.

Thompson, K. and Haigh, L. (2017). Representations of food waste in reality food television: An exploratory analysis of Ramsay's Kitchen Nightmares. *Sustainability*, *9*(7), 1139. https://doi.org/10.3390/su9071139.

Van Laer, T., Edson Escalas, J., Ludwig, S., and Van Den Hende, E. A. (2019). What happens in Vegas stays on TripAdvisor? A theory and technique to understand narrativity in consumer reviews. *Journal of Consumer Research*, *46*(2), 267–285. https://doi.org/10.1093/jcr/ucy067.

Wang, T., Wezel, F. C., and Forgues, B. (2016). Protecting market identity: When and how do organizations respond to consumers' devaluations? *Academy of Management Journal*, *59*(1), 135–162. https://doi.org/10.5465/amj.2014.0205.

Weber, K. (2005). A toolkit for analyzing corporate cultural toolkits. *Poetics*, *33*(3/4), 227–252. https://doi.org/10.1016/j.poetic.2005.09.011.

Weltevrede, E. (2016). *Repurposing digital methods: The research affordances of platforms and engines*. PhD Dissertation, University of Amsterdam.

7. Thinking of the Same Place: The Trivialisation of the Sharing Economy on Airbnb

Abstract

This chapter is dedicated to analysing how people perceive their relationship with the short-term rental platform Airbnb. The mainstream discourse emphasises how users are usually emotionally attached to social relationships developed on sharing economy platforms; we question this discourse in two ways. Firstly, we question whether Airbnb is actually a "sharing" platform by measuring the concentration of revenues for the Venice, Italy. Secondly, we analyse the imaginary of Airbnb users by focusing on all the reviews left by visitors to the city of Venice. The first step in our analysis leverages automated text analysis in order to find out clusters of discourse; then, we use qualitative content analysis in order to understand how users communicate affection. Eventually, we show that, just as the revenues concentrate in the hands of a few powerful users, the imaginary becomes increasingly standardised.

Keywords: imaginary, concentration, short-term rental, tourism, touristification

The hype that both legacy and social media have generated around the so-called sharing economy is enormous: since the late 2000s, countless newspaper articles have depicted the sharing economy as a new "gift economy" (Botsman and Rogers, 2010). While, in the social sciences, the debate on the nature of the sharing economy is ongoing (Pais and Provasi, 2015; Andreotti et al., 2017), it is impossible to deny that these narratives have accompanied the rise of digital platforms as intermediaries of distributed and digital rental markets – or pseudo-sharing, as Belk (2014) would put it. While digital platforms have always had their share of critiques (Slee,

Caliandro, A., A. Gandini, L. Bainotti, G. Anselmi, *The Platformisation of Consumer Culture: A Digital Methods Guide*. Amsterdam: Amsterdam University Press, 2024
DOI 10.5117/9789463729567_CH07

2017), we are now increasingly presented with empirical data about their negative societal impact. With respect to Airbnb, we can isolate two main issues: negative externalities and concentration. Negative externalities have to do with the damaging impact Airbnb has on the surrounding urban environment. First and foremost, Airbnb has been connected with rental price increases and housing shortages: there is empirical evidence of property increases in the US (Barron et al., 2019) and the EU (Shabrina et al., 2022; Rodriguez-Perez de Arenaza et al., 2022), which are, at the very least, connected with increased Airbnb activity. Assessing causality is a complicated endeavour in the social sciences. In this specific case, price spikes may be influenced by other factors, such as economic vitality, wage growth (or the lack of it), and demographic pressures. Nevertheless, because residential property tends to be more profitable on the short-term rental market, we can safely assume that Airbnb is contributing to price growth.

Secondly, and partially related to the previous point, Airbnb seems to be connected to the interlinked phenomena of touristification and gentrification (Sequera and Nofre, 2020). As housing units are removed from the long-term rental market, neighbourhoods (or cities) with a large presence of short-term rentals are likely to develop an economic trajectory that privileges the entertainment and hospitality sectors, eventually driving out original residents either through price increases or through the destruction of those socio-cultural patterns that regulated previous urban life. Thirdly, there is evidence of socio-cultural discrimination: for example, in the US, African Americans earn less if they are hosts and find more difficulties in finding an accommodation if they are guests (Edelman and De Luca 2014; Farmaki and Kladou, 2020). In essence, algorithmic discrimination acts as additional "weight" to drag down people who already experience societal discrimination. Far from being pure mediators resolving information asymmetries, Airbnb reputational scores reproduce patterns and prejudices that can be found in society at large (Tornberg and Chiappini, 2020) .

The specific ways in which an "actually existing" reputation economy is constructed by platforms are also at the core of the second issue: concentration. We know from both theoretical speculation and empirical research that digital platforms tend to act as monopolies (Barabasi, 2007). This has to do with, on the one hand, how human customers (or providers) interact with platforms and, on the other hand, with how platforms shape, coerce, or nudge consumers into a specific pattern of action. Platforms tend to be natural monopolies because they are extremely good at growing fast while internalising network effects (Srnicek, 2017): in its growth phase, a platform incorporates specific social ties, which, ideally, include most (if not all) transaction partners for a potential new customer. Essentially, there is no market for a clone of Facebook or Airbnb because: a) new users already find their demands at least partially satisfied by incumbent platforms and hence are unwilling to suffer reduced options; and b) platforms attract huge financial investments, leaving them with substantial funds that may be utilised to stifle competition, for example by buying (and then closing) promising competitors.

On top of "being" monopolies, platforms also "enable" monopolies: human attention and page space are the scarce resources that need to be preserved in the digital economy. A single platform may have trillions of objects for sale but human actors can only tolerate so much idle browsing: the purpose of reputation markers (e.g., review scores, stars, etc.) lies in the necessity to produce information fast enough to goad consumers into buying and eventually leading them into satisfactory transactions that may, eventually, be repeated in the future. In practice, this translates into a "Matthew effect": entities with higher scores will be visualised more (as higher scores indicate, ideally, better value for consumers), in turn leading to more positive reviews.

The combination of these factors culminates in the production of positional rents: entities with a good position within a reputation economy will "automatically" produce a stream of income. Airbnb represents a particularly interesting case, because it sits at the crossroads of multiple monopolies and rent extraction practices, as short-term rentals are simultaneously digital artefacts (hence producing rent because of their position in the digital space) and urban places, meaning that they produce rent according to their position in a spatial hierarchy, which already had its own monopolistic practices. In fact, transnational real estate capital has been using Airbnb as a strategic chokepoint to consolidate its global expansion. Real estate funds, corporations, or wealthy individuals have been buying properties with the specific intent of letting them on Airbnb for quite some time (Cocola Gant and Gago, 2021), eventually leading to a dramatic increase in wealth concentration in the platforms (Anselmi et al., 2021).

Although there is a wealth of literature exploring the issue of Airbnb concentration and its impact on society at large, we still know very little about the logics of how Airbnb shapes cultural processes; specifically, about the ways in which users behave and express themselves on the platform as well as to what extent users performances are functional to the platform's commercial scopes. To this end, given that we now know that short-term rental (hereafter, STR) platforms bear not resemblance to the ideal types mobilised in the utopian strain of sharing narratives but act as pure market intermediaries, in this chapter we investigate how "actually existing" platforms feature in users' vernaculars. Moreover, while we know that "sharing" platforms feed upon a particular cultural political economy, which requires the mobilisation of both affect (Arvidsson, 2013) and public attention, we still lack empirical insights into how this arrangement is produced by users in their everyday cultural activity.

Methods and Data

Our data source is *Inside Airbnb*,[1] which is a continually updated database of scrapes from more than sixty cities and metropolitan areas, including information on listings prices and reviews. In an initial phase, we selected 13 cities: to assess concentration patterns, we selected cities that have implemented different forms of Airbnb regulation (see Aquilera et al., 2021), ranging from very liberal ones (Milan, Naples, Venice, London, Seville, Bordeaux), to more regulated (Paris, Berlin, Amsterdam, Vienna), and highly regulated (Lisbon, Barcelona) cities, eventually also including those that do not adhere to Airbnb regulations at all (Prague). To assess one of the most important negative externalities, we followed *Inside Airbnb*'s own metrics: the number of listings that are a full home as opposed to a single room. To assess concentration, we estimated earnings from each listing (and hence for users controlling those listings) by assuming that each review corresponds to a three-day stay (see Picascia et al., 2017), eventually calculating the annual Gini coefficient for wealth distribution. Then, in order to investigate how the Airbnb user base relates to the platform, we decided to zoom in on a single city: Venice. We chose this city for a number of reasons: first and foremost, because we are familiar with the context; secondly, Venice is a global tourist hotspot, which, however, due to the relative insularity of Italian Real Estate industry (Anselmi and Vicari, 2020) has only recently been visited by transnational actors. Moreover, homeownership is dominant in Venice, as it is in Italian society generally. These conditions may, hypothetically, delimit an environment that is hostile towards capital concentration, ideally approaching the convivial stereotype of house sharing. However, this could not be further from the truth, as property concentration is rampant, both in Venice and in other cities.

Our main hypothesis was that the nature of digital platforms account for the slack between context and results, namely, that, as a platform, Airbnb actively promotes concentration as a consequence of relying on a reputational economy to function. However, being aware of concentration is only part of the dilemma. We must also be aware of how users interact

---

1   See http://insideairbnb.com/.

with the platform in producing reviews. Therefore, in this chapter we ask: *to what extent does Airbnb boost income concentration?* And, if so, *how do users relate to the reputation economy of Airbnb? Do they resist its application, or do they wholeheartedly participate in it?* To describe users' discourses, we analyse reviews for the 2011–2019 time frame (conveniently leaving out Covid) focusing on those written in English and organising them in a topic model. A "topic model" is a text analysis technique that may be employed to understand a large number of documents: in essence, without any prior knowledge of issues addressed within the group of documents, a "topic model" is able to isolate specific themes (i.e., topics) across the group of documents. Without delving into the minutiae of statistical details, it will suffice to say that topic modeling, starting from a group of documents, finds groups of words that often appear together, clusters them together (in a "topic"), and then estimates the prevalence of each topic for each document.[2]

Patterns of Concentration

In order to assess how users behave in STRs we need to understand that this kind of platform is, first and foremost, an economic intermediary: thus, its socio-technical infrastructure (our grammar here) is not necessarily designed to produce discourses or conversation. On the contrary, the combination of information about individual listings and review data produces what may be described as the grammars of STR. This gives us important insights into patterns of concentration. In all of our cities, we can witness a vertical increase in the number of listings and reviews. By looking at the data (Fig. 7.1), we can assess that (up to 2019) Airbnb is still in an exponential growth phase for both listings and reviews.

As hypothesised, these reviews flock towards a few select users controlling multiple lodgings: if we consider all sampled cities, we learn that the top users control most reviews. Understandably, this has strong repercussions for income inequality as it can be seen in Fig. 7.2.

The distribution of revenues in each and every city is becoming massively more concentrated over time: no city has a Gini index lower than .5 and

---

2   Say that we have a number of documents. Applying a topic model, we will discover that words like "tail," "fur," "whiskers," "claws" cluster together while another cluster features words like "talk," "babble," "diaper." Examining the topics, we can observe that the first topic is probably related to cats and the second one to babies. Knowing this, when we estimate that document A is strongly connected (i.e., "prevalent") with topic 1, we can safely assume it is about cats, and vice versa, documents featuring both probably talk about interactions between cats and babies.

Listings and reviews increase

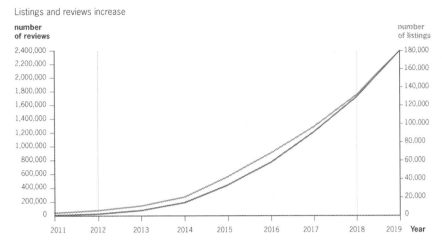

Fig. 7.1. The left axis shows the number of reviews; the right axis shows the number of listings. The black line is the number of listings; the red line is the number of reviews.

Income inequality in all cities

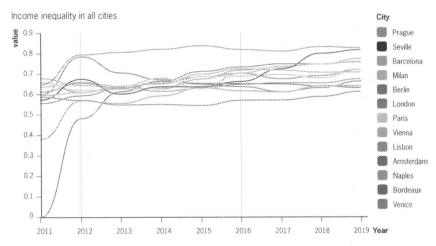

Fig. 7.2. The vertical axis reports the Gini coefficient for each city; various lines represent the different cities.

many have one higher than .65. Interestingly, regulation does not seem to have an impact on revenue concentration, as cities with widely different regulation patterns seem to have very similar trajectories. This may be due to two interlinked phenomena: on the one hand, municipalities probably have no intention (or means) of regulating away concentration (as it is already tolerated, albeit with less spectacular characteristics, in the traditional rental sector). Secondly, the juridical status of Airbnb as a platform probably eludes the range of competencies available to a municipality, as the capacity to effectively curtail Airbnb requires prerogatives and competences that are usually found in higher tiers of government. For example, laws disciplining the tourist sector are usually promulgated by regional or national governments; laws disciplining the status of digital platforms (are they content aggregators or real estate intermediaries?) are the consequence of national or transnational (read: EU level) political action. To these considerations we should add that local rentiers have the capacity of tapping into utilities of scope as well as of scale, namely, they can make a consistent effort in promoting their assets, while centralising administration and menial services (such as cleaning). The end result will, eventually, benefit from the compound reputational boost that comes from operating several listings.

The scenario is also stable if we consider negative externalities. On average, the percentage of "entire home" listings decreases from 70% in 2013 to 68% in 2019[3] (see also Anselmi et al., 2021). It is worth remembering that this issue is more "approachable" by municipalities because regulations disciplining these specific aspects of rental are usually allocated to lower tiers of governmental hierarchies. However, this capacity to regulate does not apply to "blanket" measures such as registration numbers. In fact, many dwellings remain unregistered, even in cities that have mandatory registrations in place. For example, focusing on 2019, only 42% of reviews originate from listings that display registration numbers in Paris; this percentage is 72% in Berlin and 19% in Barcelona. Specific research will be needed to understand why this is the case; however, we can assume that data ownership is critical in this process. That is to say, while cities can promulgate mandates, enforcing them (which generally means having the registration number displayed in the proper, highly visible space on the listing profile) will require either cooperation with the platform (or data scraping) or the capability to sanction violations independently, which requires associating a listing with an actual lodging within the area of the municipality. It is fairly evident how direct access to data, which is now almost universally enjoyed only by Airbnb itself, becomes a critical component of policing illegal STR offers. This kind of data policy is frequently "out of the league" of municipal government as it is something that gets discussed at national and transnational policy levels.

Standardising the Imaginary

Having shown how Airbnb enables the concentration of rent, we now need to understand how users cope with this; essentially, how the ideological imaginary of the sharing economy features in their cultural production (the

---

3   We consider 2013 as a starting point due to the very low number of listings in the previous years.

Topic model for Venice reviews

Fig. 7.3. Each square represents a single topic word; size is proportional to the importance of words in each topic.

vernacular), expressed through their reviews. Fig. 7.3 reports the results of the topic model on 518,021 reviews for the city of Venice. As can be seen, the main topic contains words that do not have strong semantic connotations per se but are, nevertheless, strong indicators of emotional warmth and enjoyment.

In essence, topic 0 seem to gather the "rules of engagement" between hosts and guests on Airbnb, which are apparently geared towards politeness and words of enthusiasm, such as "helpful," "fantastic," "great," "recommend," "amazing," and "beautiful." These are all strong indicators of the nature of this topic. Said "rules" seem to put a premium on communicating "affection," that is letting a reader (and potential next guest) feel that the short-term stay was something more than a commercial transaction: it should be noted that this kind of approach, which emphasises conviviality, is resonant with the results from Zhang (2019). The normally dry language of hotel reviews (e.g., "room was large enough, beds were clean, breakfast was so and so") is replaced by something that emphasises emotional intensity, such as the following comment:

> We absolutely LOVED our stay. Maria was the most gracious host. She made us feel at home and even invited us to be her guests at a fashion event she was part of.

We can also calculate topic prevalence for each of the reviews. Topic 0 is prevalent in 51.7% of reviews, while topic 1 is prevalent in 7% of reviews, 2 in 8%, 3 in 12.6%, 4 in 20.5%. Other topics deal with different facets of the Airbnb experience: topic 1 is probably related to some specific qualities of the lodging, namely, its connection with the city, its interaction with the channel system, and the aesthetic amenities that can be consumed while residing there ("view," "water," "channel," "overlook grand_canal," are all keywords here). Topic 2 seems related to the physical aspects of the home: words like "apartment," "flat," "kitchen," "space," "equip(ment)," "family," "kid," all seem connected to this semantic core. Topic 3 presents words associated to the experience of checking, such as "arrive," "help," "take," "leave," "check (in)," "early," and "luggage" indicate. Topic 4 addresses house amenities but mainly focuses on location, as it can be understood by looking at words like "nice," "place," "station," "train," "convenient," and "bus."

Furthermore, while the vast majority of words that are markers of affection and conviviality are within topic 0, not all of them are: in fact, we can find some sprinkled across different topics; for example, we can find "perfect" and "welcome" in topic 2 or "nice," "cosy," and "good" in topic 4. This seems to indicate that affection-signalling is even more pervasive than what emerges from a first look at the topic modeling: adjectives in reviews seem to be generally positive in nature. To further confirm this point, once having isolated adjectives through POS tagging,[4] we measured that 71% of them are positive. This is fairly consistent for a platform in which review scores are very positive: the median score for all listings is 4.6 in Venice and also fairly consistent with what we already know about the role of reputation economies in Airbnb (Anselmi et al., 2021); so, the overwhelming usage of positive adjectives reflects the actual usage of a platform in which every

---

4   We used Python Spacy to compute Parts Of Speech for any review, essentially associating each word with its role within a phrase (verb, noun, adjective, etc.); we then focused on adjectives.

stay is above average (Zervas et al., 2021). Another sign that affection is very important in the functioning of Airbnb is the frequent usage of first names within the body of a review. In fact, we have checked each review for Italian first names and found out that 63% of these contain first names: names are usually part of a larger sentence again expressing emotional connection and praising hosts for their human qualities:

> I felt at home in Annamaria's place. She is a nice warm host. I will come back to stay in her place.

> Our hosts took such good care of us, recommending places to eat, things to see, and stocking up the apartment with everything we could have needed. I would recommend this apartment to anyone visiting Venice and I would return in a heartbeat if I had the opportunity. Thanks again Daniele!

Obviously, reviews do contain information that is related to the host's professional capacity, namely, how helpful she or he was, how he or she beyond the boundaries of the "standard" to please the guests, and their adherence to rules and regulations. However, affection still acts as the main content in these reviews; names seem to act as an anchor of sorts for this process, linking the host in its role as a professional entity to the host in its role as a human being. By looking at the vernacular within Airbnb, we are presented with a more intriguing puzzle. On the one hand, quantitative analysis of the distribution of reviews (and stays/revenues) paints a picture of extreme concentration and professionalisation (Cocola Gant and Gago, 2021). Nevertheless, users seem to approach reviews with an entirely different ethos than those on, say, Amazon or Booking.com: users go out of their way to communicate affection and warmth. Oddly enough, it is also possible to find websites, tutorials, and "how-tos" dedicated to writing an "amazing" review to thank your host. In essence, Airbnb seems to have a pool of positive imaginary that it is able to tap into; now, our main research puzzle becomes essentially how to explain this.

Conclusion and Implications

The key feature we should address to understand why Airbnb reviews are so positive is, obviously, its dual review system, which ensures that as guests review hosts and lodgings, the reverse also happens; that is, guests get reviewed by hosts. We already know that platforms find their utility in resolving issues of trust in two-sided markets, namely, they deploy reputation scoring algorithms to vouch for two strangers that have no way to ascertain their reciprocal trust. Essentially, platforms are a way of avoiding "lemons" (Akerlof, 1973) in markets for goods that have non-standard conditions. However, in the hospitality business, "lemons" can also be two-sided: a host may rent a substandard dwelling or a guest may misbehave, damaging the property, hence the need for dual reviews.

Nevertheless, this need for a dual review impacts how users behave on the platform. In essence, it engenders an easily solvable, prisoner's dilemma: if host and guest cooperate, by producing mutually positive reviews and written evaluations, both will be better off. However, in the process, any meaningful content that may have been embedded in the reputational ranking gets lost. Surely, it is always possible to produce bad reviews (and to receive a bad review, in turn, as a retaliation) but it becomes undesirable and highly costly, especially for guests that receive far fewer reviews than hosts. Moreover, Airbnb has ways of enforcing this "cooperation" between hosts and guests. Firstly, at the user interface level, as the platform may use somewhat blunt incentives, such as downlisting every listing above a certain reputational threshold, hence producing a strong incentive for hosts to seek guest-written approval. Dual reviews, and the "tit-for-tat" climate they engender, may be understood as a way to avoid the worst outcomes of negative reciprocity (Bardhi and Eckhardt, 2012) while simultaneously ensuring that everyone is dutifully surveilled, and, hence, performs the whole routine of cooperation.

If we analyse the platform's native culture (and the narratives it creates), we can grasp a key piece of the puzzle, allowing us to finally understand how Airbnb solves the aforementioned prisoner's dilemma, and, by extension, why internet platforms dedicate so much effort to envelop their existence in a cocoon of ethical (*a la* Arvidsson and Peitersen, 2013) values. Airbnb, as a company, has always been super conscious about the role of buzz and about its public perception, hoping to leverage, to its advantage, part of the residual mythology embedded in Californian ideology. It has dedicated a sizable portion of its organisational effort to lobbying and, in general, to delivering (without and within) a coherent image of themselves as "change bringers," which are ultimately concerned with positive social change, and the generation of social and economic capital through enhanced connectivity, guaranteed by the Internet. One of the forms that this effort takes is that of support forums and Airbnb clubs, resources that have the explicit intent of helping hosts realise their potential as micro-entrepreneurs but also end up transmitting Airbnb's "soft power," i.e., the meaning and ethos that are attached to the otherwise crude commercial relationship linking host and platform. Premium services such as Airbnb vetted photographers also function as pivotal moments in which a given host learns to replicate the ethical (and aesthetic) stance of the platform and its core narratives.

In other words, Airbnb's effort in producing narratives is ultimately motivated by its willingness to build (or to help build in cooperation with other platforms relying on the key tropes of Californian ideology) a regime of justification (Thevenot and Boltanski, 1991) which then will get disseminated in the wider society through corporate communication and media relations and, within the platform itself, to hosts through host clubs. Eventually, the correct habitus to adopt when using the platform finds its way towards the guests, which will get a) instructed on it by hosts asking for good reviews and threatening retaliation if they don't deliver them; and b) nudged towards producing positive reviews by the constant stream of positive reviews that the platform selects for them. Furthermore, we have some empirical proof (Chung et al., 2022) that buying into that "regime of justification" holds positive outcomes for individual users; namely, those that strongly conform to this regime are able to generate more profit out of their presence on the platform, as performing their appointed role is connected to increased customer satisfaction and higher prices.

The fact that internet companies breed ethical narratives about their (supposedly super positive) role in the world should not be a surprise. Essentially, digital platforms make money by valorising attention and affect on the capital markets (Arvidsson, 2013), either because they are able to profit off the stock markets or because hype generates interest in investors, and investors' interest generates money. Obviously, there are larger trends at play here, as the hype towards platforms and "disruption" and the relevance of finance are defining features of contemporary capitalism. Nevertheless, there is something to be gained from dissecting the Airbnb case, especially in three areas. Firstly, in relation to the ambiguous connection between digital connectivity and social capital (Rainie and Wellman, 2012); secondly, in relation to the negative externalities (with capital concentration having a prominent position here) produced by platforms and the awareness of those in the general public; and thirdly, in relation to how value is produced within surveillance capitalism.

Regarding the first, it is worth noting that just a tiny minority of guests (2%) book again with the same host. This means that, unlike what has been declared in surveys by sharing economy users (Andreotti et al., 2017), review data do not support the idea that a sizable amount of social capital gets generated by short-term rental platforms. While, even in this case, transactions seem to have an ulterior dimension, namely, a sort of pleasurable interpersonal warmness, it is more likely that the rationale behind this happenstance lies in the fact that participation in a digital platform entails a performative component, one that, in this case, produces, through affective labour, the experience of something more than a commercial transaction.

Regarding the second point, it is worth noting how the layer of affection is so widespread that it is reasonable to assume that it applies to both properties managed by individual guests as well those properties managed, en masse, by commercial entities. Even in that case, affective labour is able to reproduce the ethical layer that ensures the functioning of the platform. Moreover, if we account for the recommender algorithm, and the fact that it tends to pool contacts at the top, we are on safe ground if we conclude that, ultimately, large scale rentiers are the ultimate beneficiaries of the habitus that gets promoted by Airbnb.

Thirdly, observing how Airbnb, as a platform, has spawned a corporate culture that finds life in reviews (as well as on pop and journalistic commentaries on short-term rentals), allows us to truly understand the scope and breadth of "surveillance" in surveillance capitalism (Zuboff, 2019). The short-term (as well as the stated one) goal of a platform is to solve information asymmetries by confronting the real (or assumed) preferences of a user with data gathered from other users, and, in the process, recommend the right product for the right user. Nevertheless, the emphasis on affection and on the ethical surplus that should be embedded in something that would, otherwise, be a simple commercial transaction hints at another dimension, namely, the business would not (only) be anticipating user preferences but actively causing change in behaviour. If we start from the assumption that platforms, as modern corporations, find their value in the financial sphere (Arvidsson, 2013), and if we accept that finance is, ultimately, a bet on how people will behave in the foreseeable future, then recommender algorithms and reputational economies become something more than a tool to devise any user choice pattern. Contrarily, they may act as training boxes to nudge users into behaving in a specific pattern. These behavioural shifts may then be valorised either directly on the capital markets (e.g., through share prices or investor money) or indirectly by contributing to the narrative feeding affection towards the platform.

References

Arvidsson, A. and Peitersen, N. (2013). *The ethical economy: Rebuilding value after the crisis.* Columbia University Press.

Andreotti, A., Anselmi, G., Eichhorn, T., Hoffmann, C. P., Jürss, S., and Micheli, M. (2017). European perspectives on participation in the sharing economy. *European Perspectives on Participation in the Sharing Economy (2 October 2017).* SSRN. https://ssrn.com/abstract=3046550.

Anselmi, G., Chiappini, L., and Prestileo, F. (2021). The greedy unicorn: Airbnb and capital concentration in 12 European cities. *City, Culture and Society, 27.* https://doi.org/10.1016/j.ccs.2021.100412.

Anselmi, G. and Vicari, S. (2020). Milan makes it to the big leagues: A financialized growth machine at work. *European Urban and Regional Studies, 27*(2), 106–124. https://doi.org/10.1177/0969776419860871.

Aguilera, T., Artioli, F., and Colomb, C. (2021). Explaining the diversity of policy responses to platform-mediated short-term rentals in European cities: A comparison of Barcelona, Paris and Milan. *Environment and Planning A: Economy and Space, 53*(7), 1689–1712. https://doi.org/10.1177/0308518X19862286.

Akerlof, G. A. (1978). The market for "lemons": Quality uncertainty and the market mechanism. In P. Diamond and M. Rothschild (Eds.), *Uncertainty in economics: Readings and exercises* (pp. 235–251). Academic Press.

Bardhi, F. and Eckhardt, G. M. (2012). Access-based consumption: The case of car sharing. *Journal of Consumer Research, 39*(4), 881–898. https://doi.org/10.1086/666376.

Barron, K., Kung, E., and Proserpio, D. (2019). When Airbnb listings in a city increase, so do rent prices. *Harvard Business Review, 17,* 1–62. https://ci.carmel.ca.us/sites/main/files/file-attachments/harvard_business_article_and_study.pdf.

Barabási, A. L. (2002). *Linked: the new science of networks.* Perseus Publishing.

Botsman, R. and Rogers, R. (2010). *What's mine is yours: The rise of collaborative consumption.* Harper Business.

Belk, R. (2014). Sharing versus pseudo-sharing in Web 2.0. *The anthropologist, 18*(1), 7–23. https://doi.org/10.1080/09720073.2014.11891518.

Chung, J., Johar, G. V., Li, Y., Netzer, O., and Pearson, M. (2022). Mining consumer minds: Downstream consequences of host motivations for home-sharing platforms. *Journal of Consumer Research, 48*(5), 817–838. https://doi.org/10.1093/jcr/ucab034.

Cocola-Gant, A. and Gago, A. (2021). Airbnb, buy-to-let investment and tourism-driven displacement: A case study in Lisbon. *Environment and Planning A: Economy and Space, 53*(7), 1671–1688. https://doi.org/10.1177/0308518X19869012.

Edelman, B. G. and Luca, M. (2014). Digital discrimination: The case of Airbnb. com. Harvard Business School NOM Unit Working Paper, Paper No. 14-054, SSRN. http://dx.doi.org/10.2139/ssrn.2377353.

Farmaki, A. and Kladou, S. (2020). Why do Airbnb hosts discriminate? Examining the sources and manifestations of discrimination in host practice. *Journal of Hospitality and Tourism Management, 42*, 181–189. https://doi.org/10.1016/j. jhtm.2020.01.005.

Picascia, S., Romano, A., and Teobaldi, M. (2017). The airification of cities: Making sense of the impact of peer to peer short term letting on urban functions and economy. In: Annual Congress of the Association of European Schools of Planning, Lisbon, Portugal, 11–14 July 2017. 10.31235/osf.io/vs8w3.

Rainie, H. and Wellman, B. (2012). *Networked: The new social operating system.* MIT Press.

Rodriguez-Perez de Arenaza, D., Hierro, L. Á., and Patiño, D. (2022). Airbnb, sun-and-beach tourism and residential rental prices: The case of the coast of Andalusia (Spain). *Current Issues in Tourism, 25*(20), 3261–3278. https://doi.org/10.1080/13 683500.2019.1705768.

Sequera, J. and Nofre, J. (2020). Touristification, transnational gentrification and urban change in Lisbon: The neighbourhood of Alfama. *Urban Studies, 57*(15), 3169–3189. https://doi.org/10.1177/0042098019883734.

Shabrina, Z., Arcaute, E., and Batty, M. (2022). Airbnb and its potential impact on the London housing market. *Urban Studies, 59*(1), 197–221. https://doi. org/10.1177/0042098020970865.

Slee, T. (2017). *What's yours is mine: Against the sharing economy.* Or Books.

Srnicek, N. (2017). *Platform capitalism.* Polity Press.

Thévenot, L. and Boltanski, L. (1991). *De la justification. Les économies de la grandeur.* Gallimard.

Törnberg, P. and Chiappini, L. (2020). Selling black places on Airbnb: Colonial discourse and the marketing of black communities in New York City. *Environment and Planning A: Economy and Space, 52*(3), 553–572. https://doi. org/10.1177/0308518X19886321.

Zervas, G., Proserpio, D., and Byers, J. W. (2021). A first look at online reputation on Airbnb, where every stay is above average. *Marketing Letters, 32*(1), 1–16. https:// doi.org/10.1007/s11002-020-09546-4.

Zhang, J. (2019). What's yours is mine: Exploring customer voice on Airbnb using text-mining approaches. *Journal of Consumer Marketing, 36*(5), 655–665. https:// doi.org/10.1108/JCM-02-2018-2581.

Zuboff, S. (2019). *The age of surveillance capitalism: The fight for a human future at the new frontier of power.* Profile Books.

8. Ephemeral Content and Ephemeral Consumption on TikTok

Abstract

In this chapter, we look at how TikTok's templates and algorithmic logics are incorporated into users' everyday practices of content production and of interaction within the platform itself. In doing so, we analyse how TikTok's architecture prompts practices of ephemeral consumption, here intended as forms of ephemeral digital consumption (rather than other forms of fast-paced and temporary consumption, such as fast fashion). By mixing hashtag analysis, sound analysis, and the visual analysis of TikTok videos, this chapter illustrates how platform affordances can stimulate the emergence of ephemeral consumption practices. By focusing on one TikTok challenge, the #shoechallenge, results show that ephemeral consumption on TikTok is characterised by: a) the ubiquitous display of consumption; b) the limited temporality of video clips; c) the situational nature of users' performances; and d) the attempts at attention-seeking in an algorithmically mediated and memetic platform.

Keywords: algorithms, #shoechallenge, memetic content, liquid consumption, scraping, templatability analysis

TikTok is a social media platform based on the creation of short video clips in the form of lip-syncing, viral dances, challenges, duets, and other audio-visual content. Once opening the app, users are presented with a flow of content on the so-called For You (FY) page – an algorithmically curated selection of videos ready to be almost endlessly scrolled. Immersed in a fast-paced stream of content, one cannot help but feel captivated by the seamless fusion of visual and audio elements, enriched with an abundance of dances and gestures. All these features make TikTok a peculiar platform, even when compared to other typically visual social media such as Instagram. Not surprisingly, TikTok has become one of the most downloaded apps in

Caliandro, A., A. Gandini, L. Bainotti, G. Anselmi, *The Platformisation of Consumer Culture: A Digital Methods Guide*. Amsterdam: Amsterdam University Press, 2024
DOI 10.5117/9789463729567_CH08

2020 and 2021 and now counts more than a billion monthly active users, the vast majority of whom belong to Gen Z (WeAreSocial, 2021). Moreover, it has become a central element of popular culture as well as an object of public interest and even scrutiny (Sherman, 2023).

For these reasons, TikTok is a relevant venue to study the platformisation of consumer culture and understand how social media platforms and their affordances can influence consumption practices. In this chapter, we aim to investigate how the viral, memetic, and ephemeral features of TikTok and its content go hand in hand with changes in consumer behaviour and consumption practices. The relationship between ephemerality and consumption is significant enough to investigate in a context where the presence of short-lived digital content (see e.g., Bainotti et al., 2021) is intertwined with practices of liquid and access-based consumption (Bardhi and Eckhardt, 2012; 2017) and the display thereof (Rokka and Canniford, 2016). In this chapter, we suggest that a connection can be established between TikTok's affordances and the ephemerality of content they allow users to create, and the emergence and affirmation of practices of ephemeral consumption. As explained later, ephemeral consumption is understood as a set of practices tied to the display of consumer goods, the performance of memetic activities, and the adaptation of consumer behaviours to the logic of TikTok challenges and virality. Forms of ephemeral consumption arise at the intersection of platform affordances and users' practices and can therefore be considered an expression of the platformisation of consumer culture.

TikTok content can be considered ephemeral not because it disappears after a certain amount of time, as in the case of Instagram Stories or Snapchat, but because of the specificities of the platform's affordances. As Schellewald (2021) notes, TikTok videos are transient and short-lived phenomena, as "they are only a few seconds long, often variations of a meme or trend, and distributed through an algorithmic content feed" (p. 1439). TikTok offers an enormous quantity of video content, with limited permanence on the FY page and volatile visibility due to the platform's algorithmic curation of content. The logic of the TikTok algorithm is not transparent, but we can safely say that the FY page is algorithmically generated in an attempt to provide each user with content that resonates with their interests. To do so, TikTok's algorithm takes into account what videos people watch, which kind of content they scroll through, as well as which one prompts them to like, share, re-play, or interact in any other way made possible by the platform (Schellewald, 2021; Smith, 2020). In this way, TikTok content flows through a personalised and algorithmically curated FY page and only lasts for a short span of attention. As Carah and Shaul (2016) point out when describing Instagram as an image machine, the flow of Instagram content is ephemeral, as images receive attention within the first hours of being posted and then mostly disappear from view. Similarly, in the case of TikTok, attention spans and ephemerality are strongly related.

TikTok challenges are another contributing factor to the transient nature of content on the platform. These popular activities involve users participating in various actions (often dances or gestures synchronised with specific sounds), recording, and sharing their performances on TikTok, and subsequently encouraging other users to do the same. Challenges epitomise TikTok's role as a memetic platform that thrives on imitation and replication, fostered by the platform's affordances and design (Zulli and Zulli, 2020). These challenges capture the essence of what is trending and viral. Trending and viral content is inherently fleeting, subject to evolution, dilution, and eventual disappearance over time. Therefore, challenges can be seen as the convergence point between virality and ephemerality. Due to its unique architecture and the ephemeral nature of its content, TikTok can be considered an expression of our fast-paced attention economy and short-lived consumption. We agree with Schellewald (2021) when he states that ephemeral audio-video content is not to be dismissed as short-lived entertainment, but it should rather be considered as a complex communicative form and expression of consumer behaviour.

Ephemerality not only characterises TikTok content, but also represents an increasingly important aspect of consumption. Bardhi and Eckhardt (2017) argue that ephemerality, together with access and dematerialisation, represents a core element of *liquid consumption* – a contemporary dimension of consumption that contrasts with the enduring, ownership-based, and material aspects of *solid consumption*. Liquid forms of consumption are enabled by digital media technologies and harness the advantages of fluidity, immateriality, and instantaneity that these technologies offer (Bardhi and Eckhardt, 2017). The short-lived dimension of consumption is also tied to the increasing role played by access-based consumption (Bardhi and Eckhardt, 2012). Access-based consumption presupposes that consumers get *access*, rather than *ownership*, to consumer goods and leisure activities for a defined amount of time and usually under a fee (Bardhi and Eckhardt, 2012). Practices of access-based consumption are increasingly common in the domain of social media, where the display of consumer goods is functional to gain attention and construct social status (Bainotti, 2021). As highlighted by other existing research, the display of consumption represents a way to seek micro-celebrity or to convey a sense of affluence aimed at stimulating the aspirational consumption of an online persona

(Rokka and Canniford, 2016; Marwick, 2015). The growing importance of the display also leads to deeper changes in the nature of consumption, which becomes intertwined with self-branding, and increasingly a matter of showcasing, displaying, and promoting, without actually consuming in a traditional sense (Bainotti, 2023). These behaviours are not solely exhibited by influencers and content creators, as one could think, nor do they reflect the mere need of flaunting wealth and consumer goods. On the contrary, these practices can be observed among a variety of TikTok users, including "regular" ones (i.e., those who use the platform to share their everyday life without the explicit or implicit intention of achieving micro-celebrity or turning their activity into a profession).

Despite the wide variety of literature just discussed, an analysis of how the process of platformisation is influencing consumption practices and their ephemeral dimension is still missing. In this chapter, we will show how ephemeral consumption emerges at the intersection of platform affordances and users' practices, and because of the penetration of the logic of platforms into our everyday lives (Helmond, 2015). As mentioned in the Introduction, the expansion of digital platforms' economic and infrastructural logics into the web and society, affects the production and circulation of cultural content, as well as its status (Poell et al., 2022). As a consequence, cultural commodities become "contingent," that is, malleable, informed by datafied user feedback, and open to constant revision and circulation (Nieborg and Poell, 2018). Consumption practices and digital consumer imaginaries, we argue, are contingent as well, as they are increasingly influenced by, and reliant upon, data flows, algorithms' rankings and recommendations, platforms' affordances and the participatory culture and vernaculars they foster (see e.g., Airoldi and Rokka, 2022; Rocamora, 2022). In a similar way to the platformisation of cultural production, consumer culture, too, is ever more dependent upon platforms, in that how consumers think, act, and relate to consumption is influenced by the ways in which platforms operate. If consumption is contingent, meaning, dependent on and influenced by the conditions and circumstances set by platforms, we can arguably say that it also includes an element of ephemerality. Ephemerality, here, refers to the short-lived and transient nature of consumption, as well as the ways in which it is perceived and performed in the context of algorithmically curated and memetic social media environments such as TikTok. The nature of consumption becomes entangled with the creation and reception of fast-paced, viral, and memetic content, which increasingly relies on practices of displays of consumption. These aspects are strongly intertwined with the transient nature of content and practices afforded by social media platforms' architectures. To understand how ephemeral consumption emerges, and the specific forms it assumes, the chapter focuses on the analysis of a specific TikTok challenge, known as the #shoechallenge.

Data Collection and Techniques for the Analysis

As anticipated, the main purpose of this chapter is to understand in what ways TikTok's affordances, as well as the ephemerality of content they allow users to create, influence consumption practices. Therefore, we seek to answer the following research questions: *What is the role of TikTok affordances in prompting practices of ephemeral consumption? What are the main practices and templates through which ephemeral consumption unfolds on TikTok?* The first research question allows us to focus on how TikTok affordances contribute to the formation of specific platform grammars, which in turn can be considered as the infrastructural skeleton of ephemeral consumption practices. The analysis of templates, instead, will be more focused on the vernaculars promoted by the platform's material architecture and collective cultural practices (Gibbs et al., 2015), and adopted by TikTok users. Ultimately, by answering the research questions and looking at the intersection of grammars and vernaculars, it will be possible to better understand the relationship between the platformisation of consumer culture and the emergence of ephemeral consumption.

The empirical research focuses on a TikTok challenge, as this kind of content is particularly apt to study the platform's affordances, as well as issues of virality and ephemerality, in reciprocal interaction. The challenge chosen for this study is the "#shoechallenge," which has reached 1.5 billion views at the time of writing. As mentioned on the TikTok page dedicated to the challenge,[1] users are invited to answer the question "What kind of shoes do you like?" by frequently changing shoes in front of the camera and showing their talent in flipping content and using transition effects. Besides gestures, sounds, and trending content, TikTok challenges are associated with hashtags. For the data collection, we focused on the data labelled with the hashtag #shoechallenge, which refers to, and categorises, content in line with the challenge under study. In this way, we were able to "repurpose" this feature for social media research, in a Digital Method fashion (Rogers, 2019), and find an entry point for the empirical research.

---

1   https://www.tiktok.com/tag/shoechallenge?lang=en.

There are at least two types of challenges posed by TikTok analysis. The first is technical, as the collection of TikTok data has proved to be difficult due to the absence of public APIs. Secondly, the interpretation of this kind of data can be troubling because it entails considering the multimodality of the platform, as well as the different levels of signification it offers. Another critical point related to the study of TikTok content lies in its expressive dimension, given that visual elements are functional to vehiculate performative and expressive messages and not only aesthetically pleasing and curated representations. So far, existing research has mostly been based on qualitative approaches inspired by digital ethnography (Schellewald, 2021) and visual content analysis (Vizcaíno-Verdú and Abidin, 2022), or by means of the walkthrough method technique (Zulli and Zulli, 2020). The method we propose, instead, follows a rather unexplored Digital Methods perspective (with a few exceptions, see e.g., Bainotti et al., 2022; Geboers et al., 2022) and it is, therefore, experimental and iterative.

For the data collection procedure, we used the Firefox extension "Zeeschuimer," developed in the context of the Digital Methods Initiative (Peeters, 2022).[2] The extension allows the researcher to collect TikTok data in a "scrolling and scraping" fashion by capturing data directly from the TikTok web interface. By scrolling down the #shoechallenge page, we were able to collect data about the video displayed and then import them directly to the 4CAT Capture and Analysis Toolkit for preliminary analysis (Peeters and Hagen, 2022).[3] The use of the Zeeschuimer extension is helpful for collecting the metadata about the object of study by mimicking users' behaviours and experiences of the platforms – which also includes the algorithmic curation of content. To limit the biases related to content personalisation, we set up a research profile on Firefox by cleaning the browsing history and deactivating the tracking of cookies.[4] With this procedure, we were able to collect a dataset of 1,800 TikTok posts, from September 2019 to January 2022. This is a small-medium size set of data, which allows us to take into consideration the granularity and complexity of audio-video content, without losing the broader picture.

The data collection procedure presents some critical points that are worthy of being addressed, which regard the ethical issues related to scraping

2   Further information on how to install and use the Zeeschuimer extension is available at this link: https://github.com/digitalmethodsinitiative/zeeschuimer.
3   To access and use the 4CAT Capture and Analysis Toolkit see the following website: https://4cat.oilab.nl/.
4   For further detail see the following tutorial: 'The research browser' https://www.youtube.com/watch?v=bj65Xr9GkJMandt=15s.

as a technique and in the use of individual data for doing research (see also Chapter 6). First, we are aware that scraping represents a contested research technique, which is here considered a "necessary evil" to perform social media research in an age of API curtailing (Venturini and Rogers, 2018). Moreover, in the chapter, we will analyse data in an aggregated way, and we will not disclose information that could potentially harm the individuals represented in TikTok videos.

The data analysis is articulated on different levels, following the specificity of the platform and its affordances. The first step focused on the textual metadata, which comes with TikTok content, specifically hashtags. We performed a co-hashtag analysis to account for the relationships among hashtags and the thematic clusters emerging from hashtags co-occurrences (Marres and Gerlitz, 2016). The network was created with Table2Net[5] and visualised with Gephi. In order to simplify the network and increase its significance, only the hashtags with more than three occurrences were included. We then applied the community detection algorithm to detect different clusters and highlight the themes which emerge in relation to the challenge.

Secondly, we paid attention to the "sound" feature, to understand which audio elements are associated with the challenge. We selected the ten top-used sounds and created a temporal bump chart with RawGraph[6] to display the presence, absence, and change of sound over time.

Finally, we delved deeper into TikTok audio-visual content by performing an ethnographic content analysis (Altheide, 1987), which considers the visual elements of each video (Rose, 2016), their textual elements (i.e., captions) as well as paratextual information (i.e., the layers of text added to TikTok video), to better understand the practices and contexts wherein #shoechallenge posts are created. In this part of the analysis, we paid particular attention to the various templates that characterise a TikTok challenge, that is, the organising principles and aesthetic norms that guide users in the creation of video content on the platform (Leaver et al., 2020). The analysis of templates is particularly useful in this research because it allows us to grasp how grammars and vernaculars intersect in the creation of memetic content and its variations (Caliandro and Anselmi, 2021). Therefore, content analysis is coupled with what can be called "templatability analysis," which consists of the analysis of templates by interpreting scene-by-scene timelines. Scene-by-scene timelines can be considered as a specific kind of composite

5   https://medialab.github.io/table2net/.
6   https://rawgraphs.io/.

image (Colombo, 2018) and are created by extracting the frames of different video clips and juxtaposing them next to each other. In this way, the entire content of a TikTok video can be taken into account. For the creation of the scene-by-scene timelines, we selected the two most engaged TikToks in each category found with the content analysis. We used VLC Media Player to extract the video frames (one frame every three seconds) and save them as images.[7] The output is a folder of images, which we visualised with the help of Figma, a web-based vector graphics editor.[8]

TikTok Hashtag and Sound Analysis

As it appears clear from TikTok's description, the #shoechallenge collects content aimed at showcasing consumer goods, as well as showing one's ability to create engaging video clips. The display of clothing items and shoes is at the very core of this challenge. Yet, it is important to unravel how these consumption practices blend with the platform's affordances and viral logic, as well as how and to what extent they can be considered forms of ephemeral consumption. To do so, the analysis starts with an investigation of hashtags and sounds, to unravel the ways in which these affordances organise and influence TikTok users' practices. In this way, it is possible to start grasping the grammars underpinning ephemeral consumption.

The Use of Hashtags

The first step of the analysis is to understand the ways in which users connect their content to hashtags and, more generally, how hashtags are used in relation to the challenge under study.

The co-hashtag network (Fig. 8.1) is very dense, meaning that nodes are highly connected with each other and, therefore, that hashtags are often co-occurring (that is, they are used in similar combinations). Moreover, the network appears to be homogeneous, with the presence of four, highly connected, clusters, detected by the community detection algorithm. Delving deeper into the network, the following clusters clearly emerge:

7   There are different possible ways in which scene-by-scene timelines can be created. One could replicate our analysis by using VLC Media Player, which is an intuitive and easy programme to use. For more information on how to extract images from video clips, see e.g., https://www. raymond.cc/blog/extract-video-frames-to-images-using-vlc-media-player/. As an alternative, it is possible to create scene-by-scene timelines directly with 4CAT (https://4cat.oilab.nl/).
8   https://www.figma.com/.

Co-hashtag network

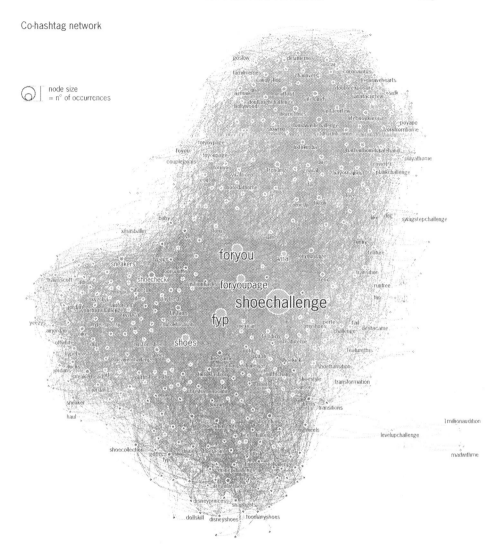

Fig. 8.1. The co-hashtag network was created using Table2Net and visualised with Gephi. The community detection algorithm has been used to identify clusters of related videos, which Gephi marks with different colours. The size of the nodes represents the number of times (occurrences) each hashtag appears in the dataset. Hashtags with less than three occurrences are excluded from the network.

- **Attention-seeking hashtags (green):** These hashtags reflect users' attempts at seeking visibility and producing trending content in order to appear on the FY page (e.g., #fy; #foryoupage; #trending). As the size of the nodes in Fig. 8.1 shows, these hashtags are the most frequent ones in terms of occurrence count.

- **Shoe hashtags (orange):** The hashtags used in this cluster are mostly aimed at connecting the content to the challenge and the topic of shoes (e.g., #shoes, #shoechek). These hashtags are related to sneakers and sneaker brands, such as #Nike, #Converse, #Jordan etc.
- **Fashion hashtags (light blue):** This cluster focuses on fashion, with hashtags such as #oodt and #fashion inspiration. Hashtags referring to other types of shoes, especially high heels (#highheelschallenge) and fashion brands, which are mostly luxury ones, (#louisvuitton; #gucci) are present.
- **Covid-19 hashtags (purple):** In this cluster, it is possible to find Covid-19-related hashtags, such as #handwashchallenge, #homefitness, and #safehands. The presence of this cluster is justified by the fact that the challenge gained popularity during the Covid-19 pandemic. The content linked to the hashtags, however, is unrelated to both pandemic and the #shoechallenge. This cluster can be interpreted as an example of hashtag hijacking, whereby users make use of popular, issue-related hashtags for a different purpose than the one originally intended, in an attempt of boosting the visibility of their content and appear on the FY page. In this part of the network, it is also possible to find an Indian sub-cluster (e.g., #tiktokindia; #foryouindia, #punjabi), which, again, is not directly linked to the #shoechallenge. We can interpret the mix of #shoechallenge, Covid-19, and Indian-TikTok hashtags as attention-seeking behaviours peculiar to a specific niche of the platform (TikTok India, before the platform was banned from this country, see e.g., Levine, 2023).

The network reflects a behaviour that is becoming increasingly popular, which consists of hashtags being used primarily to label the different elements present in each post and, most importantly, to attract attention, rather than grouping similar topics and issues (a phenomenon that has also been called "hashtag stuffing," see e.g., Rogers, 2017; Tuters and Willaert, 2022). This style of hashtag usage is evident on platforms like Instagram, but it is taken to the extreme on TikTok where, as the network shows, hashtags are predominantly employed as a means to engage with challenges, garner attention, and pursue popularity, rather than connecting to various topics.

The use of hashtags just presented points to a first grammar useful for understanding the relationship between ephemerality and consumption. In the #shoechallenge, hashtags are mostly used to mark a connection with an imitation public (Zulli and Zulli, 2020), a social formation wherein "networks form through processes of imitation and replication, not interpersonal connections, expressions of sentiment, or lived experiences" (Zulli and Zulli, 2020, p. 2). Hashtags, therefore, mediate the participation in an imitation public that is limited and fluctuating in time, as it is based more on imitative (consumption) practices and affective drives than a shared sense of identity or belonging (as also seen with the concept of brand publics and influencer hybrid formations in Chapter 5). Moreover, hashtags are predominantly used to seek attention and make content viral, in the context of fast-paced and transient spans of attention fostered by the TikTok platform. Hence, we can see the emergence of a mediated and temporary connection between hashtags and consumption practices, which is aimed at increasing the visibility of content within the #shoechallenge.

The Use of Sounds

The second feature fundamental to understanding TikTok data is the sound indexing feature. Not only do sounds represent one of the most important components of TikTok content, but they are also useful for understanding how one challenge deploys and appears on the platform, as well as the various templates associated with it (as explained later). The bump chart in Fig. 8.2 shows the evolution over time of the top eight sounds with more than 20 occurrences in the dataset: Original Sounds (n=357), Run Free (Original Mix) (n= 281), 23 Island (n= 243), Original Sound_user[9] (n=56), I like shoes (n=38), Fat Joe – All the Way Up (n=22), and Kismet (N=21).

Leaving aside, for the moment, the Original Sound category, the most frequent sound associated with the challenge is the song Run Free, by Deep Chills feat. IVIE, which was released in 2017 and then adapted and re-used as a TikTok sound. In the data, this sound is present from 2018 to 2020, with a peak of 126 occurrences in 2018. Therefore, it is possible to say that the development of the challenge goes hand in hand with the use of this sound, especially at its inception. Although the lyrics do not relate to the theme of the challenge itself, the rhythm of the sound appears to be functional to mark the shoe changes in front of the camera. The chorus "If you do it just the way I like, maybe I could waste my time on you" is followed by a series of beats that mark the transition to different scenes and the display of different shoes, outfits, or other items. The ways in which frames are transitioned show the personal and creative touch added

---

9   To preserve users' privacy, the username embedded in the name of the sound has been substituted with "user."

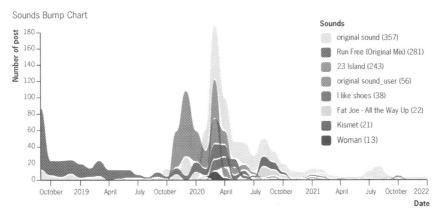

Fig.8.2. The Bump Chart was created with RAWGraph to visualise the top eight most recurring sounds under the hashtag "#shoechallenge." In this way, it is possible to analyse the most popular sounds and how their use evolves over time.

by each user. At its inception, in 2018 and 2019, the challenge and the use of the sound "Run Free" remain homogenous. The focus of the videos is in line with the general spirit of the challenge, based on the display of shoes and extended to the display of outfits, clothing items, or other consumer goods. The third most relevant sound in terms of occurrences (n=122) is the song "23 Island" by JayDaYoungan. This sound appears in 2019, the same year the song was released, and was still popular in 2020 (n=116), and slightly in 2021. This sound introduces a different song in the #shoechallenge, which, however, remains the same at its core, maintaining the display of shoes and outfits as the main focus. In terms of content, as we will see more in-depth later, there is almost no difference between the two sounds and the two versions of the challenge, with only some small changes in the ways in which the video scenes are transitioned. While, in the first case, the transitions follow the rhythm of the sound, in the second version, users display their consumption items by slowly parading in front of the camera.

Starting from mid-2020, instead, we can see the emergence of a wider variety of sounds, which attests to the evolution of the challenge over time. One of the variants of the challenge shows users tossing one of their shoes in the air and, the moment their foot catches it, they are seen wearing a different outfit, usually with the "Fat Joe" or "Kismet" sounds (from the name of this song, this variation is also known as "Kismet shoe transitions," Know Your Meme, 2020). However, such a variant represents only a small portion of how the challenge develops and therefore will not be considered in depth in the rest of the analysis. Moreover, in the same time frame,

Original Sounds sees an enormous rise, with a peak of 180 occurrences in March 2020. These sounds are directly created by singular users by recording their voices, playing songs from other devices, remixing already existing TikTok sounds, etc. It is then no surprise that such a category is extremely varied, which makes it difficult to identify common patterns and templates. What is relevant here is that, after a more homogeneous and memetic phase, the use of sounds becomes messier, leaving space for forms of appropriation, reappropriation, and alteration of the challenge (Bainotti et al., 2022).

Therefore, the analysis of sounds is relevant to understanding the duration and evolution of a challenge over time and, in turn, its ephemeral dimension. Sounds reach their peak only to then slowly disappear and be replaced by more recent and popular ones. Moreover, as time passes, sounds become more contaminated, the memetic component of the challenge diminishes, and new variants start to appear until they become the predominant content. Consumption practices involving the display of consumer goods are embedded into this flow of sounds and content and become a constitutive part of the trend. These practices become ephemeral in that they follow the momentary hype of joining the challenge and are then substituted by other, more recent trends. In the next part of the analysis, we delve deeper into the different variants of the trend in order to understand the various ways in which users appropriate and make sense of the #shoechallenge, as well as the visual templates associated with it.

TikTok Content and Templatability Analysis

As previously highlighted, the #shoechallege assumes different forms over time and in relation to the sound feature. Although the core of the challenge remains mostly the same, by means of an ethnographic content analysis (Altheide, 1987), we were able to identify three main groups of practices through which the challenge is used and appropriated: challenge *replication*, *variation*, and *alteration*, as shown in Table 8.1. The forms in which the challenge unfolds on TikTok are expressions of how the grammars previously outlined intersect with specific platform vernaculars. For each use of the challenge, numerous unique templates emerge, which incorporate hashtags, sounds, and the distinctive stylistic elements and language inherent to TikTok.

Table 8.1.   Content analysis

Use of the challenge	Type of content
Challenge replication	– Memetic
Challenge variation	– Ironic
	– Self-branding
	– Situational
Challenge alteration	– Shoe hacks
	– Do-it-yourself
	– Flaunting consumption

Challenge Replication

As previously seen, a substantial amount of content shares a similar template characterised by the display of consumer goods in front of the camera, although it differs in how the transition between one item and the other is performed. Users tend to "follow the trend" in what can be called a process of *challenge replication*. These replication practices are characterised by uniformity and regularity in the content and templates used, and therefore by the predominance of memetic behaviours (Caliandro and Anselmi, 2021; Zulli and Zulli, 2020) (Fig. 8.3).

To further interpret these practices, it is convenient to look at the captions related to the videos. In most cases, the challenge is replicated to showcase a collection of shoes before an imagined audience, as it emerges from captions such as "check out my shoe collection," or "my Nike shoe collection." In other cases, users express a sort of fear of missing out (FOMO), and their willingness to keep up with TikTok trends: "finally did this challenge too" or "couldn't skip this TikTok trend." The engagement with users' audience becomes apparent in captions such as: "What do you prefer?" "Which one?" or "Should I do my heels next?" and "You asked for another outfit change ... here it is." In these cases, users directly interact with the public by asking for feedback or suggestions for the creation of other content.

The analysis of challenge replication templates and practices shows that consumption is ephemeral as it responds to the logic of self-branding and attention-seeking (as already seen in the hashtag analysis) and is oriented by the requests of imagined publics. In this way, consumption practices function as both a display and a performance, and their duration is contingent upon following the trend, attracting attention with the hope of getting viral and establishing a connection with the audience.

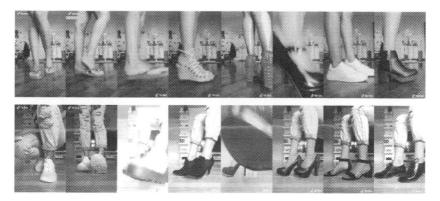

Fig. 8.3. The scene-by-scene timelines were created with VLC Media Player and visualised with the vector graphic editor Figma. The scene-by-scene timelines were then anonymised by obscuring the username displayed in the watermark of each frame. The visualisation showcases the recurring use of the same template that defines the initial and most popular characteristics of the #shoechallenge.

Challenge Variation

The analysis of the #shoechallenge's templates also shows practices of *challenge variation.* In this case, TikTok content partly shares a common template, and partly puts forward unexpected visual patterns and vernaculars, with some changes related to the different messages that users want to convey with their versions of the challenge. Forms of challenge variation are indicative of expressions of vernacular creativity (Burgess, 2006) and show how users take advantage of the platform's affordances (e.g., sounds, hashtags, but also stickers and captions) to add compositional, original changes to a template that is repeated from user to user. Furthermore, TikTok audio-visual elements are functional to vehiculate performative and expressive messages, and not only aesthetically pleasing and curated representations. In challenge variations, the expressive dimension of TikTok content clearly emerges in parallel with the memetic aspects of the trend. From the analysis, three main variations can be found, each one pointing to a specific kind of content: ironic, trend surfing, and situational (see Table 8.1).

Firstly, challenge variations appear in the form of ironic content. The videos in this category poke fun at the processes of content production in the context of the challenge, as well as the time and effort that some users invest in it. Ironic content follows different templates that mimic the moves typically associated with the challenge, with captions such as "These transitions are hard" or that they "Only have 2 pairs of shoes". Occasionally, ironic content portrays mishaps or failures within the challenge. For example, a TikTok video deliberately showcasing a phone dropping during transition shots, accompanied by the caption "Let's start a new trend." As already highlighted in previous research (Schellewald, 2021), people use the challenge in a comedic way, parodying the way others use it.

Secondly, the #shoechallenge includes what can be called *self-branding* content. In these cases, the challenge is used as a means to brand the self, in order to increase users' visibility, create trending content, or promote different products, companies, and activities. In one of the videos in this category, the user replicates the template of the challenge to promote a new collection of sunglasses they designed and produced. In this and similar cases, the main template of the challenge remains the same, but the messages conveyed by participating in the trend differ from the original one. This type of content differs from other attention-seeking ones in that there is a purposeful intention to appropriate the trend for branding the self and/or sponsoring products.

Lastly, and more importantly for this research, in the case of the *situational* type of content, users connect the display of consumer goods to specific, everyday situations. The trend is used to present viewers with different shoes for various occasions, as can be seen in Fig. 8.4. Such occasions can be very simple, such as "what I wear to go to school," or more articulated, such as "coffee with the girls" and "afternoon brunch," or ironic, such as "See you in court" or "to the latina clubs." In these cases, (mostly female) TikTokers try on and display their mothers' shoes, making fun of their choices and style. Moreover, through the display of shoes, users narrate the different steps and challenges of women's lives, moving from "single," which is usually represented by the display of high heels, to "mom," which, on the contrary, shows comfortable and unsightly slippers. These insights also point out that TikTok content is often a mix of different components, such as situational and ironic content. The presence of such a variety of content reflects users' practices of navigating, integrating, and adapting TikTok's platform vernaculars to their communicative and expressive needs.

To further prove this point, the analysis reveals the emergence of a template that includes text labels representing different situations for shoe usage (Fig. 8.4). Such a template marks a change in the message conveyed by TikTok videos and suggests users' participation in a slightly different imitation public. This type of content highlights the situational dimension of consumption (Airoldi et al., 2016; Caliandro and Anselmi, 2021), by showcasing its reliance on specific contextual occasions and moods (as also shown in the case of the platformisation of music taste, see Chapter 3). In this type of challenge variation, the situational use and

Fig. 8.4. The scene-by-scene timelines showcase how the original template of the #shoechallenge has been appropriated by different users. The result is a variation in the challenge. The change in the template emerges clearly in the use of stickers, which add a textual layer to the video clips, as well as a new and situational meaning to the consumption practices displayed.

display of consumption are related to specific contexts and occasions, limited in time and space, thus hinting at another aspect that makes consumption ephemeral. More generally, the analysis of challenge variations shows that consumption is ephemeral as it becomes functional to adapt to various formats and templates, as well as to follow the logic of the challenge prompted by the platform affordances. Moreover, the display of consumption is used in an expressive way to create and vehiculate a variety of messages, which only lasts for the short duration of the video and the limited temporality of the challenge and its variation form. The combination of the display of consumption and its expressive dimension is one more sign of the volatility of consumption. This is even more true if we consider the situational dimension of consumption, which adds a specific spatiality and temporality to the use and display of consumer behaviours in relation to TikTok trends.

Challenge Alteration

The last use of the #shoechallenge is that of challenge alteration, which emerges specifically around 2020, in correspondence to the rise of different sounds and original sounds in the data. The homogeneity of the trend starts to diminish and we can see the emergence of three types of content: shoe hacks, "do-it-yourself" content, and practices aimed at explicitly flaunting consumption (see Table 8.1). All three categories are related to the #shoechallenge simply by the fact that they are associated with the challenge's official hashtag and maintain a focus on shoes.

With *shoe hacks*, users share tricks on how to clean and take care of sneakers, as well as tips to make high heels more comfortable. These hacks often become more related to creativity and leave the floor to "do-it-yourself" content. The TikTok videos in this category show users who create their

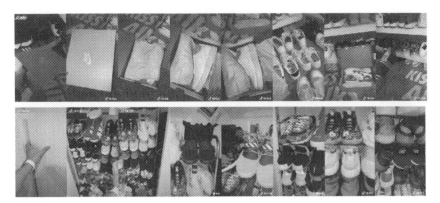

Fig. 8.5. The scene-by-scene timelines show that the original template of the challenge has been completely altered over time. A new template emerges showing the conspicuous display of consumer goods, in particular, sneakers.

own designs, harvest, and readjust old shoes, decorate sneakers, etc. As a sign of challenge alteration, in these two categories, there is no uniform template organising users' content and no prevailing sound. On the contrary, individual practices and original sounds prevail, reducing to the minimum the memetic component of the challenge.

In the case of the third type of content, *consumption flaunting*, a new template characterised by users showcasing their collection of sneakers emerges (Fig. 8.5). These videos portray a large number of shoe boxes in the background or, alternatively, shoe racks full of sneakers, usually from the same brands (frequently, Nike). TikTokers then show their last purchase or gift and accompany the video content with captions such as "oops I did it again" or "I might have an obsession ... another one!," referring to another pair of Air Jordans. This type of video also exemplifies what kind of content can be found in the "shoe hashtags" cluster of the co-hashtag network previously shown (Fig. 8.1). In these clips, the display of consumption is taken to the extreme, so much so that it represents the main content as well as the main message of the videos. The display of consumption assumes the form of more explicit showing off behaviours, aimed at building an aspirational persona (Marwick, 2015), as well as creating and signalling social status (Bainotti, 2021).

Generally, the display of consumption, the core element of the #shoe-challenge, emerges across the various uses and templates of the trend. The challenge relies not only on the display of consumption, but also on its accumulation, sometimes exceeding mere necessity. Therefore, the analysis also shows examples of displays of overconsumption – a common trait of all three uses of the trend. These practices challenge the concept of access-based consumption (Bardhi and Eckhardt, 2012), reinstating ownership and accumulation as ways of joining memetic publics, building a self-brand, and participating in the logic of TikTok. Ephemeral consumption on TikTok is therefore not so much related to the role of access, as Bardhi and Eckhart (2012) argue; rather, it is characterised by the relevance of imitation and repetition, the temporality of a performance lasting only a few seconds, and the logic of attention-seeking in an algorithmically mediated and memetic platform.

Conclusion

The aim of this chapter is to understand the role that TikTok affordances play in the emergence of ephemeral consumption, as well as the practices and templates through which such forms of consumption unfold on the platform. By looking at the intersections of grammars and vernaculars, we can see how TikTok's affordances introduce a specific type of ephemeral content, which is tightly connected with practices of ephemeral consumption. Hashtags, sounds, and challenges, in particular, serve as more than compositional elements to create TikTok content. They act as mediators for the formation of imitation publics (Zully and Zulli, 2020) and facilitate attention-seeking endeavours as well as the creation of viral content. Given the temporary nature of imitation publics and the fast-paced feature of attention and virality on TikTok, the grammars provided by hashtags and sounds reinforce the ephemerality of content and consumption practices on the platforms. Furthermore, the grammars created by hashtags and sounds intersect with platform vernaculars to generate specific templates. The templates associated with the #shoechallenge highly rely on practices of display of consumption and include expressions of situational consumption (in the case of challenge variation) as well as forms of overconsumption (in the case of challenge alteration). Moreover, the ways in which grammars and vernaculars can be combined showcase the variability of the #shoechallenge and the emergence of appropriation and alteration strategies. The dynamics of ephemeral consumption are further amplified by the memetic behaviours encouraged by the platform through challenges, which increase the circulation of short-lived variations of similar templates. In summary, the results show that TikTok provides users with an infrastructure that favours imitative as well as ephemeral practices, which blend perfectly with behaviours aligned with liquid consumption (Bardhi and Eckhardt, 2017) and consumption as a display (Bainotti, 2023). Collectively, these elements underscore the inherently transient nature of consumption within the TikTok ecosystem.

What, then, is ephemeral consumption, and how does this phenomenon relate to the platformisation of consumer culture? Firstly, consumption is ephemeral due to the pervasive influence of digital platforms' logics on society (Poell et al., 2022). Like cultural commodities, consumer culture too becomes contingent upon the infrastructural and economic models of digital platforms (Nieborg and Poell, 2018), resulting in increased malleability, variability, and transience of consumption practices and digital consumer imaginaries. This contingency introduces elements of changeability and ephemerality to the domain of consumption. Notably, this emphasis on contingency distinguishes ephemeral consumption from other practices that focus on liquidity and dematerialisation, such as the concept of liquid consumption (Bardhi and Eckhardt, 2017). More precisely, we could argue that contemporary consumption encompasses both liquidity, immateriality, and access, while also being deeply intertwined with the logics of digital platforms. In this sense, a reflection on ephemeral consumption contributes to complexifying the dichotomy between empowerment and datafication discussed in the Introduction (Airoldi and Rokka, 2022). Indeed, ephemeral consumption presents some elements of access and dematerialisation that enable consumer empowerment, yet it is also intricately connected to the logic of datafication and the influence exerted by data and algorithms in shaping users' practices.

Furthermore, the role of platformisation clearly emerges in the memetic behaviours that characterise hashtag and sound use, as well as challenge reproduction practices. The main features of the platform, which afford mimesis and replication (Zulli and Zulli, 2020), together with the algorithmically created For You page, influence the use of hashtags, sounds, and visual templates. The result is a platform populated by content that ends up being aesthetically and structurally similar, yet having different expressive dimensions and messages, as shown in the case of challenge appropriation practices. Mimesis and templatability are not only the results of the interaction between users and the platform affordances but also two elements useful to the TikTok platform itself. As Zulli and Zulli (2020) argue, "mimesis is an advantageous strategy for both the users and the platform, as imitation and replication engender content production and spreadability in unparalleled ways" (p. 13). The production and spreadability of content play a crucial role in fuelling platforms' business models and increasing the possibilities for capitalising on consumers' practices. Interestingly, the growing standardisation of content introduces an element of ephemerality:

the memetic nature of a trend is not perpetual, and the same applies to the consumption practices on which it relies. As the results made clear, mimesis and imitation intertwine with virality, further amplifying the transient nature of consumption.

Limitations and Future Research

Among the limitations of the research, it is important to acknowledge that the data collected and analysed reflects the algorithmic functioning of the TikTok platform. By capturing data directly from the TikTok web interface through tools such as the Zeeschuimer extension, the algorithmic rankings of the platforms are replicated and embedded in the resulting dataset. Consequently, the research might tend to analyse content that receives visibility and (in theory) conforms to the algorithmic requirements dictated by the platform, thus losing sight of the long tail of other content. Researchers should be aware of how tools and techniques for data collection might shape the outcomes of the research. To overcome this issue and focus on less visible content, particular attention should be put on the query design process (see e.g., Pilipets, 2023). Furthermore, this chapter focused on a specific challenge that centres around consumption practices. However, it is important to note that in other challenges or types of content, this dimension of consumption may vary or present different nuances. Additionally, it would be worthwhile to explore how the concept of ephemeral consumption can be applied to other forms of fast-paced consumption that were not considered in this study, such as the phenomenon of fast fashion.

References

Airoldi, M., Beraldo D. and Gandini, A. (2016). Follow the algorithm: An exploratory investigation of music on YouTube. *Poetics, 57,* 1–13. https://doi.org/10.1016/j.poetic.2016.05.001.

Airoldi, M., and Rokka, J. (2022). Algorithmic consumer culture. *Consumption Markets and Culture, 25*(5), 411–428. https://doi.org/10.1080/10253866.2022.2084726.

Altheide, D. (1987). Reflections: Ethnographic content analysis. *Qualitative Sociology, 10,* 65–77. https://doi.org/10.1007/BF00988269.

Arvidsson, A. and Caliandro, A. (2016). Brand public. *Journal of Consumer Research, 42*(5), 727–748. https://doi.org/10.1093/jcr/ucv053.

Bainotti, L. et al. (2022). Tracing the geology and change of TikTok audio memes. Research Report. Digital Methods Summer School, University of Amsterdam. https://wiki.digitalmethods.net/Dmi/WinterSchool2022TikTokAudioMemes.

Bainotti, L. (2021), Striving for conspicuousness: How micro-influencers construct and display social status on Instagram (PhD dissertation). University of Milan – University of Turin.

Bainotti, L. (2023). How conspicuousness becomes productive on social media. *Marketing Theory.* https://doi.org/10.1177/14705931231202435.

Bainotti, L., Caliandro, A., and Gandini, A. (2021). From archive cultures to ephemeral content, and back: Studying Instagram Stories with digital methods. *New Media and Society, 23*(12), 3656–3676. https://doi.org/10.1177/1461444820960071.

Bardhi, F. and Eckhardt, G. M. (2012). Access-Based Consumption: The case of car sharing. *Journal of Consumer Research, 39*(4), 881–898. https://doi.org/10.1086/666376.

Bardhi, F. and Eckhardt, G.M. (2017). Liquid consumption. *Journal of Consumer Research,* 44(3), 582–97. https://doi.org/10.1093/jcr/ucx050.

Burgess, J. (2006). Hearing ordinary voices: Cultural studies, vernacular creativity and digital storytelling. *Continuum: Journal of media and cultural studies, 20*(2), 201–214. https://doi.org/10.1080/10304310600641737.

Caliandro, A. and Anselmi, G. (2021). Affordances-based brand relations: An inquiry on memetic brands on Instagram. Social Media+ Society, 7(2). https://doi.org/10.1177/20563051211021367.

Colombo, G. (2018). The design of composite images: Displaying digital visual content for social research (PhD dissertation). Politecnico di Milano.

Geboers et al. (2022). How (long) do we #standwithukraine? Summer School report. https://wiki.digitalmethods.net/Dmi/Summerschool2022Howlongdowestand-withukraine.

Gibbs, M., Meese, J., Arnold, M., Nansen, B., and Carter, M. (2015). #Funeral and Instagram: Death, social media, and platform vernacular. *Information, Communication and Society, 18*(3), 255–268. https://doi.org/10.1080/1369118X.2014.987152.

Know Your Meme (2020). https://knowyourmeme.com/memes/kismet-shoe-transitions.

Leaver, T., Highfield, T., and Abidin, C. (2020). *Instagram: Visual social media cultures.* Polity Press.

Levine, A.S. (2023, May 21). India banned TikTok in 2020: TikTok still has access to years of Indians' data. *Forbes.* https://www.forbes.com/sites/alexandralevine/2023/03/21/tiktok-india-ban-bytedance-data-access/?sh=7a8866a12eca.

Marres, N. and Gerlitz, C. (2016). Interface methods: Renegotiating relations between digital social research, STS and sociology. *The Sociological Review, 64*(1), 21–46. https://doi.org/10.1111/1467-954X.12314.

Marwick, A. E. (2015). Instafame: Luxury selfies in the attention economy. *Public Culture, 27*(1/75), 137–160. https://doi.org/10.1215/08992363-2798379.

Nieborg, D. B. and Poell, T. (2018). The platformization of cultural production: Theorizing the contingent cultural commodity. *New Media and Society. 20*, 4275–4292. https://doi.org/10.1177/1461444818769694.

Peeters, S. (2022). Zeeschuimer [browser extension]. https://doi.org/10.5281/zenodo.6826878

Peeters, S. and Hagen, S. (2022). The 4CAT capture and analysis toolkit: A modular tool for transparent and traceable social media research. *Computational Communication Research, 4*(2). https://computationalcommunication.org/ccr/article/view/120.

Pilipets, E., (2023). Hashtagging, duetting, sound-linking: TikTok gestures and methods of (in)distinction. *The Journal of Media Art Study and Theory, 4*(1), 109–135. https://doi.org/10.59547/26911566.4.1.07.

Poell, T., Nieborg, D.B., and Duffy, B.E. (2021). *Platforms and cultural production*. Polity Press.

Rocamora, A. (2016). Mediatization and digital media in the field of fashion. *Fashion Theory, 21*(5), 505–522. https://doi.org/10.1080/1362704X.2016.1173349.

Rokka, J. and Canniford, R. (2016). Heterotopian selfies: How social media destabilizes brand assemblages. *European Journal of Marketing, 50*(9/10), 1789–1813. https://doi.org/10.1108/EJM-08-2015-0517.

Rogers, R. (2019). *Doing digital methods*. Sage.

Rogers, R. (2017). Digital methods for cross-platform analysis. In J. Burgess, T. Poell, and A. Marwick (Eds.), *The SAGE handbook of social media* (pp. 91–110). Sage

Rose, G. (2016). *Visual Methodologies: An introduction to researching with visual materials*. Sage.

Schellewald, A. (2021). Communicative forms on TikTok: Perspectives from digital ethnography. *International Journal of Communication, 15*, 1437–1457. https://ijoc.org/index.php/ijoc/article/view/16414.

Sherman, J. (2023, March 31). What just about everyone is getting wrong about banning TikTok. Slate. https://slate.com/technology/2023/03/tiktok-ban-debate-broken-congress-biden.html.

Smith, A. (2020, June 19). TikTok explains how its algorithm actually works. *The Independent*. https://www.independent.co.uk/tech/tiktok-algorithm-videos-explained-likes-comments-a9574696.html.

Tuters, M. and Willaert, T. (2022). Deep state phobia: Narrative convergence in coronavirus conspiracism on Instagram. *Convergence, 28*(4), 1214–1238. https://doi.org/10.1177/13548565221118751.

Venturini, T. and Rogers, R. (2019). "API-based research" or how can digital sociology and journalism studies learn from the Facebook and Cambridge Analytica

data breach. *Digital Journalism*, *7*(4), 532–540. https://doi.org/10.1080/216708
11.2019.1591927.

Vizcaíno-Verdú, A. and Aguaded, I. (2022). #ThisIsMeChallenge and music for
empowerment of marginalized groups on TikTok. *Media and Communication*,
10(1), 157–172. https://doi.org/10.17645/mac.v10i1.4715.

WeAreSocial (2021, October 21). Social media users pass the 4.5 billion mark. https://
wearesocial.com/jp/blog/2021/10/social-media-users-pass-the-4-5-billion-mark/.

Zulli, D. and Zulli, D. J. (2020). Extending the internet meme: Conceptualizing
technological mimesis and imitation publics on the TikTok platform. *New
Media and Society*, *24*(8), 1872–1890. https://doi.org/10.1177/1461444820983603.

III. Conclusion: Platforms and Consumer Research. What Next?

Through a variety of case studies and topics, employing a multiplicity of techniques and approaches within the digital methods tradition, this book has illustrated the key dimensions concerning what we have described as the platformisation of consumer culture, providing examples of how to approach this phenomenon empirically. In doing so, we have outlined what we believe is the necessary array of tools and heuristics that consumer culture scholars are required to handle and be familiar with if they wish to study consumer practices and cultures and their relationship with platforms in a non-dualistic approach (cf. Caliandro and Gandini, 2017); that is, seeing online and offline consumption practices and cultures as processes that cannot be artificially separated. Indeed, the relevance of platformisation processes in consumption studies is not limited to what happens in the online domain but demands consideration of the offline–online dimensions as a continuum of practices whereby users – aka, consumers – position themselves according to individual needs and desires, taking advantage of social media in various ways to engage with brands, products, and services.

The multifaceted nature of the process of platformisation of consumption practices and cultures inevitably renders this selection of case studies a non-exhaustive one: different platforms, cases, and techniques could (and perhaps should) have been considered. Almost certainly, some important aspects have been overlooked in this text. This process, after all, is evolving by the day, and the relationship between platforms and consumer cultures continues to develop as new apps appear, new demographics enter the consumer arena, and existing lifestyles and habits change. Yet, taken together, the snapshots presented here are evidence of what we believe are some key elements of continuity that characterise platformisation as a process, and which allow us to further elaborate on its nature and boundaries from a theoretical perspective. Thus, as a conclusion to the book, in the following sections we develop this argumentation further, aiming to answer the following question: *what is the platformisation of consumer culture, after all?*

Caliandro, A., A. Gandini, L. Bainotti, G. Anselmi, *The Platformisation of Consumer Culture: A Digital Methods Guide*. Amsterdam: Amsterdam University Press, 2024
DOI 10.5117/9789463729567_CON

Platforms and CCT

It may be argued that the platformisation of consumer culture represents the byproduct and consolidation of three main theoretical concepts that concern the relationship between digital (and social) media, on the one hand, and consumption processes, on the other. These have been widely discussed in consumer culture theory – yet, so far, they have been observed somewhat in isolation from one another. Today, as platforms become the infrastructural model that re-mediates social and cultural processes surrounding consumption, these dimensions coexist and reciprocally influence each other (Caliandro et al., 2024). The first one concerns the historical notion of *prosumption* (Ritzer and Jurgenson, 2010). In 2009, at the dawn of the platform era, Declev Zwick and Janice Denegri Knott published an article entitled "Manufacturing customers: The database as new means of production," in which they argued that: "the recent increase in available consumer data, computational power, and analytical skills leads to a reorganisation of the gaze of marketers and increasingly reverses the Fordist articulation of production and consumption. More specifically, instead of flexibly adjusting production regimes to shifting consumption patterns, database marketers collapse the production–consumption dichotomy *by manufacturing customers as commodities*" (Zwick and Knott, 2009, p. 221, emphasis in original).

Today, 25 years later, this process finds its culmination in platforms, here considered as a technological model for the (re)organisation of social relations, built on an algorithmic infrastructure that serves the capture and circulation of data about users and, in turn, the monetisation of the former by the companies who own them. The nature of platforms, as outlined by Poell et al. (2021, p. 5), is that of being "data infrastructures, that facilitate, aggregate, monetise, and govern interactions between end-users and content and service providers." In doing so, they continue, platforms operate as institutional actors, reconfiguring the logics of cultural production by re-fencing the practices of production, distribution, and monetisation, which are now being subdued to their own logic (Zwick and Knott, 2009; see also Gandini, 2021). In relation to consumption, platforms ultimately produce personalised social environments for individual consumers, engaging, on the one hand, in the *concentration* of user behaviour for prediction purposes (as data is transformed into targeted recommendations) and, subsequently, in their *fragmentation*, as consumers are grouped for similar interests as a result of their activity on the platform. Thus, as Zwick and Denegri-Knott (2009) envisaged, consumers ultimately become commodities in the form of data, traded in what Shoshana Zuboff (2019) calls "surveillance capitalism," considered the main business model of the social media economy (as articulated in the Introduction). As shown in Chapters 3 and 7, digital platforms may act as concentration flywheels or as prisms that disperse or regroup their audiences into different subdivisions. Understanding how (and why) different socio-technical setups embedded into platforms cause one or the other is one of the central points in digital research, mainly because it allows empirically grounded efforts to interface with larger macro-social and political economic issues (see Chapter 7 in particular).

This second aspect – *fragmentation* – already finds space in consumer culture theory through the notion of *brand public* (Arvidsson and Caliandro, 2016). Brand publics, Arvidsson and Caliandro contend, are social formations that are not based on interaction but rather on a continuous focus of interest and mediation, whereby participation is not structured by discussion or deliberation but by an affective, i.e., emotional dimension. As algorithmic infrastructures, platforms render this affect productive once it becomes visible – mainly in the form of metrics – and thus (re)start the cycle of datafication and personalisation illustrated earlier. By way of their affordances, platforms organise, coordinate, and standardise the processes of formation of publics around brands, consumer objects, or goods. At the same time, as argued by Caliandro and Anselmi (2021), users engage in activity around brands and consumption objects by way of templates, which enable them to express their vernacular creativity in relation to them. These templates serve to standardise the datafication process and optimise its output.

Consequently, and thirdly, platforms represent efficient devices in producing, organising, and monetising *contingent* consumer attention. The notion of contingent consumer attention is related to the definition of contingent commodities (Nieborg and Poell, 2018), which points to how cultural products and services become increasingly "malleable, modular in design, and informed by datafied user feedback, open to constant revision and recirculation" (Nieborg and Poell, 2018, p. 2) due to processes of platformisation. Following a similar logic, consumers' practices and attention can be considered contingent, too, in that they are increasingly dependent on the production of content that is temporary, multi-modal, and optimised for platform monetisation (Nieborg and Poell, 2018). Furthermore, consumer attention becomes contingent in the encounter with liquid, ephemeral, access-based, and dematerialised forms of consumption (Bardhi and Eckhardt 2012; 2017) (as also seen in Chapters 3 and 8). Throughout this process, platforms become the main milieu of consumer discourse, offering a variety of affordances and formats for users to share their views and express their feelings in relation to consumption objects or brands. In doing so, they produce cultural rankings and hierarchies (Rieder et al., 2018), reshaping the cultural conceptions of value by which users approach and discuss them. Metrics emphasise popularity and, in tandem with personalisation and imitation, determine a perimeter for engagement in status games, wherein consumption also becomes an important reputational device. This is the case of social media influencers, who engage in what Bainotti (2021) calls "circles of prosumption," whereby performative displays of consumption are repurposed as productive activities aimed at creating and signalling social status (see also Eckhardt and Bardhi, 2020). It is from this complex set of practices that the key dimensions of the platformisation of consumer culture emerge: we illustrate them in greater detail in the next section through the notion of the *digital consumer imaginary*.

Digital Consumer Imaginary and Platformised Imaginaries

A good way to define a *digital consumer imaginary* is to start from the general concept of socio-technical imaginary. A socio-technical imaginary is a "powerful cultural resource for making sense of and enacting new technologies" (Jasanoff and Kim, 2013, p. 190). Scholars use the term "socio-technical" because such a "cultural resource" is not really the product of the imaginative mind of the individual, but rather the combined product of the inherent properties of a technological device and the norms of use that society constructs around it (Sörum and Fuentes, 2023; Caliandro et al., 2024). Similarly, we could argue that a digital consumer imaginary is a cultural resource for making sense of and enacting consumption practices that social groups construct around brands, products, or services within digital environments. However, conceived as such, this sounds more like the definition of a *digitised* consumer imaginary (Rogers, 2009), rather than a *natively digital* consumer imaginary. On the contrary, as illustrated in the Introduction and through the case studies presented in the book, a digital consumer imaginary has some specific features. In particular, we contend that it is a cultural artefact that: a) is co-created by human and non-human actors populating digital environments; b) is shaped by the affordances of digital environments (technical architectures + online participatory cultures); c) vehiculates general discourses about consumption (e.g., authenticity, belonging, affectivity, etc.), rather than opinions about brands, products, and services; d) is (re)assembled by the very digital tools of data collection, analysis, and visualisation that the researcher uses to investigate digital environments.

Moreover, by specifically focusing on digital platforms, in this book we showed how this kind of imaginary is also *platformised*. The implications of this statement are twofold. First, the digital consumer imaginary is platformised because it does not assume "random forms" but is deeply shaped by the *grammars* and *vernaculars* of digital platforms. For example, in Chapter 1 we have seen that Facebook's nostalgic imaginary does not manifest as an undistinguished sentimental magma, but it is specifically shaped by the grammars of *celebration*, *memorialisation*, and *techno-longing* – on top of which users construct their own vernaculars, which coalesce into three main narrations: *reminiscent*, *playful*, and *experiential*. Second, the digital consumer imaginary can be considered platformised insofar as the platform logic seems to be incorporated in the mentality and practices of those users that create such imaginary (Van Es and Poell, 2020; Caliandro et al., 2021). We provided various examples in which users do not talk so much about brands per se, but rather employ brands *as platforms* to vehicle, amplify, and circulate their personal identities, experiences, and worldviews. In Chapter 4, for instance, we have seen how both human users and bots piggyback on brand-related fake news to promote their own "agendas" (political for the former and commercial for the latter), rather than bashing brands' reputation or value. These various platformised imaginaries, which we analysed through different case studies across different platforms, substantiate the phenomenon of the *platformisation of consumer culture* and capture the various tensions that characterise this process.

The Platformisation of Consumer Culture and Its Tensions

A first element that is peculiar to the platformisation of consumer culture, which can be drawn by looking at the empirical cases illustrated throughout the book, is the tension between the necessity to, at once, "standardise" and "de-standardise" consumer practices of cultural production (as we discussed, for instance, in the conclusions of Chapter 2). Building on the tension between *datafication* vs *liquification* (identified by Airoldi and Rokka, 2022), we can identify two related, and perhaps even contradictory, dimensions of the platformisation of consumer culture: *standardisation* and *ephemerality*.

Standardisation means that practices, imaginaries, and vernaculars are conformed to, and oriented by, the mechanisms through which platforms operate and the standards they set. The notion of standardisation is useful to account for how the penetration of digital platforms and their logics (Helmond, 2015; Poell et al., 2021) has impacted the ways in which consumption is performed, imagined, and discussed. On the one hand, as said, platforms need to standardise users' behaviours in order to better (and more efficiently) track and convert them into data. These forms of standardisation create a sort of path dependency: platforms and their logics define what is deemed relevant, visible, or viral, while relegating all the rest to the threat of invisibility (Bucher, 2012). Although resistance is possible (see e.g., O'Meara, 2019), standardisation means conformity and adaptation to digital platforms and the requirements they set in terms of the practices and content deemed appropriate or successful. From the perspective of standardisation, grammars could thus be interpreted not only as units of action, but also as the building blocks of a platformised consumer culture whereby consumer interests can assume multiple forms and change in multiple ways. The combination of these building blocks, and their intersection with platform vernaculars, fuels processes of *replication* and *imitation*, as clearly emerged in the presence of the "#shoechallenge" templates (Chapter 8). Templates mirror the memetic practices and imitative publics promoted by platforms like TikTok (Zulli and Zulli, 2020), but also represent principles that orient the relationships between users, on the one hand, and goods, services, and brands, on the other (Caliandro and Anselmi, 2021).

Notably, the growing standardisation of content and practices also introduces a significant element of *ephemerality*. While certain content and trends may enjoy a moment of popularity and widespread replication, they eventually fade away quickly as new trends emerge. This continuous, rapid cycle of memetic behaviours and the extenuating pursuit of virality contribute to the transient nature of content, practices, and digital consumer imaginaries. Ephemerality does not necessarily lie in the type of content shared (i.e., TikTok videos do not formally disappear after a certain amount of time), but at the level of the platform's affordances and participatory culture. As a result, ephemerality expands to consumption practices as these become an integral part of a trend and an effective device to seek attention and "go viral" through forms of display, and increasingly entail a situational component. As seen, for example, in Chapter 3, practices of music consumption – and the role of music genres in orienting listening preferences – increasingly get tied to temporary situations, moods, and specific occasions of consumption.

The idea of ephemerality in relation to standardisation also brings forward a component of *variability*. The combination of the standardised building blocks described above, with their ephemerality, leaves some space for vernacular creativity (Burgess, 2006) and free forms of expression. This is why the concept of vernacular is particularly suitable to complement that of grammars, as it allows to grasp the various ways in which users/consumers personalise their expressions online within the structure of opportunities set by platforms. It is important to underline that digital platforms do need to grant users some space for freedom, in order to foster their continued engagement and avoid excessive monotony. If this attempt at retaining users admittedly responds to a logic of empowerment (and thus aligns with the idea of liquification (Airoldi and Rokka, 2022)), it is also true that the ultimate scope of social media platforms is to push users and consumers to continuously generate more and fresh data.[1]

Cutting right across the tension between standardisation and ephemerality, imitation and variability is the *hybridisation* of the dimensions of *interaction* and *mediation*. Building on the concepts of brand publics (Arvidsson and Caliandro, 2016) and imitation publics (Zulli and Zulli, 2020), as well as on the analysis of hybrid influencer publics deployed in Chapter 5, it may be argued that consumer practices and digital consumer imaginaries constitute an example of the increasing combination of interactions among users and practices of mediation by means of socio-technical affordances (e.g., hashtags) – and, as a result, should be seen as the byproduct of this blending process. As shown in Chapter 5, online social formations are hybrid in that they combine elements of communities and publics, and are formed around temporary, affective drives, and a mediated sense of identity. Notably, the hybrid nature of influencer publics also presents an element of ephemerality, as these social formations are formed around temporary drives of affect mediated by the influencer persona. This perspective of hybridisation between interaction and mediation can also be applied to future research aimed at understanding the emergence and features of digital consumer imaginaries. Lastly, while the process of platformisation of consumer culture may be seen as inherently *immaterial*, we should not forget the *material* dimension this continues to entail: as seen in Chapter 1, for instance, the articulation of a nostalgic discourse around consumption on Facebook takes place as users mobilise a variety of material objects. Put

---

1   Curiously, this tension echoes a key economic logic underpinning the business model of all digital platforms, which Nick Srnicek (2017) calls "cross-subsidisation." On the one hand, platforms offer paid services to certain kinds of users (e.g., Facebook Advertising), thereby contrasting some groups of users. On the other hand, platforms provide some free services to other kinds of users (e.g., all the networking tools available on Facebook), de facto making some other groups of users more "free."

differently, the platformisation of consumer culture neither excludes –nor renders useless paying attention to the material cultures that pertain to consumption practices, which maintain significant relevance. Indeed, the relationship between the platformisation of consumer culture and (old and new forms of) materiality represents a potentially insightful avenue for future research on this topic.

Ultimately, while we discourage understanding the platformisation of consumer culture in terms of strict dichotomies, such as datafication vs liquification or standardisation vs ephemerality, we argue that a deep and nuanced understanding of this phenomenon primarily lies at the intersections and overlapping of these dimensions. It is from these primal and basic tensions that we can see the dynamics that characterise consumer culture being deployed on digital platforms.

Methodological Conclusions

Finally, from a methodological point of view, the definition of platformisation of consumer culture as elaborated in the previous paragraphs results from our operationalisation of the key dimensions here described into the notions of platform grammars and vernaculars and the observation of their interaction. Throughout the book, *grammars* have been understood as patterns of content production driven by the technical architecture of platforms (e.g., see the use of hashtags and sounds to create memetic videos on TikTok, as shown in Chapter 8). *Vernaculars*, instead, are here understood as those linguistic conventions, stemming from ordinary creativity, that users build on top of platform grammars (e.g., consider the vernaculars through which users decline possible patterns of radicalisation of vegetarian consumption presented in Chapter 2). Building on these definitions and on the analysis of the eight case studies related to eight different platforms, we can provide some considerations that may be useful to advance the methodological understanding of grammars and vernaculars in consumer studies.

On the one hand, we can argue that, although profoundly rooted in the technical infrastructure of platforms, grammars do not depend entirely on platforms' technicalities, but also on the manipulation of those technicalities by users. A sheer example can be found in Chapter 1, where we encountered three different grammars of nostalgia: *celebration, memorialisation, techno-longing*. Certainly, those grammars are shaped by the Facebook infrastructure, in terms of post format as well as the format of those few highly circulating images within Pages dedicated to the '80s.

Yet, the specific grammars of *celebration, memorialisation, techno-longing* are also the byproduct of the specific intent of Pages' administrators, who compose posts (using certain texts and images) to elicit emotional reactions from followers (as testified by the numerous comments accompanying such posts). On the other hand, it may be said that vernaculars are not random and unruly manifestations of users' creativity, but tend to follow specific (and sometimes very repetitive) patterns of cultural production. More specifically, vernaculars tend to be shaped by both grammars and platform rhetorics. We found a clear example of this phenomenon in Chapter 6. The narrations that customers articulate on Tripadvisor present a structure that seems very much modelled on the interface of the comment section itself. Moreover, customers create ad hoc narrations that seem strongly influenced by: a) common rhetorics circulating on TripAdvisor (i.e., "the food expert rhetoric"); and b) the specific topic of conversation, in our case Kitchen Nightmares (to this end, see the rhetorics: "the Cannavacciuolo cure," "Kitchen Nightmares effect," "Nothing Changed," "A Missed Opportunity").

These considerations lead us to develop some further methodological speculations, which we hope will inspire future research on platformisation of consumer culture based on digital methods. First, it may be argued that the analysis of grammars and vernaculars is neither qualitative nor quantitative; on the contrary, it can be only proficiently done by combining qualitative and quantitative techniques (Caliandro and Gandini, 2017). Second, due to their repetitive and standardised nature, grammars and vernaculars can be easily traced and measured. Thus, it is intriguing to note how "cultural modules" of content production have a *quantifiable* nature as well (Manovich, 2017). Finally, if one had the capacity to precisely identify, trace, and quantify grammars and vernaculars, and follow them over time, they would be able to explore some *dynamics* of platformisation of consumer culture – and not only snapshots of its "static" nature, as we did in this book. Specifically, we hypothesise three possible dynamics:

1) *Platforming*: a scenario in which grammars and vernaculars repeat consistently over time, with few or no changes. In this case, we have a consumer culture that is relatively standardised and compliant with the logics of platforms: a condition that renders consumers and their imaginaries mere objects of data extraction.
2) *De-platforming*: a scenario in which heterogeneous grammars and vernaculars multiply over time. In this case, we have a consumer culture that is de-standardised and somehow "resistant" towards platforms'

logics: a condition in which consumers are more free, and their imaginaries more liquid.

3) *Re-platforming*: a scenario in which heterogeneous grammars and vernaculars recompose after a certain period of time. In this case, we have some initial consumer practices and imaginaries that are deviant from platforms' logics, but then, at a second moment, are (re)apportioned by the platform itself. Drawing on Gerlitz et al. (2019), we used the prefix "re-" to signal a sort of advantage that platforms have over consumers. In fact, thanks to their surveillance mechanisms (which are opaque and invisible), platforms have always had the capacity to translate users' eccentric "languages" into their "official" grammar[2] (Gerlitz and Rieder, 2018). More generally, re-platforming could also signal an ongoing struggle between consumers' liberating drive and platforms' surveillance imperative.

We believe that the analysis of the dynamics of platformisation of consumer culture, based on a *quantification of qualitative entities* (Caliandro and Bennato, 2022), could be properly done in the future by taking advantage of advanced computational techniques, such as image recognition (Caliandro and Anselmi, 2021; Omena et al., 2021), machine learning (Borch and Hee Min, 2022), or even AI applications (Rieder et al., 2022; Querubín and Niederer, 2022). Unfortunately, we could not explore this possibility in the present book; however, we hope that further research will follow this path and give new impetus to the study of digital consumer culture.

A Final Note

While we fully share the overarching goal of a "multiplication of the frames of reference" (Poell et al., forthcoming) which inhabits platform studies in its current state, and maintain the necessity to de-centre Western culture and re-provincialise its significance – in the context of a global society where the West is only one of many possible contexts to observe and study – this book inevitably maintains a Western-centric disposition and gaze. In admitting this drawback, we also seek to underline that we

---

2   The most infamous example in this sense is that of hashtags. Hashtags (#) were born as a vernacular convention amongst (earlier) Twitter users, who used them to signal a thread of conversation. Soon after, this vernacular convention was adopted by Twitter, which made it an integral part of its public interface (Marres and Weltevrede, 2013).

are fully conscious of it, and, in so doing, we reiterate the call to extend the study of global processes of platformisation – of consumer culture and generally – beyond the Western scenario, which continues to suffer from the hegemonic significance of the Californian Ideology (Barbrook and Cameron, 1996) after several decades.

References

Airoldi, M., and Rokka, J. (2022). Algorithmic consumer culture. *Consumption Markets and Culture, 25*(5), 411–428. https://doi.org/10.1080/10253866.2022.20 84726.

Arvidsson, A. and Caliandro, A. (2016). Brand public. *Journal of Consumer Research, 42*(5), 727–748. https://doi.org/10.1093/jcr/ucv053.

Caliandro A. and Gandini A. (2017), *Qualitative research in digital environments: A research toolkit.* Routledge.

Caliandro, A. and Anselmi, G. (2021). Affordances-based brand relations: An inquiry on memetic brands on Instagram. *Social Media+ Society, 7*(2). https://doi.org/10.1177/20563051211021367.

Caliandro, A. and Bennato, D. (2022). Cultural Machines: Unlocking the power of digital methods and computational techniques for understanding socio-cultural processes in digital environments. *Mediascapes Journal, 20*(2), I–VII. https://rosa.uniroma1.it/rosa03/mediascapes/article/view/18266.

Caliandro, A., Garavaglia, E., and Anselmi, G. (2021a). Studying ageism on social media: An exploration of ageing discourses related to Covid-19 in the Italian Twittersphere. *Rassegna Italiana di Sociologia, 62*(2), 343–375. 10.1423/101848.

Caliandro, A., Gandini, A., Bainotti, L., and Anselmi, G. (2024). The platformization of consumer culture: A theoretical framework. *Marketing Theory.* https://journals.sagepub.com/doi/10.1177/14705931231225537

Bainotti, L. (2021). Striving for conspicuousness: How micro-influencers construct and display social status on Instagram (PhD dissertation). NASP, University of Turin-Milan.

Bardhi, F. and Eckhardt, G. M. (2012). Access-based consumption: The case of car sharing. *Journal of Consumer Research, 39*(4), 881–898. https://doi.org/10.1086/666376.

Bardhi, F. and Eckhardt, G. M. (2017). Liquid consumption. *Journal of Consumer Research, 44*(3), 582–597. https://doi.org/10.1093/jcr/ucx050.

Borch, C. and Hee Min, B. (2022). Toward a sociology of machine learning explainability: Human–machine interaction in deep neural network-based automated trading. *Big Data and Society, 9*(2). https://doi.org/10.1177/20539517221111361.

Burgess, J. (2006). Hearing ordinary voices: Cultural studies, vernacular creativity and digital storytelling. *Continuum: Journal of Media and Cultural Studies*, 20(2), 201–214. https://doi.org/10.1080/10304310600641737.

Bucher, T. (2012). Want to be on the top? Algorithmic power and the threat of invisibility on Facebook. *New Media and Society*, 14(7), 1164–1180. https://doi.org/10.1177/1461444812440159.

Eckhardt, G. M. and Bardhi, F. (2020). New dynamics of social status and distinction. *Marketing Theory*, 20(1), 85–102. https://doi.org/10.1177/1470593119856650.

Gerlitz, C. and Rieder, B. (2018). All tweets are not created equal: Investigating Twitter's client ecosystem. *International Journal of Communication*, 12, 528–547. 1932–8036/20180005.

Gerlitz, C., Helmond, A., Van der Vlist, F. N., and Weltevrede, E. (2019). Regramming the platform: Infrastructural relations between apps and social media. *Computational Culture: A Journal of Software Studies*, 7. ISSN: 2047-2390.

Helmond, A. (2015). The platformisation of the web: Making web data platform ready. *Social Media+ Society*, 1(2), https://doi.org/10.1177/2056305115603080.

Jasanoff, S. and Kim, S. H. (2013). Sociotechnical imaginaries and national energy policies. *Science as Culture*, 22(2), 189–196. https://doi.org/10.1080/09505431.2013.786990.

Manovich, L. (2017). Instagram and contemporary image. Manovich.net. http://manovich.net/index.php/projects/instagram-and-contemporary-image.

Marres, N. and Weltevrede, E. (2013). Scraping the social? Issues in real-time social research. *Journal of Cultural Economy*, 6(3), 313–335. https://doi.org/10.1080/17530350.2013.772070.

Nieborg, D. B. and Poell, T. (2018). The platformization of cultural production: Theorizing the contingent cultural commodity. *New Media and Society*, 20(11), 4275–4292. https://doi.org/10.1177/1461444818769694.

O'Meara, V. (2019). Weapons of the chic: Instagram influencer engagement pods as practices of resistance to Instagram platform labor. *Social Media+ Society*, 5(4), https://doi.org/10.1177/2056305119879671.

Omena, J. J., Pilipets, E., Gobbo, B., and Chao, J. (2021). The potentials of Google Vision API-based networks to study natively digital images. *Diseña*, 19, 1–25. 10.7764/disena.19.Article.1.

Poell, T., Duffy B.E., Nieborg, D., Sun, P., Arriagada, A., Mutsvairo, B., Tse, T., and De Kloet, J. (forthcoming). Global perspectives on platforms and cultural production. *International Journal of Cultural Studies*.

Poell, T., Nieborg, D. B., and Duffy, B. E. (2021). *Platforms and cultural production*. John Wiley and Sons.

Querubín, N. S. and Niederer, S. (2022). Climate futures: Machine learning from cli-fi. *Convergence*, https://doi.org/10.1177/13548565221135715.

Rieder, B., Gordon, G., and Sileno, G. (2022). Mapping value (s) in AI: Methodological directions for examining normativity in complex technical systems. *Sociologica, 16*(3), 51–83. https://doi.org/10.6092/issn.1971-8853/15910.

Rieder, B., Matamoros-Fernández, A., and Coromina, Ò. (2018). From ranking algorithms to "ranking cultures": Investigating the modulation of visibility in YouTube search results. *Convergence, 24*(1), 50–68. https://doi.org/10.1177/1354856517736982.

Rogers, R. (2009). *The end of the virtual: Digital methods.* Amsterdam University Press.

Srnicek, N. (2017). *Platform capitalism.* Polity Press.

Sörum, N. and Fuentes, C. (2023). How sociotechnical imaginaries shape consumers' experiences of and responses to commercial data collection practices. *Consumption Markets and Culture, 26*(1), 24–46. https://doi.org/10.1080/10253 866.2022.2124977.

Van Es, K. and Poell, T. (2020). Platform imaginaries and Dutch public service media. *Social Media+ Society, 6*(2), https://doi.org/10.1177/2056305120933289.

Zuboff, S. (2019). *The age of surveillance capitalism: The fight for a human future at the new frontier of power.* Profile Books.

Zulli, D. and Zulli, D. J. (2020). Extending the Internet meme: Conceptualizing technological mimesis and imitation publics on the TikTok platform. *New Media and Society, 24*(8), 1872–1890. https://doi.org/10.1177/1461444820983603.

Zwick, D. and Denegri Knott, J. (2009). Manufacturing customers: The database as new means of production. *Journal of Consumer Culture, 9*(2), 221–247. https://doi.org/10.1177/1469540509104375.

Bibliography

Abidin, C. (2015). Communicative intimacies: Influencers and perceived interconnectedness. *Ada: A Journal of Gender, New Media, and Technology, 8*. https://adanewmedia.org/2015/11/issue8–abidin/.

Abidin. C. (2016). Aren't these just young, rich women doing vain things online?: Influencer selfies as subversive frivolity. *Social Media + Society. 2*(2), 1–17. https://doi.org/10.1177/2056305116641342.

Abidin, C. (2018). *Internet celebrity: Understanding fame online*. Emerald Publishing.

Abidin, C. (2021). Singaporean influencers and Covid-19 on Instagram stories. *Celebrity Studies, 12*(4), 693–698. https://doi.org/10.1080/19392397.2021.1967604.

Abidin, C. and de Seta, G. (2020). Doing digital ethnography: Private messages from the field. *Journal of Digital Social Research, 2*(1), 1–19. http://doi.org/10.33621/jdsr.

Adler-Nissen, R., Eggeling, K. A., and Wangen, P. (2021). Machine anthropology: A view from international relations. *Big Data & Society, 8*(2). https://doi.org/10.1177/20539517211063690.

Agre, P. E. (1994). Surveillance and capture: Two models of privacy. *The Information Society, 10*(2), 101–127. https://doi.org/10.1080/01972243.1994.9960162.

Aguilera, T., Artioli, F., and Colomb, C. (2021). Explaining the diversity of policy responses to platform-mediated short-term rentals in European cities: A comparison of Barcelona, Paris and Milan. *Environment and Planning A: Economy and Space, 53*(7), 1689–1712. https://doi.org/10.1177/0308518X19862286.

Airoldi, M. (2021a). Digital traces of taste: Methodological pathways for consumer research. *Consumption Markets and Culture, 24*(1), 97–117. https://doi.org/10.1080/10253866.2019.1690998.

Airoldi, M. (2021b). The techno-social reproduction of taste boundaries on digital platforms: The case of music on YouTube. *Poetics, 89*. https://doi.org/10.1016/j.poetic.2021.101563.

Airoldi, M., Beraldo, D., and Gandini, A. (2016). Follow the algorithm: An exploratory investigation of music on YouTube. *Poetics, 57*, 1–13. https://doi.org/10.1016/j.poetic.2016.05.001.

Airoldi, M. and Rokka, J. (2022). Algorithmic consumer culture. *Consumption Markets and Culture, 25*(5), 411–428. https://doi.org/10.1080/10253866.2022.2084726.

Akerlof, G. A. (1978). The market for "lemons": Quality uncertainty and the market mechanism. In P. Diamond and M. Rothschild (Eds.), *Uncertainty in economics: Readings and exercises* (pp. 235–251). Academic Press.

Alexander, V. D., Blank, G., and Hale, S. A. (2018). TripAdvisor reviews of London museums: A new approach to understanding visitors. *Museum International, 70*(1/2), 154–165. https://doi.org/10.1111/muse.12200.

Allen, K. and Mendick, H. (2013). Keeping it real? Social class, young people and "authenticity" in reality TV. *Sociology, 47*(3), 460–476. https://doi. org/10.1177/0038038512448563.

Altheide, D. (1987). Reflections: Ethnographic content analysis. *Qualitative Sociology, 10*, 65–77. https://doi.org/10.1007/BF00988269.

Anderson, W. (1997). *The future of the self: Inventing the postmodern person.* Penguin Putnam Inc.

Andreotti, A., Anselmi, G., Eichhorn, T., Hoffmann, C. P., Jürss, S., and Micheli, M. (2017). European perspectives on participation in the sharing economy. *European Perspectives on Participation in the Sharing Economy (October 2, 2017)*. SSRN. https://ssrn.com/abstract=3046550.

Anselmi, G., Chiappini, L., and Prestileo, F. (2021). The greedy unicorn: Airbnb and capital concentration in 12 European cities. *City, Culture and Society, 27*. https:// doi.org/10.1016/j.ccs.2021.100412.

Anselmi G., Maneri M., and Quassoli F. (2020). "Un attentato quasiterroristico." Macerata, Twitter e le opportunità politiche dell'arena pubblica. *Comunicazione punto doc. 23*, 17–36. https://hdl.handle.net/10281/295220.

Anselmi, G. and Vicari, S. (2020). Milan makes it to the big leagues: A financialized growth machine at work. *European Urban and Regional Studies, 27*(2), 106–124. https://doi.org/10.1177/0969776419860871.

Appadurai, A. (1996). *Modernity at large: Cultural dimensions of globalization.* University of Minnesota Press.

Arditi, D. (2015). The new distribution oligopoly: Beats, iTunes, and digital music distribution. *Media Fields, 10*. http://mediafieldsjournal.squarespace.com/ the-new-distribution-oligopoly/2015/11/14/the-new-distribution-oligopoly- beats-itunes-and-digital-musi.html;jsessionid=8BE275AEDEDF1B7F0A3FB8B 9DE000697.v5-web016.

Arnould, E. J., Arvidsson, A., and Eckhardt, G. M. (2021). Consumer collectives: A history and reflections on their future. *Journal of the Association for Consumer Research, 6*(4), 415–428. https://doi.org/10.1086/716513.

Arnould, E. J. and Thompson, C. J. (2005). Consumer culture theory (CCT): Twenty years of research. *Journal of Consumer Research, 31*(4), 868–882. https://doi. org/10.1086/426626.

Arnould, E. J., and Thompson, C. J. (2018). *Consumer culture theory.* Sage.

Arvidsson, A. (2005). Brands: A critical perspective. *Journal of Consumer Culture, 5*(2), 235–258. https://doi.org/10.1177/1469540505053093.

Arvidsson, A. (2016). Facebook and finance: On the social logic of the derivative. *Theory, Culture and Society, 33*(6), 3–23. https://doi.org/10.1177/0263276416658104.

Arvidsson, A (2019). *Changemakers: The industrious future of the digital economy.* Polity Press.

Arvidsson, A. and Caliandro, A. (2016). Brand public. *Journal of Consumer Research*, *42*(5), 727–748. https://doi.org/10.1093/jcr/ucv053.

Arvidsson, A., Caliandro, A., Airoldi, M., and Barina, S. (2016). Crowds and value: Italian directioners on Twitter. *Information, Communication and Society*, *19*(7), 921–939. https://doi.org/10.1080/1369118X.2015.1064462.

Arvidsson, A. and Peitersen, N. (2013). *The ethical economy: Rebuilding value after the crisis*. Columbia University Press.

Atton, C. (2001). The mundane and its reproduction in alternative media. *Journal of Mundane Behavior*, *2*(1), 122–137. http://researchrepository.napier.ac.uk/id/eprint/3620.

Audrezet, A., De Kerviler, G., and Moulard, J. G. (2020). Authenticity under threat: When social media influencers need to go beyond self-presentation. *Journal of Business Research*, *117*, 557–569. https://doi.org/10.1016/j.jbusres.2018.07.008.

Audy Martínek, P., Caliandro, A., and Denegri-Knott, J. (2023). Digital practices tracing: Studying consumer lurking in digital environments. *Journal of Marketing Management*, *39*(3/4), 244–274. https://doi.org/10.1080/0267257X.2022.2105385.

Bainotti, L. (2021), Striving for conspicuousness. How micro-influencers construct and display social status on Instagram (PhD dissertation), University of Milan – University of Turin.

Bainotti, L. (2023). How conspicuousness becomes productive on social media. *Marketing Theory*. https://doi.org/10.1177/14705931231202435.

Bainotti, L. et al. (2022). Tracing the geology and change of TikTok audio memes. Research Report. Digital Methods Summer School, University of Amsterdam. https://wiki.digitalmethods.net/Dmi/WinterSchool2022TikTokAudioMemes.

Bainotti, L., Caliandro, A., and Gandini, A. (2021). From archive cultures to ephemeral content, and back: Studying Instagram Stories with digital methods. *New Media and Society*, *23*(12), 3656–3676. https://doi.org/10.1177/1461444820960071.

Bajde, D. (2012). Mapping the imaginary of charitable giving. *Consumption Markets and Culture*, *15*(4), 358–373. https://doi.org/10.1080/10253866.2012.659433.

Barabási, A. L. (2002). *Linked: The new science of networks*. Perseus Pub.

Bardhi, F. and Eckhardt, G. M. (2012). Access-based consumption: The case of car sharing. *Journal of Consumer Research*, *39*(4), 881–898. https://doi.org/10.1086/666376.

Bardhi, F. and Eckhardt, G. M. (2017). Liquid consumption. *Journal of Consumer Research*, *44*(3), 582–597. https://doi.org/10.1093/jcr/ucx050.

Barron, K., Kung, E. and Proserpio, D. (2019). When Airbnb listings in a city increase, so do rent prices. *Harvard Business Review*, *17*, 1–62. https://ci.carmel.ca.us/sites/main/files/file-attachments/harvard_business_article_and_study.pdf.

Bastian, M., Heymann, S., and Jacomy, M. (2009). Gephi: An open-source software for exploring and manipulating networks. In Proceedings of the international AAAI conference on web and social media (vol. 3, no. 1, pp. 361–362).

Bauman, Z. (2017). *Retrotopia*. Polity.

BBC (2020). BAME we're not the same: Indian. https://www.bbc.co.uk/creative-diversity/nuance-in-bame/indian/#:~:text=Made%20up%20of%201.4%20million,within%20the%20global%20Indian%20diaspora.

Beer, D. (2017). The social power of algorithms. *Information, Communication and Society, 20*(1), 1–13. https://doi.org/10.1080/1369118X.2016.1216147.

Beer, D. (2019). *The Quirks of Digital Culture*. Emerald Group Publishing.

Berthon, P. R. and Pitt, L. F. (2018). Brands, truthiness and post-fact: Managing brands in a post-rational world. *Journal of Macromarketing, 38*, 218–227. https://doi.org/10.1177/0276146718755869.

Belk, R. W. (2013). Extended self in a digital world. *Journal of Consumer Research, 40*(3), 477–500. https://doi.org/10.1086/671052.

Belk, R. (2014). Sharing versus pseudo-sharing in Web 2.0. *The anthropologist, 18*(1), 7–23. https://doi.org/10.1080/09720073.2014.11891518.

Berger, J., Humphreys, A., Ludwig, S., Moe, W. W., Netzer, O., and Schweidel, D. A. (2020). Uniting the tribes: Using text for marketing insight. *Journal of Marketing, 84*(1), 1–25. https://doi.org/10.1177/0022242919873106.

Bessi, A. and Ferrara, E. (2016). Social bots distort the 2016 US Presidential election online discussion. *First Monday, 21*(11/7), https://doi.org/10.5210/fm.v21i11.7090.

Bishop, S. (2019). Managing visibility on YouTube through algorithmic gossip. *New Media and Society, 21*(11/12), 2589–2606. https://doi.org/10.1177/1461444819854731.

Bonini, T., and Gandini, A. (2019). First week is editorial, second week is algorithmic: Platform gatekeepers and the platformisation of music curation. *Social Media+ Society, 5*(4). https://doi.org/10.1177/2056305119880006.

Bonini, T. and Gandini, A. (2020). The field as a black box: Ethnographic research in the age of platforms. *Social Media+ Society, 6*(4). https://doi.org/10.1177/2056305120984477.

Borch, C. and Hee Min, B. (2022). Toward a sociology of machine learning explainability: Human–machine interaction in deep neural network-based automated trading. *Big Data and Society, 9*(2). https://doi.org/10.1177/20539517221111361.

Botsman, R. and Rogers, R. (2010). *What's mine is yours: The rise of collaborative consumption*. Harper Business.

Boudreau, K. J. (2017). Platform boundary choices and governance: Opening-up while still coordinating and orchestrating. In J. Furman, A. Gawer, B. S. Silverman, and S. Stern (Eds.), *Entrepreneurship, innovation, and platforms* (pp. 227–297). Emerald Publishing Limited.

Bounegru L., Gray J., Venturini T., and Mauri, M. (2018). *A field guide to "fake news" and other information disorders*. Public Data Lab.

Bourdieu, P. (1984). *Distinction: A social critique of the judgement of taste*. Harvard University Press.

boyd, d. (2011). Social networking sites as networked publics: Affordances, dynamics and implication. In Z. Papacharissi (Ed.), *A networked self: Identity community and culture on social network sites* (pp. 39–58). Routledge.

Brigida, M. and Pratt, W. R. (2017). Fake news. *North American Journal of Economics and Finance. 42*, 564–573. 10.1016/j.najef.2017.08.012.

Bristow, J. (2016). *The sociology of generations: New directions and challenges.* Springer.

Brodie, R. J., Ilic, A., Juric, B., and Hollebeek, L. (2013). Consumer engagement in a virtual brand community: An exploratory analysis. *Journal of Business Research, 66*(1), 105–114. https://doi.org/10.1016/j.jbusres.2011.07.029.

Bruns, A. (2019a). After the "APIcalypse": Social media platforms and their fight against critical scholarly research. *Information, Communication and Society, 22*(11), 1544–1566. https://doi.org/10.1080/1369118X.2019.1637447.

Bruns, A. (2019b). *Are filter bubbles real?* John Wiley and Sons.

Bruns, A., Harrington, S. and Hurcombe, E. (2020). <? covid19?>'Corona? 5G? or both?': The dynamics of COVID-19/5G conspiracy theories on Facebook. *Media International Australia, 177*(1), 12–29. https://doi.org/10.1177/1329878X20946113.

Bruns, A., Moon, B., Paul, A., and Münch, F. (2016). Towards a typology of hashtag publics: A large-scale comparative study of user engagement across trending topics. *Communication Research and Practice, 2*(1), 20–46.

Bucher, T. (2012). Want to be on the top? Algorithmic power and the threat of invisibility on Facebook. *New Media and Society, 14*(7), 1164–1180. https://doi.org/10.1177/1461444812440159.

Bucher, T. (2016). Neither black nor box: Ways of knowing algorithms. In S. Kubitschko and A. Kaun (Eds.), *Innovative methods in media and communication research* (pp. 81–98). Palgrave Macmillan.

Bucher, T. and Helmond, A. (2017). The Affordances of Social Media Platforms. In J. Burgess, T. Poell and A. Marwick (Eds.), *The SAGE handbook of social media* (pp. 233–253). Sage.

Burgess, J. (2006). Hearing ordinary voices: Cultural studies, vernacular creativity and digital storytelling. *Continuum: Journal of Media and Cultural Studies, 20*(2), 201–214. https://doi.org/10.1080/10304310600641737.

Caliandro, A. (2014). Ethnography in digital spaces: Ethnography of virtual worlds, netnography, and digital ethnography. In R. Denny and P. Sunderland (Eds.), *Handbook of anthropology in business* (pp. 658–680). Left Coast Press.

Caliandro, A. (2018). Digital methods for ethnography: Analytical concepts for ethnographers exploring social media environments, *Journal of Contemporary Ethnography, 47*(5), 551–578. https://doi.org/10.1177/0891241617702.

Caliandro, A. (2021). Repurposing digital methods in a post-API research environment: Methodological and ethical implications. *Italian Sociological Review*, *11*(4S), 225–225. https://doi.org/10.13136/isr.v11i4S.433.

Caliandro, A. (2022). Digital Ethnography. In A. Ceron (Ed), *Elgar encyclopedia of technology and politics* (pp. 122–126). Edward Elgar Publishing.

Caliandro, A. and Anselmi, G. (2021). Affordances-based brand relations: An inquiry on memetic brands on Instagram. *Social Media+ Society*, *7*(2). https://doi.org/10.1177/20563051211021367.

Caliandro, A. and Bennato, D. (2022). Cultural Machines: Unlocking the power of digital methods and computational techniques for understanding socio-cultural processes in digital environments. *Mediascapes journal*, *20*(2), I–VII. https://rosa.uniroma1.it/rosa03/mediascapes/article/view/18266.

Caliandro A. and Gandini A. (2017), *Qualitative research in digital environments: A research toolkit*. Routledge.

Caliandro, A., Garavaglia, E., and Anselmi, G. (2021a). Studying ageism on social media: An exploration of ageing discourses related to Covid-19 in the Italian Twittersphere. *Rassegna Italiana di Sociologia*, *62*(2), 343–375. 10.1423/101848.

Caliandro, A., Garavaglia, E., Sturiale, V., and Di Leva, A. (2021b). Older people and smartphone practices in everyday life: An inquiry on digital sociality of Italian older users. *The Communication Review*, *24*(1), 47–78. https://doi.org/10.1080/10714421.2021.1904771.

Caliandro, A., Gandini, A., Bainotti, L., and Anselmi, G. (2024). The platformization of consumer culture: A theoretical framework. *Marketing Theory*. https://journals.sagepub.com/doi/10.1177/14705931231225537

Cambrosio, A., Cointet, J. P., and Abdo, A. H. (2020). Beyond networks: Aligning qualitative and computational science studies. *Quantitative Science Studies*, *1*(3), 1017–1024. https://doi.org/10.1162/qss_a_00055.

Canavan, B. (2021). Post-postmodern consumer authenticity, shantay you stay or sashay away? A netnography of RuPaul's Drag Race fans. *Marketing Theory*, *21*(2), 251–276. https://doi.org/10.1177/1470593120985144.

Canniford, R. (2011). A typology of consumption communities. In R.W Belk, K. Grayson, A.M. Muñiz, and J.H. Schau (Eds.), *Research in Consumer Behavior* (pp. 57–75). Emerald Group Publishing Limited.

Canniford, R. and Bajde, D. (2015). *Assembling consumption: Researching actors, networks and markets*. Routledge.

Carah, N. and Angus, D. (2018). Algorithmic brand culture: Participatory labour, machine learning and branding on social media. *Media, Culture and Society*, *40*(2), 178-194. https://doi.org/10.1177/016344371875464.

Carrieri, V., Madio, L., and Principe, F. (2019). Vaccine hesitancy and (fake) news: Quasi-experimental evidence from Italy. *Health economics*, *28*(11), 1377–138. https://doi.org/10.1002/hec.3937.

Charmaz, K. (2000). *Grounded theory: Objectivist and constructivist methods*. In N. Denzin and Y. Lincoln (Eds.), *Handbook of qualitative research* (pp. 509–535). Sage.

Cheng, Y. and Chen, Z. F. (2021). The influence of presumed fake news influence: Examining public support for corporate corrective response, media literacy interventions, and governmental regulation. In D. Pompper and L. Hoffman (Eds.) *What IS news?* (pp. 103–127). Routledge.

Chung, J., Johar, G. V., Li, Y., Netzer, O., and Pearson, M. (2022). Mining consumer minds: Downstream consequences of host motivations for home-sharing platforms. *Journal of Consumer Research, 48*(5), 817–838. https://doi.org/10.1093/jcr/ucab034.

Cochoy, F., Licoppe, C., McIntyre, M. P., and Sörum, N. (2020). Digitalizing consumer society: Equipment and devices of digital consumption. *Journal of Cultural Economy, 13*(1), 1–11. https://doi.org/10.1080/17530350.2019.1702576.

Cocola-Gant, A. and Gago, A. (2021). Airbnb, buy-to-let investment and tourism-driven displacement: A case study in Lisbon. *Environment and Planning A: Economy and Space, 53*(7), 1671–1688. https://doi.org/10.1177/0308518X19869012.

Colleoni, E., Rozza, A., and Arvidsson, A. (2014). Echo chamber or public sphere? Predicting political orientation and measuring political homophily in Twitter using big data. *Journal of communication, 64*(2), 317–332. https://doi.org/10.1111/jcom.12084.

Colombo, G. (2018). The design of composite images: Displaying digital visual content for social research (PhD dissertation). Politecnico di Milano.

Corchia, L. (2022). Digital trace data analysis. In A. Ceron (Ed.), *Elgar encyclopedia of technology and politics* (pp. 72–77). Edward Elgar Publishing.

Cotter, K. (2019). Playing the visibility game: How digital influencers and algorithms negotiate influence on Instagram. *New Media and Society, 21*(4), 895–913. https://doi.org/10.1177/1461444818815684.

Cova, B. (1997). Community and consumption: Towards a definition of the "linking value" of product or services. *European Journal of Marketing, 31*(3/4), 297–316. https://doi.org/10.1108/03090569710162380.

Cova, B. and Dalli, D. (2009). Working consumers: The next step in marketing theory? *Marketing Theory, 9*(3), 315–339. https://doi.org/10.1177/1470593109338414.

Cross, G. (2015). *Consumed nostalgia: Memory in the age of fast capitalism*. Columbia University Press.

Dajem, Z. A. S. and Alyousef, H. S. (2020). An analysis of mood and modality in workplace discourse and the impact of power differentials: Ramsay's *Kitchen Nightmares*. *Advances in Language and Literary Studies, 11*(4), 48–61. https://doi.org/10.7575/aiac.alls.v.11n.4p.48.

Darmody, A. and Zwick, D. (2020). Manipulate to empower: Hyper-relevance and the contradictions of marketing in the age of surveillance capitalism. *Big Data and Society, 7*(1). https://doi.org/10.1177/2053951720909041.

Deighton, J. (2019). Big data. *Consumption Markets and Culture*, 22(1), 68–73. https://doi.org/10.1080/10253866.2017.1422902.

DeLanda, M. (2006). *A new Philosophy of Society: Assemblage Theory and Social Complexity*. Continuum.

Denegri-Knott, J., Jenkins, R., and Lindley, S. (2020). What is digital possession and how to study it: A conversation with Russell Belk, Rebecca Mardon, Giana M. Eckhardt, Varala Maraj, Will Odom, Massimo Airoldi, Alessandro Caliandro, Mike Molesworth, and Alessandro Gandini. *Journal of Marketing Management*, 36(9/10), 942–971. https://doi.org/10.1080/0267257X.2020.1761864.

Denegri-Knott, J. and Molesworth, M. (2010). Concepts and practices of digital virtual consumption. *Consumption, Markets and Culture*, 13(2), 109–132. https://doi.org/10.1080/10253860903562130.

De Veirman, M., Cauberghe, V., and Hudders, L. (2017). Marketing through Instagram influencers: The impact of number of followers and product divergence on brand attitude. *International Journal of Advertising*, 36(5), 798–828. https://doi.org/10.1080/02650487.2017.1348035.

Developer Mozilla (2023). Introduction to the DOM. Developer.mozilla.org. https://developer.mozilla.org/en-US/docs/Web/API/Document_Object_Model/Introduction.

Di Domenico, G., Sit, J., Ishizaka, A., and Nunan, D. (2021). Fake news, social media and marketing: A systematic review. *Journal of Business Research*, 124, 329–341. https://doi.org/10.1016/j.jbusres.2020.11.037.

Di Domenico, G. and Visentin, M. (2020). Fake news or true lies? Reflections about problematic contents in marketing. *International Journal of Market Research*, 62(4), 409–417. https://doi.org/10.1177/147078532093471.

Dolbec, P. Y. and Fischer, E. (2015). Refashioning a field? Connected consumers and institutional dynamics in markets. *Journal of Consumer Research*, 41(6), 1447–1468. https://doi.org/10.1086/680671.

Doughty, M., Rowland, D., and Lawson, S. (2011). Co-viewing live TV with digital backchannel streams. In *Proceedings of the 9th European Conference on Interactive TV and Video* (pp. 141–144). https://doi.org/10.1145/2000119.2000147.

Duffy, B. E. (2017). (*Not*) *getting paid to do what you love: Gender, social media, and aspirational work*. Yale University Press.

Duffy, B. E. and Hund, E. (2019). Gendered visibility on social media: Navigating Instagram's authenticity bind. *International Journal of Communication*, 13, 4983–5002. https://ijoc.org/index.php/ijoc/article/view/11729.

Duffy, B. E., Poell, T., and Nieborg, D. B. (2019). Platform practices in the cultural industries: Creativity, labor, and citizenship. *Social Media+ Society*, 5(4). https://doi.org/10.1177/2056305119879672.

Duguay, S. (2019). Running the numbers: Modes of microcelebrity labor in queer women's self-representation on Instagram and Vine. *Social Media+ Society, 5*(4). https://doi.org/10.1177/2056305119894002.

Eckhardt, G. M. and Bardhi, F. (2020). New dynamics of social status and distinction. *Marketing Theory, 20*(1), 85–102. https://doi.org/10.1177/1470593119856650.

Edelman, B. G. and Luca, M. (2014). Digital discrimination: The case of Airbnb. com. *Harvard Business School NOM Unit Working Paper*, Paper No. 14-054, SSRN. http://dx.doi.org/10.2139/ssrn.2377353.

Elder, B. (2022, July 7). Rule books alone cannot govern the rise of the robots. *Financial Times*. https://www.ft.com/content/973efb17-6b8b-420e-a89d-dbddee06adf4.

Eriksson, M., Fleischer, R., Johansson, A., Snickars, P., and Vonderau, P. (2019). *Spotify teardown: Inside the black box of streaming music*. MIT Press.

Etter, M., Ravasi, D., and Colleoni, E. (2019). Social media and the formation of organizational reputation. *Academy of Management Review, 44*(1), 28–52. https://doi.org/10.5465/amr.2014.0280.

Faddoul, M., Chaslot, G., and Farid, H. (2020). A longitudinal analysis of YouTube's promotion of conspiracy videos. *ArXiv*. http://arxiv.org/abs/2003.03318.

Fan, C. (2022). *Understanding and citing CrowdTangle data*. https://help.crowdtangle. com/en/articles/4558716-understanding-and-citing-crowdtangle-data.

Farmaki, A. and Kladou, S. (2020). Why do Airbnb hosts discriminate? Examining the sources and manifestations of discrimination in host practice. *Journal of Hospitality and Tourism Management, 42*, 181–189. https://doi.org/10.1016/j. jhtm.2020.01.005.

Fernández-Ardèvol, M., Belotti, F., Ieracitano, F., Mulargia, S., Rosales, A., and Comunello, F. (2020). "I do it my way": Idioms of practice and digital media ideologies of adolescents and older adults. *New Media and Society, 24*(1), 31–49. https://doi.org/10.1177/1461444820959298.

Ferrara, E. (2020). Bots, elections, and social media: A brief overview. In K. Shu, S. Wang, D. Lee, and H. Liu (Eds.), *Disinformation, misinformation, and fake news in social media: Emerging research challenges and opportunities* (pp. 95–114). Springer.

Fiesler, C., Beard, N., and Keegan, B. C. (2020). No robots, spiders, or scrapers: Legal and ethical regulation of data collection methods in social media terms of service. In *Proceedings of the international AAAI conference on web and social media* (Vol. 14, pp. 187–196). https://doi.org/10.1609/icwsm.v14i1.7290.

Figueiredo, B. and Scaraboto, D. (2016). The systemic creation of value through circulation in collaborative consumer networks. *Journal of Consumer Research, 43*(4), 509–533. https://doi.org/10.1093/jcr/ucw038.

Fong, A. (2010). The influence of online reviews: Case study of TripAdvisor and the effect of fake reviews. In *Digital Research and Publishing* (pp. 106–113). The University of Sydney.

Freelon, D. (2018). Computational research in the post-API age. *Political Communica-tion*, *35*(4), 665–668. https://doi.org/10.1080/10584609.2018.1477506.

Fredborg, B., Clark, J., and Smith, S. D. (2017). An examination of personality traits associated with autonomous sensory meridian response (ASMR). *Frontiers in Psychology*, *8*(247). https://doi.org/10.3389/fpsyg.2017.00247.

Füller, J., Jawecki, G. and Mühlbacher, H. (2007). Innovation creation by online basketball communities. *Journal of Business Research*, *60*(1), 60–71. https://doi.org/10.1016/j.jbusres.2006.09.019.

Galov, N. (2023, May 20). Where is TripAdvisor going? 39+ signpost statistics. https://review42.com/resources/tripadvisor-statistics/.

Gandini, A. (2020). *Zeitgeist nostalgia: On populism, work and the "good life"*. Zero Books.

Gandini, A. (2021). P2P (Peer-to-peer). *The Blackwell encyclopedia of sociology*. https://doi.org/10.1002/9781405165518.wbeosp204.pub2.

Geboers, M., Stolero, N., Scuttari, A., Van Vliet, L., and Ridley, A. (2020). Why buttons matter: Repurposing Facebook's reactions for analysis of the social visual. *International Journal of Communication*, *14*, 1564–1585. 1932–8036/20200005.

Geboers et al. (2022). How (long) do we #standwithukraine? Summer School report. https://wiki.digitalmethods.net/Dmi/Summerschool2022Howlongdowestand-withukraine.

Geertz, C. (1973). *The interpretation of cultures*. Basic books.

Gelfert, A. (2018). Fake news: A definition. *Informal Logic*, *38*(1), 84–117. 10.22329/il.v38i1.5068.

Georgakopoulou, A. (2017). Small stories research: A narrative paradigm for the analysis of social media. In L. Sloan and A. Quan-Haase (Eds.), *The SAGE handbook of social media research methods* (pp. 266–281). Sage.

Georgakopoulou, A. (2021). Small stories as curated formats on social media: The intersection of affordances, values and practices. *System*, *102*. https://doi.org/10.1016/j.system.2021.102620.

Gerlitz, C. and Helmond, A. (2013). The like economy: Social buttons and the data-intensive web. *New Media and Society*, *15*(8), 1348–1365. https://doi.org/10.1177/1461444812472322.

Gerlitz, C., Helmond, A., van der Vlist, F. N., and Weltevrede, E. (2019). Regram-ming the platform: Infrastructural relations between apps and social media. *Computational Culture: A Journal of Software Studies*, *7*. ISSN: 2047-2390.

Gerlitz, C. and Rieder, B. (2013). Mining one percent of Twitter: Collections, baselines, sampling. *M/C Journal*, *16*(2). https://doi.org/10.5204/mcj.620.

Gerlitz, C. and Rieder, B. (2018). AI Tweets are not created equal: Investigating Twitter's client ecosystem. *International Journal of Communication*, *12*, 528–547. 1932–8036/20180005.

Gibbs, M., Meese, J., Arnold, M., Nansen, B., and Carter, M. (2015). #Funeral and Instagram: Death, social media, and platform vernacular. *Information, Communication and Society*, *18*(3), 255–268. https://doi.org/10.1080/1369118X.2014.987152.

Gielens, K. and Steenkamp, J. B. E. (2019). Branding in the era of digital (dis) intermediation. *International Journal of Research in Marketing*, *36*(3), 367–384. https://doi.org/10.1016/j.ijresmar.2019.01.005.

Giglietto, F., Righetti, N., Rossi, L., and Marino, G. (2020). It takes a village to manipulate the media: Coordinated link sharing behavior during 2018 and 2019 Italian elections. *Information, Communication and Society*, *23*(6), 867–891. https://doi.org/10.1080/1369118X.2020.1739732.

Gillespie, T. (2010). The politics of "platforms". *New Media and Society*, *12*(3), 347–364. https://doi.org/10.1177/1461444809342273.

Giorgi, G. (2022). *Memeing generations: Studying meme cultures and generational identities*. PhD dissertation, NASP, University of Milan-Turin.

Golovchenko, Y., Hartmann, M., and Adler-Nissen, R. (2018). State, media and civil society in the information warfare over Ukraine: Citizen curators of digital disinformation. *International Affairs*, *94*(5), 975–994. https://doi.org/10.1093/ia/iiy148.

Goulding, C. (2002). An exploratory study of age-related vicarious nostalgia and aesthetic consumption. In S. M. Broniarczyk and K. Nakamoto (Eds.), *ACR North American advances* volume *29* (pp. 542–546). Association for Consumer Research.

Graham, T., Bruns, A., Zhu, G., and Campbell, R. (2020). *Like a virus: The coordinated spread of coronavirus disinformation*. Centre for Responsible Technology.

Gray, J., Bounegru, L., and Venturini, T. (2020). "Fake news" as infrastructural uncanny. *New Media and Society*, *22*(2), 317–341. https://doi.org/10.1177/1461444819856912.

Greenebaum, J. (2012). Veganism, identity and the quest for authenticity. *Food, Culture and Society*, *15*(1), 129–144. https://doi.org/10.2752/175174412X13190510222101.

Grosglik, R. and Lerner, J. (2020). Gastro-emotivism: How MasterChef Israel produces therapeutic collective belongings. *European Journal of Cultural Studies*, *24*(5), 1053–1070. https://doi.org/10.1177/1367549420902801.

Gruzd, A. and Roy, J. (2014). Investigating political polarization on Twitter: A Canadian perspective. *Policy and Internet*, *6*(1), 28–45. https://doi.org/10.1002/1944-2866.POI354.

Guarino, S., Pierri, F., Di Giovanni, M., and Celestini, A. (2021). Information disorders during the COVID-19 infodemic: The case of Italian Facebook. *Online Social Networks and Media*, *22*. https://doi.org/10.1016/j.osnem.2021.100124.

Gurrieri, L. and Drenten, J. (2019), Visual storytelling and vulnerable health care consumers: Normalising practices and social support through Instagram. *Journal of Services Marketing*. *33*(6), 702–720. https://doi.org/10.1108/JSM-09-2018-0262.

Hamilton, J. (2021, October 6). Spotify has made all music into background music. *The Atlantic*. https://www.theatlantic.com/magazine/archive/2021/11/kelefa-sanneh-major-labels-music/620178/.

Hartmann, B. J. and Brunk, K. H. (2019). Nostalgia marketing and (re-) enchantment. *International Journal of Research in Marketing*, *36*(4), 669–686. https://doi.org/10.1016/j.ijresmar.2019.05.002.

Hall, S. (1980). Encoding/decoding. In S. Hall, D. Hobson, A. Lowe, and P. Willis (Eds). *Culture, Media, Language* (pp. 128–38). Hutchinson.

Hagberg, J. and Kjellberg, H. (2020). Digitalized markets. *Consumption Markets and Culture*, *23*(2), 97–109. https://doi.org/10.1080/10253866.2020.1694209.

Hallinan, B., Kim, B., Scharlach, R., Trillò, T., Mizoroki, S., and Shifman, L. (2023). Mapping the transnational imaginary of social media genres. *New Media and Society*, *25*(3), 559–583. https://doi.org/10.1177/14614448211012372.

Heilweil, R. (2022, May 11). Twitter now labels misleading coronavirus tweets with misleading label. *Vox*. https://www.vox.com/recode/2020/5/11/21254889/twitter-coronavirus-covid-misinformation-warnings-labels.

Helmond, A. (2015). The platformisation of the web: Making web data platform ready. *Social Media+ Society*, *1*(2), https://doi.org/10.1177/2056305115603080.

Herkes, E. and Redden, G. (2017). Misterchef? Cooks, chefs and gender in MasterChef Australia. *Open Cultural Studies*, *1*(1), 125–139. https://doi.org/10.1515/culture-2017-0012.

Hesmondhalgh, D. and Baker, S. (2008). Creative work and emotional labour in the television industry. *Theory, Culture and Society*, *25*(7/8), 97–118. https://doi.org/10.1177/0263276408097798.

Hesmondhalgh, D. and Meier, L. M. (2018). What the digitalisation of music tells us about capitalism, culture and the power of the information technology sector. *Information, Communication and Society*, *21*(11), 1555–1570. https://doi.org/10.1080/1369118X.2017.1340498.

Higgins, M., Montgomery, M., Smith, A., and Tolson, A. (2012). Belligerent broadcasting and makeover television: Professional incivility in Ramsay's Kitchen Nightmares. *International Journal of Cultural Studies*, *15*(5), 501–518. https://doi.org/10.1177/1367877911422864.

Hochschild, A. R. (1983). *The managed heart. Commercialization of human feeling*. University of California Press.

Hoffman, D. L. and Novak, T. P. (2018). Consumer and object experience in the internet of things: An assemblage theory approach. *Journal of Consumer Research*, *44*(6), 1178–1204. https://doi.org/10.1093/jcr/ucx105.

Hosseinmardi, H., Ghasemian, A., Clauset, A., Mobius, M., Rothschild, D. M., and Watts, D. J. (2021). Examining the consumption of radical content on YouTube. *Proceedings of the National Academy of Sciences*, *118*(32), e2101967118. https://doi.org/10.1073/pnas.2101967118.

Holbrook, M. B. (1993). Nostalgia and consumption preferences: Some emerging patterns of consumer tastes. *Journal of Consumer research*, *20*(2), 245–256. https://doi.org/10.1086/209346.

Holbrook, M. B. and Schindler, R. M. (1991). Echoes of the dear departed past: Some work in progress on nostalgia. In R. H. Holman and M. R. Solomon (Eds.), *ACR North American advances in consumer research, volume 18* (pp. 330–333). Association for Consumer Research.

Holbrook, M. B. and Schindler, R. M. (2003). Nostalgic bonding: Exploring the role of nostalgia in the consumption experience. *Journal of Consumer Behaviour: An International Research Review*, *3*(2), 107–127. https://doi.org/10.1002/cb.127.

Humphreys, A. and Wang, R. J. H. (2018). Automated text analysis for consumer research. *Journal of Consumer Research*, *44*(6), 1274–1306. https://doi.org/10.1093/jcr/ucx104.

Hutchinson, J. (2016). An introduction to digital media research methods: how to research and the implications of new media data. *Communication Research and Practice*, *2*(1), 1–6. https://doi.org/10.1080/22041451.2016.1155307.

Integrity Transparency (2022). *How do you calculate overperforming scores?* https://help.crowdtangle.com/en/articles/2013937-how-do-you-calculate-overperforming-scores.

Jacomy, M., Venturini, T., Heymann, S., and Bastian, M. (2014). ForceAtlas2, a continuous graph layout algorithm for handy network visualization designed for the Gephi software. *PloS one*, *9*(6), e98679. https://doi.org/10.1371/journal.pone.0098679.

Janda, S. and Trocchia, P. J. (2001). Vegetarianism: Toward a greater understanding. *Psychology and Marketing*, *18*(12), 1205–1240. https://doi.org/10.1002/mar.1050.

Jasanoff, S. and Kim, S. H. (2013). Sociotechnical imaginaries and national energy policies. *Science as Culture*, *22*(2), 189–196. https://doi.org/10.1080/09505431.2013.786990.

Jenkins, H. (2006). *Convergence culture: Where old and new media collide*. New York University Press.

Khamis, S., Ang, L. and Welling, R. (2017). Self-branding, "micro-celebrity" and the rise of social media influencers. *Celebrity Studies*, *8*(2), 191–208. https://doi.org/10.1080/19392397.2016.1218292.

Kim, D.Y. and Kim, H.-Y. (2022). Social media influencers as human brands: An interactive marketing perspective. *Journal of Research in Interactive Marketing*, *17*(1), 94–109. https://doi.org/10.1108/JRIM-08-2021-0200.

Know Your Meme (2020). https://knowyourmeme.com/memes/kismet-shoe-transitions.

Kozinets, R. V., Ferreira, D. A., and Chimenti, P. (2021). How do platforms empower consumers? Insights from the affordances and constraints of Reclame Aqui. *Journal of Consumer Research*, *48*(3), 428–455. https://doi.org/10.1093/jcr/ucab014.

Kozinets, R., Patterson, A. and Ashman, R. (2017). Networks of desire: How technology increases our passion to consume. *Journal of Consumer Research*, *43*(5), 659–682. https://doi.org/10.1093/jcr/ucw061.

Krause, M. (2019). What is Zeitgeist? Examining period-specific cultural patterns. *Poetics*, *76*, https://doi.org/10.1016/j.poetic.2019.02.003.

Krippendorff, K. (2012). *Content analysis: An introduction to its methodology.* Sage.

Ladeira, W. J., Dalmoro, M., Santini, F. D. O., and Jardim, W. C. (2022). Visual cognition of fake news: The effects of consumer brand engagement. *Journal of Marketing Communications*, *28*(6), 681–701. https://doi.org/10.1080/13527266.2021.1934083.

Lala, K. (2022, August 11). The hidden economy of spam. https://integrityinstitute. org/our-ideas/hear-from-our-fellows/the-hidden-economy-of-spam.

Landers, R. N., Brusso, R. C., Cavanaugh, K. J., and Collmus, A. B. (2016). A primer on theory-driven web scraping: Automatic extraction of big data from the Internet for use in psychological research. *Psychological methods*, *21*(4), 475–492. https:// doi.org/10.1037/met0000081.

Langley, P. and Leyshon, A. (2017). Platform capitalism: The intermediation and capitalization of digital economic circulation. *Finance and society*, *3*(1), 11–31. https://doi.org/10.2218/finsoc.v3i1.1936.

Lasaleta, J. D., Werle, C. O., and Yamim, A. P. (2021). Nostalgia makes people eat healthier. *Appetite*, *162*, ttps://doi.org/10.1016/j.appet.2021.105187.

Latour, B. (2005). *Reassembling the social: An introduction to actor-network theory.* Oxford University Press.

Latour, B., Jensen, P., Venturini, T., Grauwin, S., and Boullier, D. (2012). The whole is always smaller than its parts: A digital test of Gabriel Tardes' monads. *The British journal of sociology*, *63*(4), 590–615. https://doi.org/10.1111/j.1468-4446.2012.01428.x.

Lawler, R. (2022, June 23). Meta reportedly plans to shut down CrowdTangle. *The Verge*. https://www.theverge.com/2022/6/23/23180357/meta-crowdtangle-shut-down-facebook-misinformation-viral-news-tracker.

Lawrenson, E. (2023, June 13). What is mukbang? And why is it so popular? https:// www.qustodio.com/en/blog/what-is-mukbang/.

Lazer, D., Kennedy, R., King, G., and Vespignani, A. (2014). Google flu trends still appears sick: An evaluation of the 2013–2014 flu season. *SSRN*. http://dx.doi. org/10.2139/ssrn.2408560.

Lazer, D. , Baum, M. A., Benkler, Y., Berinsky, A. J., Greenhill, K. M., Menczer, F., and Zittrain, J. L. (2018). The science of fake news. *Science*, *359*(6380), 1094–1096. DOI: 10.1126/science.aao2998.

Leaver, T., Highfield, T. and Abidin, C. (2020). *Instagram: Visual social media cultures.* Polity Press.

Leung, E., Paolacci, G., and Puntoni, S. (2018). Man versus machine: Resisting automation in identity-based consumer behavior. *Journal of Marketing Research*, *55*(6), 818–831. https://doi.org/10.1177/0022243718818423.

Levine, A.S. (2023, May 21). India banned TikTok in 2020. TikTok still has access to years of Indians' data. *Forbes*. https://www.forbes.com/sites/alexandralevine/2023/03/21/tiktok-india-ban-bytedance-data-access/?sh=7a8866a12eca.

Lewis, B. (2018). Alternative influence: Broadcasting the reactionary right on YouTube. Data and Society Research Institute. https://datasociety.net/wp-content/uploads/2018/09/DS_Alternative_Influence.pdf.

Lewis, S. C., Zamith, R., and Hermida, A. (2013). Content analysis in an era of big data: A hybrid approach to computational and manual methods. *Journal of broadcasting and electronic media*, 57(1), 34–52. https://doi.org/10.1080/08838151.2012.761702.

Li, B., Forgues, B., and Jourdan, J. (2022). The consequences of status loss on the evaluation of market actors. *Academy of Management Proceedings*, 2022(1). https://doi.org/10.5465/AMBPP.2022.15910abstract.

Lury, C. (1996). *Consumer culture*. Rutgers University Press.

Mancosu, M. and Vegetti, F. (2020). What you can scrape and what is right to scrape: A proposal for a tool to collect public Facebook data. *Social Media+ Society*, 6(3). https://doi.org/10.1177/20563051209407.

Maneri, M., Pogliano, A., Anselmi, G., and Piccoli, F. (2022). Migration narratives in traditional and social media: The case of Italy. BRIDGES Working Papers, October 2022.

Mangold, W. G. and Faulds, D. J. (2009). Social media: The new hybrid element of the promotion mix. *Business horizons*, 52(4), 357–365. https://doi.org/10.1016/j.bushor.2009.03.002.

Manovich, L. (2017). Instagram and contemporary image. Manovich.net. http://manovich.net/index.php/projects/instagram-and-contemporary-image.

Mardon, R., Cocker, H., and Daunt, K. (2023). When parasocial relationships turn sour: Social media influencers, eroded and exploitative intimacies, and anti-fan communities. *Journal of Marketing Management*, 1–31. https://doi.org/10.1080/0267257X.2022.2149609.

Mardon, R., Denegri-Knott, J., and Molesworth, M. (2022). "Kind of mine, kind of not": Digital possessions and affordance misalignment. *Journal of Consumer Research*, 50(2), 255–281. https://doi.org/10.1093/jcr/ucac057.

Maheshwari, S. (2018, November 11) Are you ready for the nanoinfluencers? *The New York Times*. https://www.nytimes.com/2018/11/11/business/media/nanoinfluencers-instagram-influencers.html?smtyp=curandsmid=tw-nytimes.

Markham, A. (2012). Fabrication as Ethical Practice. *Information, Communication and Society*, 15(3), 334–353. https://doi.org/10.1080/1369118X.2011.641993.

Markham, A. and Buchanan, E. (2012). Ethical decision-making and internet research: Recommendations from the AoIR Ethics Working Committee (Version 2.0). *Association of Internet Researchers*, 1–19. https://aoir.org/reports/ethics2.pdf.

Marres, N. (2017). *Digital sociology: The reinvention of social research*. John Wiley and Sons.

Marres, N. and Gerlitz, C. (2016). Interface methods: Renegotiating relations between digital social research, STS and sociology. *The Sociological Review, 64*(1), 21–46. https://doi.org/10.1111/1467-954X.12314.

Marres, N. and Weltevrede, E. (2013). Scraping the social? Issues in real-time social research. *Journal of Cultural Economy, 6*(3), 313–335. https://doi.org/10.1080/17 530350.2013.772070.

Marwick, A. E. (2015). Instafame: Luxury selfies in the attention economy. *Public culture, 27*(1/75), 137–160. https://doi.org/10.1215/08992363-2798379.

Matamoros-Fernandez, A., Gray, J. E., Bartolo, L., Burgess, J., and Suzor, N. (2021). What's "up next"? Investigating algorithmic recommendations on YouTube across issues and over time. *Media and Communication, 9*(4), 234–249. https://doi.org/10.17645/mac.v9i4.4184.

Mawer, R. (2023, November 7). The ketogenic diet: A detailed beginner's guide to keto. https://www.healthline.com/nutrition/ketogenic-diet-101#:~:text=%3E-,Keto%20 basics,a%20metabolic%20state%20called%20ketosis.

McLachlan, S. and Cooper, P. (2023, April 18). How the YouTube algorithm works in 2023: The complete guide. Hootsuite. https://blog.hootsuite.com/ how-the-youtube-algorithm-works/.

McQuarrie, E. F., Miller, J. and Phillips, B. J. (2013). The megaphone effect: Taste and audience in fashion blogging. *Journal of Consumer Research, 40*(1), 136–158. https://doi.org/10.1086/669042.

Moe, H. (2019). Comparing platform "ranking cultures" across languages: The case of Islam on YouTube in Scandinavia. *Social Media+ Society, 5*(1), https://journals. sagepub.com/doi/full/10.1177/2056305118817038.

Moufahim, M., Wells, V., and Canniford, R. (2018). The consumption, politics and transformation of community. *Journal of Marketing Management, 34*(7/8), 557–568. https://doi.org/10.1080/0267257X.2018.1479506.

Mehta, I and Singh, M. (2023, February 2). Twitter to end free access to its API in Elon Musk's latest monetization push. TechCrunch+. https://techcrunch. com/2023/02/01/twitter-to-end-free-access-to-its-api/?guce_referrer=aHR0cH M6Ly93d3cuZ29vZ2xlLmNvbS8andguce_referrer_sig=AQAAALa-1teLuMQH- mTRzKDMQSh67Oxqjx4GMhdj7lQMQbzcn-nQBoTZn-VMj7m5eeGvwz1V1k- osOKYGl3nHn_t18WaEbakGDMDwodwrKcpN3OpocXdVf-xhJxuE1SyQnXe- CouLDoUWA7zpd1M5R3VYoLM-5r1Lg23A4D4qblugWgcVC8andguccounter=2.

Merton, R. K. (1968). The Matthew effect in science: The reward and communica- tion systems of science are considered. *Science, 159*(3810), 56–63. DOI: 10.1126/ science.159.3810.56.

Mettier, K. (2016, November 15). We live in crazy times: Neo-Nazis have declared New Balance the "Official Shoes of White People." *Washington Post* https://www. washingtonpost.com/news/morning-mix/wp/2016/11/15/the-crazy-reason-neo- nazis-have-declared-new-balance-the-official-shoes-of-white-people/.

Michael, J. (2015). It's really not hip to be a hipster: Negotiating trends and authenticity in the cultural field. *Journal of Consumer Culture*, 15(2), 163–182. https://doi.org/10.1177/1469540513493206.

Miles, C. (2022a). What data is CrowdTangle tracking? https://help.crowdtangle.com/en/articles/1140930-what-data-is-crowdtangle-tracking.

Miles. C. (2022b). Using CrowdTangle's historical data. https://help.crowdtangle.com/en/articles/1194215-using-crowdtangle-s-historical-data.

Miles, C. (2022c). FAQ: Followers. https://help.crowdtangle.com/en/articles/4797890-faq-followers.

Mills, A.J., Pitt, C., and Ferguson, S. L. (2019). The relationship between fake news and advertising: Brand management in the era of programmatic advertising and prolific falsehood. *Journal of Advertising Research*, 59(1), 3–8. https://doi.org/10.2501/JAR-2019-007.

Mills, A.J. and Robson, K. (2020). Brand management in the era of fake news: Narrative response as a strategy to insulate brand value. *Journal of Product and Brand Management*, 29(2), 159–167. https://doi.org/10.1108/JPBM-12-2018-2150.

Mittiga, C. (2022, November 16). Copyright protection: A content creator's guide to YouTube. https://legalvision.com.au/content-creators-guide-youtube/.

Mukhopadhyay, S. (2021, August 31). The girlboss is dead. Long live the girlboss. *The Cut*. https://www.thecut.com/2021/08/demise-of-the-girlboss.html.

Mulligan, M. (2022, January 18). Music subscriber market shares Q2. Midia Research. https://www.midiaresearch.com/blog/music-subscriber-market-shares-q2-2021.

Muñiz, A. M., and O'Guinn, T. C. (2001). Brand community. *Journal of Consumer Research*, 27(4), 412–432. https://doi.org/10.1086/319618.

Muñiz, A. M. and Schau, H. J. (2005). Religiosity in the abandoned Apple Newton brand community. *Journal of Consumer Research*, 31(4), 737–747. https://doi.org/10.1086/426607.

Munger, K. and Phillips, J. (2022). Right-wing YouTube: A supply and demand perspective. *The International Journal of Press/Politics*, 27(1), 186–219. https://doi.org/10.1177/1940161220964767.

Munk, A. K., Olesen, A. G., and Jacomy, M. (2022). The thick machine: Anthropological AI between explanation and explication. *Big Data and Society*, 9(1). https://doi.org/10.1177/20539517211069891.

Negra, D., Pike, K., and Radley, E. (2013). Gender, nation, and reality TV. *Television and New Media*, 14(3), 187–193. https://doi.org/10.1177/1527476412458163.

Negus, K. and Pickering, M. (2004). *Creativity, communication and cultural value*. Sage.

Nelson, L. K. (2020). Computational grounded theory: A methodological framework. *Sociological Methods and Research*, 49(1), 3–42. https://doi.org/10.1177/0049124117729703.

Newsroom Spotify (2021, February 25). How to sort your favorite songs with Spotify's new genre and mood filters. https://newsroom.spotify.com/2021-02-25/how-to-sort-your-favorite-songs-with-spotifys-new-genre-and-mood-filters/.

Nicoll, B. and Nansen, B. (2018). Mimetic production in YouTube toy unboxing videos. *Social Media + Society*, *4*(3). https://doi.org/10.1177/2056305118790761.

Nieborg, D. B., Duffy, B. E., and Poell, T. (2020). Studying platforms and cultural production: Methods, institutions, and practices. *Social Media+ Society*, *6*(3), https://doi.org/10.1177/2056305120943273.

Nieborg, D.B. and Poell, T. (2018). The platformization of cultural production: Theorizing the contingent cultural commodity. *New Media and Society*, *20*, 4275–4292. https://doi.org/10.1177/1461444818769694.

Niedeer, S. and Colombo, G. (2019). Visual methodologies for networked images: Designing visualizations for collaborative research, cross-platform analysis, and public participation. *Diseña*, *14*, 40–67. https://doi.org/10.7764/disena.14.40-67.

Niemeyer, K. (2014). *Media and nostalgia: Yearning for the past, present and future*. Springer.

Nyilasy, G. (2019). Fake news: When the dark side of persuasion takes over. *International Journal of Advertising*, *38*(2), 336–342. https://doi.org/10.1080/02650487.2019.1586210.

Obadă, R. (2019). Sharing fake news about brands on social media: A new conceptual model based on flow theory. *Argumentum: Journal of the Seminar of Discursive Logic, Argumentation Theory and Rhetoric*, *17*(2), 144–166. https://philpapers.org/rec/OBASFN.

O'Callaghan, D., Greene, D., Conway, M., Carthy, J., and Cunningham, P. (2015). Down the (white) rabbit hole: The extreme right and online recommender systems. *Social Science Computer Review*, *33*(4), 459–478. https://doi.org/10.1177/0894439314555329.

O'Meara, V. (2019). Weapons of the chic: Instagram influencer engagement pods as practices of resistance to Instagram platform labor. *Social Media+ Society*, *5*(4), https://doi.org/10.1177/2056305119879671.

Omena, J. J., Pilipets, E., Gobbo, B., and Chao, J. (2021). The potentials of Google Vision API-based networks to study natively digital images. *Diseña*, *19*, 1–25. 10.7764/disena.19.Article.1.

Papacharissi, Z. (2014). *Affective Publics: Sentiment, Technology, Politics*. Oxford University Press.

Parmentier, M. A., and Fischer, E. (2015). Things fall apart: The dynamics of brand audience dissipation. *Journal of Consumer Research*, *41*(5), 1228–1251. https://doi.org/10.1177/2056305119879671.

Pasquale, F. (2015). *The black box society: The secret algorithms that control money and information*. Harvard University Press.

Peeters, S. (2022). Zeeschuimer [browser extension]. https://doi.org/10.5281/zenodo.6826878.

Peeters, S. and Hagen, S. (2022). The 4CAT capture and analysis toolkit: A modular tool for transparent and traceable social media research. *Computational Communication Research*, *4*(2). https://computationalcommunication.org/ccr/article/view/120.

Perren, R. and Kozinets, R. V. (2018). Lateral exchange markets: How social platforms operate in a networked economy. *Journal of Marketing*, *82*(1), 20–36. https://doi.org/10.1509/jm.14.0250.

Perriam, J., Birkbak, A., and Freeman, A. (2020). Digital methods in a post-API environment. *International Journal of Social Research Methodology*, *23*(3), 277–290.

Peters, J. (2023, June 6). It's not just Apollo: Other Reddit apps are shutting down, too. *The Verge*. https://www.theverge.com/2023/6/8/23754616/reddit-third-party-apps-api-shutdown-rif-reddplanet-sync.

Peterson, R. A. (1992). Understanding audience segmentation: From elite and mass to omnivore and univore. *Poetics*, *21*(4), 243–258. https://doi.org/10.1016/0304-422X(92)90008-Q.

Pfeffer, J., Zorbach, T., and Carley, K. M. (2014). Understanding online firestorms: Negative word-of-mouth dynamics in social media networks. *Journal of Marketing Communications*, *20*(1/2), 117–128. https://doi.org/10.1080/13527266.2013.797778.

Phillipov, M. (2013). Mastering obesity: MasterChef Australia and the resistance to public health nutrition. *Media, Culture and Society*, *35*(4), 506–515. https://doi.org/10.1177/0163443712474615.

Picascia, S., Romano, A., and Teobaldi, M. (2017). The airification of cities: Making sense of the impact of peer-to-peer short-term letting on urban functions and economy. In: Annual Congress of the Association of European Schools of Planning, Lisbon, Portugal, 11–14 July 2017. 10.31235/osf.io/vs8w3.

Pilipets, E., (2023). Hashtagging, duetting, sound-linking: TikTok gestures and methods of (in)distinction. *The Journal of Media Art Study and Theory*, *4*(1), 109–135. https://doi.org/10.59547/26911566.4.1.07.

Pine, J. and Gilmore, J.H. (2011). *The experience economy: Work is theater and every business a stage*. Harvard Business Review Press.

Pink, S., Horst, H., Postill, J., Hjorth, L., Lewis, T., and Tacchi, J. (2015). *Digital ethnography: Principles and practice*. Sage.

Poell, T., Duffy B.E., Nieborg, D., Sun, P., Arriagada, A., Mutsvairo, B., Tse and T., de Kloet, J. (forthcoming). Global perspectives on platforms and cultural production. *International Journal of Cultural Studies*.

Poell, T., Nieborg, D.B., and Duffy, B.E. (2021). *Platforms and cultural production*. Polity Press.

Poell, T., Nieborg, D., and Van Dijck, J. (2019). Platformisation. *Internet Policy Review*, *8*(4), 1–13. doi:10.14763/2019.4.1425.

Porter, J. (2023, March 30). Twitter announces new API pricing, posing a challenge for small developers. *The Verge*. https://www.theverge.com/2023/3/30/23662832/twitter-api-tiers-free-bot-novelty-accounts-basic-enterprice-monthly-price.

Prey, R. (2020). Locating power in platformization: Music streaming playlists and curatorial power. *Social Media+ Society*, 6(2). https://doi.org/10.1177/2056305120933291.

Prey, R., Esteve Del Valle, M., and Zwerwer, L. (2022). Platform pop: Disentangling Spotify's intermediary role in the music industry. *Information, Communication and Society*, 25(1), 74–92. https://doi.org/10.1080/1369118X.2020.1761859.

Punziano, G., Trezza, D., and Acampa, S. (2022). Russian-Ukraine war and institutional use of memetic communication: Methodological opportunities and challenges. *Mediascapes Journal*, 20(2), 70–90. https://rosa.uniroma1.it/rosa03/mediascapes/article/view/18036.

Qaiser, S. and Ali, R. (2018). Text mining: Use of TF-IDF to examine the relevance of words to documents. *International Journal of Computer Applications*, 181(1), 25–29. 10.5120/ijca2018917395.

Querubín, N. S. and Niederer, S. (2022). Climate futures: Machine learning from cli-fi. *Convergence*, https://doi.org/10.1177/13548565221135715.

Rainie, H. and Wellman, B. (2012). *Networked: The new social operating system*. MIT Press.

Rama, I., Bainotti, L., Gandini, A., Giorgi, G., Semenzin, S., Agosti, C., Corona, G., and Romano, S. (2022). The platformization of gender and sexual identities: an algorithmic analysis of Pornhub. *Porn Studies*, 10(2), 154–173. https://doi.org/10.1080/23268743.2022.2066566.

Rauchfleisch, A. and Kaiser, J. (2020). The false positive problem of automatic bot detection in social science research. *PloS one*, 15(10), e0241045. https://doi.org/10.1371/journal.pone.0241045.

Reynolds, S. (2011). *Retromania: Pop culture's addiction to its own past*. Macmillan.

Ribeiro, M. H., Ottoni, R., West, R., Almeida, V. A. F, and Meira, W. (2020). Auditing radicalization pathways on YouTube. In M. H. Ribeiro, R. Ottoni, R. West, and V. A. F. Almeida, W. Meira (Eds.), *Proceedings of the 2020 conference on fairness, accountability, and transparency* (pp. 131–141). ACM.

Rieder, B. (2015, May 4). Introducing YouTube data tools: The politics of systems. http://thepoliticsofsystems.net/?s=youtube.

Rieder, B. (2023, May 3). YouTube data tools: Overview (May 2023). https://www.youtube.com/watch?v=TmF4mWZYnbkandt=39s.

Rieder, B., Borra, E., Coromina, Ò., and Matamoros-Fernández, A. (2023). Making a living in the creator economy: A large-scale study of linking on YouTube. *Social Media+ Society*, 9(2), https://doi.org/10.1177/20563051231180628.

Rieder, B., Coromina, O., and Matamoros-Fernandez, A. (2020). Mapping YouTube: A quantitative exploration of a platformed media system. *First Monday*, 25(8). 0.5210/fm.v25i8.10667.

Rieder, B., Gordon, G., and Sileno, G. (2022). Mapping value(s) in AI: Methodological directions for examining normativity in complex technical systems. *Sociologica*, *16*(3), 51–83. https://doi.org/10.6092/issn.1971-8853/15910.

Rieder, B., Matamoros-Fernández, A., and Coromina, O. (2018). From ranking algorithms to "ranking cultures": Investigating the modulation of visibility in YouTube search results. *Convergence*, *24*(1), 50–68. https://doi.org/10.1177/1354856517736982.

Rimoldi, L. (2015). How to show a national cuisine: Food and national identities in the *MasterChef* kitchen. *Academic Journal of Interdisciplinary Studies*, *4*(2), 257–262. https://dx.doi.org/10.5901/ajis.2015.v4n2p257.

Rocamora, A. (2016). Mediatization and digital media in the field of fashion. *Fashion Theory*, *21*(5), 505–522. https://doi.org/10.1080/1362704X.2016.1173349.

Rodriguez-Perez de Arenaza, D., Hierro, L. Á., and Patiño, D. (2022). Airbnb, sun-and-beach tourism and residential rental prices: The case of the coast of Andalusia (Spain). *Current Issues in Tourism*, *25*(20), 3261–3278. https://doi.org/10.1080/13683500.2019.1705768.

Rogers, R. (2009). *The end of the virtual: Digital methods*. Amsterdam University Press.

Rogers, R. (2010). Internet research: The question of method. A keynote address from the YouTube and the 2008 election cycle in the United States conference. *Journal of Information Technology and Politics*, *7*, 241–260. https://doi.org/10.1080/19331681003753438.

Rogers, R. (2013). *Digital methods*. MIT press.

Rogers, R. (2017). Foundations of digital methods: Query design. In M. T. Schäfer and K. van Es (Eds.), *The datafied society: Studying culture through data* (pp. 75–94). Amsterdam University Press.

Rogers, R. (2018). Otherwise engaged: Social media from vanity metrics to critical analytics. *International Journal of Communication*, *12*, 23. 1932–8036/20180005.

Rogers, R. (2019). *Doing digital methods*. Sage.

Rogers, R. (2020). Deplatforming: Following extreme Internet celebrities to Telegram and alternative social media. *European Journal of Communication*, *35*(3), 213–229. https://doi.org/10.1177/0267323120922066.

Rogers, R. and Giorgi, G. (2023). What is a meme, technically speaking?. *Information, Communication and Society*, 1–19, https://doi.org/10.1080/1369118X.2023.2174790.

Rogers, R., and Niederer, S. (2020). *The politics of social media manipulation*. Amsterdam University Press.

Rogers, R., Sánchez-Querubín, N., and Kil, A. (2015). *Issue mapping for an ageing Europe*. Amsterdam University Press.

Rokka, J. (2021). Consumer culture theory's future in marketing. *Journal of Marketing Theory and Practice*, *29*(1), 114–124. https://doi.org/10.1080/10696679.2020.1860685.

Rokka, J. and Canniford, R. (2016). Heterotopian selfies: How social media destabilizes brand assemblages. *European Journal of Marketing*, *50*(9/10), 1789–1813. https://doi.org/10.1108/EJM-08-2015-0517.

Romano, S., Polidoro, A., Corona, G, Kerby, N., Rama, I., and Giorgi, G. (3 July 2022). Non-logged-in children using YouTube. How does YouTube use data about non-logged-in under 18 users? What adverts, and potentially harmful content, are they exposed to?. Tracking Exposed Special Report. https://tracking.exposed/ pdf/youtube-non-logged-kids-03July2022.pdf.

Rose, G. (2016). *Visual methodologies: An introduction to researching with visual material*s. Sage.

Rose, R. L. and Wood, S. L. (2005). Paradox and the consumption of authenticity through reality television. *Journal of Consumer Research*, *32*(2), 284–296. https:// doi.org/10.1086/432238.

Ruckenstein, M. and Granroth, J. (2020). Algorithms, advertising and the intimacy of surveillance. *Journal of Cultural Economy*, *13*(1), 12–24. https://doi.org/10.108 0/17530350.2019.1574866.

Ruppert, E., Law, J., and Savage, M. (2013). Reassembling social science methods: The challenge of digital devices. *Theory, Culture and Society*, *30*(4), 22–46. https:// doi.org/10.1177/0263276413484941.

Salganik, M. J. (2019). *Bit by bit: Social research in the digital age*. Princeton University Press.

Salmons, J. (2016). *Doing qualitative research online*. Sage.

Savage, M. (2009). Contemporary sociology and the challenge of descriptive assemblage. *European Journal of Social Theory*, *12*(1), 155–174. https://doi. org/10.1177/1368431008099650.

Schau, H. J. (2000). Consumer imagination, identity and self-expression. In S. J. Hoch and R. J. Mayer (Eds.), *NA – Advances in Consumer Research*, *27* (pp. 50–56). Association for Consumer Research.

Schau, H. J. and Gilly, M. C. (2003). We are what we post? Self-presentation in personal web space. *Journal of Consumer Research*, *30*(3), 385–404. https://doi. org/10.1086/378616.

Schau, H. J., Muñiz, A. M., and Arnould, E. J. (2009). How brand community practices create value. *Journal of Marketing*, *73*(5), 30–51. https://doi.org/10.1509/ jmkg.73.5.30.

Schellewald, A. (2021). Communicative forms on TikTok: Perspectives from digital ethnography. *International Journal of Communication*, *15*, 1437–1457. https://ijoc. org/index.php/ijoc/article/view/16414.

Schellewald, A. (2022). Theorizing "stories about algorithms" as a mechanism in the formation and maintenance of algorithmic imaginaries. *Social Media+ Society*, *8*(1), https://doi.org/10.1177/20563051221077025.

Sherman, J. (2023, March 31). What just about everyone is getting wrong about banning TikTok. *Slate*. https://slate.com/technology/2023/03/tiktok-ban-debate-broken-congress-biden.html.

Schiermer, B. (2014). Late-modern hipsters: New tendencies in popular culture. *Acta sociologica*, *57*(2), 167–181. https://doi.org/10.1177/0001699313498263.

Schöps, J. D. (2022). *Digital markets as performative assemblages* (PhD dissertation), Leopold-Franzens-Universität Innsbruck.

Schöps, J. D., Kogler, S., and Hemetsberger, A. (2020). (De-)stabilizing the digitized fashion market on Instagram-dynamics of visual performative assemblages. *Consumption Markets and Culture*, *23*(2), 195–213. https://doi.org/10.1080/1025 3866.2019.1657099.

Schöps, J. D., Reinhardt, C., and Hemetsberger, A. (2022). Sticky market webs of connection–human and nonhuman market co-codification dynamics across social media. *European Journal of Marketing*, *56*(13), 78–104. https://doi.org/10.1108/ EJM-10-2020-0750.

Schouten, J. W. and McAlexander, J. H. (1995). Subcultures of consumption: An ethnography of the new bikers. *Journal of Consumer Research*, *22*(1), 43–61. https://doi.org/10.1086/209434.

Scott, M. (2017). "Hipster capitalism" in the age of austerity? Polanyi meets Bourdieu's new petite bourgeoisie. *Cultural Sociology*, *11*(1), 60–76. https://doi. org/10.1177/1749975516681226.

Seale, K. (2012). *MasterChef*'s amateur makeovers. *Media International Australia*, *143*(1), 28–35. https://doi.org/10.1177/1329878X1214300105.

Seaver, N. (2018). What should an anthropology of algorithms do? *Cultural anthropology*, *33*(3), 375–385. http://orcid.org/0000-0002-3913-1134.

Sequera, J. and Nofre, J. (2020). Touristification, transnational gentrification and urban change in Lisbon: The neighbourhood of Alfama. *Urban Studies*, *57*(15), 3169–3189. https://doi.org/10.1177/0042098019883734.

Severson, P. (2019). How critical digital method development can strengthen studies of media and terrorism. In R. de La Brosse and K. Holt (Eds.), *Media and Journalism in an Age of Terrorism* (pp. 168–184). Cambridge Scholars Publishing.

Shabrina, Z., Arcaute, E., and Batty, M. (2022). Airbnb and its potential impact on the London housing market. *Urban Studies*, *59*(1), 197–221. https://doi. org/10.1177/0042098020970865.

Shao, C., Ciampaglia, G. L., Varol, O., Flammini, A., and Menczer, F. (2017). The spread of fake news by social bots. arXiv preprint arXiv:1707.07592, *96*, 104.

Shifman, L. (2014). The cultural logic of photo-based meme genres. *Journal of Visual Culture*, *13*(3), 340–358. https://doi.org/10.1177/1470412914546577.

Simon, F. M. and Camargo, C. Q. (2023). Autopsy of a metaphor: The origins, use and blind spots of the "infodemic". *New Media and Society*, *25*(8), 2219–2240. https://doi.org/10.1177/14614448211031908.

Singh, V. (2019, April 10). How Google reviews is crushing TripAdvisor. https://www. hospitalitynet.org/opinion/4092845.html.

Slee, T. (2017). *What's yours is mine: Against the sharing economy*. Or Books.

Smith, A. (2020, June 19). TikTok explains how its algorithm actually works. *The Independent*. https://www.independent.co.uk/tech/tiktok-algorithm-videos-explained-likes-comments-a9574696.html.

Sörum, N. and Fuentes, C. (2023). How sociotechnical imaginaries shape consumers' experiences of and responses to commercial data collection practices. *Consumption Markets and Culture*, 26(1), 24–46. https://doi.org/10.1080/10253866.2022.2124977.

Spink, A. and Jansen, B. J. (2004). *Web search: Public searching of the Web*. Springer Netherlands.

Srnicek, N. (2017). *Platform capitalism*. Polity Press.

Stewart, M. (2020). Live tweeting, reality TV and the nation. *International Journal of Cultural Studies*, 23(3), 352–367. https://doi.org/10.1177/1367877919887757.

Talwar, S., Dhir, A., Kaur, P., Zafar, N., and Alrasheedy, M. (2019). Why do people share fake news? Associations between the dark side of social media use and fake news sharing behavior. *Journal of Retailing and Consumer Services*, 51, 72–82. https://doi.org/10.1016/j.jretconser.2019.05.026.

Tandoc Jr, E. C., Lim, Z. W., and Ling, R. (2018). Defining "fake news": A typology of scholarly definitions. *Digital journalism*, 6(2), 137–153. https://doi.org/10.108 0/21670811.2017.1360143.

Tanner, G. (2020). *The circle of the snake: Nostalgia and utopia in the age of big tech*. John Hunt Publishing.

Täuscher, K. and Laudien, S.V. (2018). Understanding platform business models: A mixed methods study of marketplaces. *European Management Journal*, 36(3), 319–329. https://doi.org/10.1016/j.emj.2017.06.005.

Thévenot, L. and Boltanski, L. (1991). *De la justification. Les économies de la grandeur*. Gallimard.

Thompson, C. J. (2014). The politics of consumer identity work. *Journal of Consumer Research*, 40(5), iii–vii. ttps://doi.org/10.1086/673381.

Thompson, C. J. (2019). The "big data" myth and the pitfalls of 'thick data' opportunism: On the need for a different ontology of markets and consumption. *Journal of Marketing Management*, 35(3/4), 207–230. https://doi.org/10.1080/02 67257X.2019.1579751.

Thompson, K. and Haigh, L. (2017). Representations of food waste in reality food television: An exploratory analysis of Ramsay's *Kitchen Nightmares*. *Sustainability*, 9(7), 1139. https://doi.org/10.3390/su9071139.

Thomson, C. (2020, September 18). YouTube's plot to silence conspiracy theories. https://www.wired.com/story/youtube-algorithm-silence-conspiracy-theories/.

Thurlow, C., Aiello, G., and Portman, L. (2020). Visualizing teens and technology: A social semiotic analysis of stock photography and news media imagery. *New Media and Society*, 22(3), 528–549. https://doi.org/10.1177/1461444819867318.

Törnberg, P. and Chiappini, L. (2020). Selling black places on Airbnb: Colonial discourse and the marketing of black communities in New York City. *Environment and Planning A: Economy and Space*, *52*(3), 553–572. https://doi.org/10.1177/0308518X19886321.

Timmer, J. (2021, August 8). If YouTube algorithms radicalize users, data doesn't show it. https://www.wired.com/story/youtube-algorithms-radicalization-data-doesnt-show-it/.

Treré, E. and Bonini, T. (2022). Amplification, evasion, hijacking: Algorithms as repertoire for social movements and the struggle for visibility. *Social Movement Studies*, 1–17. https://doi.org/10.1080/14742837.2022.2143345.

Tromble, R. (2021). Where have all the data gone? A critical reflection on academic digital research in the post-API age. *Social Media+ Society*, *7*(1). https://doi.org/10.1177/2056305121988929.

Tufekci, Z. (2018, March 10). YouTube, the great radicalizer. *New York Times*. https://www.nytimes.com/2018/03/10/opinion/sunday/youtube-politics-radical.html.

Tuters, M. and Willaert, T. (2022). Deep state phobia: Narrative convergence in coronavirus conspiracism on Instagram. *Convergence*, *28*(4), 1214–1238. https://doi.org/10.1177/13548565221118751.

Tuten, T. L. and Solomon, M. R. (2017). *Social media marketing*. Sage.

Twitter (2021, January 8). Permanent suspension of @realDonaldTrump. https://blog.twitter.com/en_us/topics/company/2020/suspension.

Van Dijck, J. (2014). Datafication, dataism and dataveillance: Big data between scientific paradigm and ideology. *Surveillance and Society*, *12*(2), 197–208. https://doi.org/10.24908/ss.v12i2.4776.

Van Dijck, J. and Poell, T. (2013). Understanding social media logic. *Media and Communication*, *1*(1), 2–14. https://ssrn.com/abstract=2309065.

Van Dijck, J., Poell, T., and De Waal, M. (2018). *The platform society: Public values in a connective world*. Oxford University Press.

Van Es, K. and Poell, T. (2020). Platform imaginaries and Dutch public service media. *Social Media+ Society*, *6*(2), https://doi.org/10.1177/2056305120933289.

Van Laer, T., Edson Escalas, J., Ludwig, S., and Van Den Hende, E. A. (2019). What happens in Vegas stays on TripAdvisor? A theory and technique to understand narrativity in consumer reviews. *Journal of Consumer Research*, *46*(2), 267–285. https://doi.org/10.1093/jcr/ucy067.

Venturini, T., Bounegru, L., Gray, J., and Rogers, R. (2018). A reality check (list) for digital methods. *New Media and Society*, *20*(11), 4195–4217. https://doi.org/10.1177/1461444818769236.

Venturini, T., Jacomy, M., and Jensen, P. (2021). What do we see when we look at networks: Visual network analysis, relational ambiguity, and force-directed layouts. *Big Data and Society*, *8*(1), https://doi.org/10.1177/20539517211018488.

Venturini, T. and Munk, A. K. (2021). *Controversy mapping: A field guide*. John Wiley and Sons.

Venturini, T. and Rogers, R. (2019). "API-based research" or how can digital sociology and journalism studies learn from the Facebook and Cambridge Analytica data breach. *Digital Journalism*, *7*(4), 532–540. https://doi.org/10.1080/216708 11.2019.1591927.

Vicari, S. and Kirby, D. (2023). Digital platforms as socio-cultural artifacts: Developing digital methods for cultural research. *Information, Communication and Society*, *26*(9), 1733–1755. https://doi.org/10.1080/1369118X.2022.2027498.

Visentin, M., Pizzi, G., and Pichierri, M. (2019). Fake news, real problems for brands: The impact of content truthfulness and source credibility on consumers' behavioral intentions toward the advertised brands. *Journal of Interactive Marketing*, *45*, 99–112. https://doi.org/10.1016/j.intmar.2018.09.001.

Vizcaíno-Verdú, A. and Aguaded, I. (2022). #ThisIsMeChallenge and music for empowerment of marginalized groups on TikTok. *Media and Communication*, *10*(1), 157–172. https://doi.org/10.17645/mac.v10i1.4715.

Von Hippel, E. (2005). *Democratizing innovation*. MIT Press.

Vosoughi, S., Roy, D., and Aral, S. (2018). The spread of true and false news online. *Science*, *359*(6380), 1146–1151. 10.1126/science.aap9559.

Wallendorf, M. and Arnould, E. J. (1988). "My favorite things": A cross-cultural inquiry into object attachment, possessiveness, and social linkage. *Journal of Consumer Research*, *14*(4), 531–547. https://doi.org/10.1086/209134.

Wang, T., Wezel, F. C., and Forgues, B. (2016). Protecting market identity: When and how do organizations respond to consumers' devaluations? *Academy of Management Journal*, *59*(1), 135–162. https://doi.org/10.5465/amj.2014.0205.

WeAreSocial (2021, October 21). Social media users pass the 4.5 billion mark. https://wearesocial.com/jp/blog/2021/10/social-media-users-pass-the-4-5-billion-mark/.

WeAreSocial (2023). Digital 2023: Your ultimate guide to the evolving digital world. WeAreSocial.com. https://wearesocial.com/uk/blog/2023/01/digital-2023/.

Weber, K. (2005). A toolkit for analyzing corporate cultural toolkits. *Poetics*, *33*(3/4), 227–252. https://doi.org/10.1016/j.poetic.2005.09.011.

Weinswig, D. (2016, October 5). Influencers are the new brands. *Forbes*. https://www.forbes.com/sites/deborahweinswig/2016/10/05/influencers-are-the-new-brands/?sh=20e0345b7919.

Weiss, G. (2019, October 23). *Penn State study posits YouTube's algorithm isn't to blame for far-right radicalization*. https://www.tubefilter.com/2019/10/23/penn-state-study-youtube-algorithm-isnt-to-blame/.

Weltevrede, E. (2016). *Repurposing digital methods: The research affordances of platforms and engines* (PhD dissertation), University of Amsterdam.

Wichmann, J. R., Wiegand, N,. and Reinartz, W. J. (2022). The platformization of brands. *Journal of Marketing*, *86*(1), 109–131. https://doi.org/10.1177/00222429211054073.

Wiggins, B. E. and Bowers, G. B. (2015). Memes as genre: A structurational analysis of the memescape. *New Media and Society, 17*(11), 1886–1906. https://doi.org/10.1177/1461444814535194.

Wilson, J. L. (2005). *Nostalgia: Sanctuary of meaning.* Bucknell University Press.

Wischnewski, M., Ngo, T., Bernemann, R., Jansen, M., and Krämer, N. (2022). "I agree with you, bot!" How users (dis)engage with social bots on Twitter. *New Media and Society.* https://doi.org/10.1177/14614448211072307.

Youn, S. and Jin, S. V. (2017). Reconnecting with the past in social media: The moderating role of social influence in nostalgia marketing on Pinterest. *Journal of Consumer Behaviour, 16*(6), 565–576. https://doi.org/10.1002/cb.1655.

YouTube. (n.d.). How does YouTube provide more quality information to users? https://www.youtube.com/intl/ALL_au/howyoutubeworks/our-commitments/fighting-misinformation/#raising-quality-info.

YouTube (n.d.). Search: list. https://developers.google.com/youtube/v3/docs/search/list.

Yu, Y., Duan, W., and Cao, Q. (2013). The impact of social and conventional media on firm equity value: A sentiment analysis approach. *Decision support systems, 55*(4), 919–926. https://doi.org/10.1016/j.dss.2012.12.028.

Zervas, G., Proserpio, D., and Byers, J. W. (2021). A first look at online reputation on Airbnb, where every stay is above average. *Marketing Letters, 32*(1), 1–16. https://doi.org/10.1007/s11002-020-09546-4.

Zhang, J. (2019). What's yours is mine: Exploring customer voice on Airbnb using text-mining approaches. *Journal of Consumer Marketing, 36*(5), 655–665. https://doi.org/10.1108/JCM-02-2018-2581.

Zhu, F. and Furr, N. (April 2016). Products to platforms: Making the leap. *Harvard Business Review, 94*(4), 72–78. https://hbr.org/2016/04/products-to-platforms-making-the-leap.

Zuboff, S. (2015). Big other: Surveillance capitalism and the prospects of an information civilization. *Journal of Information Technology, 30*(1), 75–89. https://doi.org/10.1057/jit.2015.5.

Zuboff, S. (2019). *The age of surveillance capitalism: The fight for a human future at the new frontier of power.* Profile Books.

Zulli, D. and Zulli, D. J. (2020). Extending the Internet meme: Conceptualizing technological mimesis and imitation publics on the TikTok platform. *New Media and Society, 24*(8), 1872–1890. https://doi.org/10.1177/1461444820983603.

Zwick, D., Bonsu, S. K., and Darmody, A. (2008). Putting consumers to work: Co-creation and new marketing govern-mentality. *Journal of Consumer Culture, 8*(2), 163–196. https://doi.org/10.1177/1469540508090089.

Zwick, D. and Denegri Knott, J. (2009). Manufacturing customers: The database as new means of production. *Journal of Consumer Culture, 9*(2), 221–247. https://doi.org/10.1177/1469540509104375.

About the Authors

Alessandro Caliandro (PhD, University of Milan) is an Associate Professor in Sociology of Culture and Communication at the Department of Political and Social Sciences at the University of Pavia. His current research focuses on digital methods, digital consumer culture, platformisation of culture, surveillance capitalism, ageing and digital media. He is Scientific Coordinator of V-DATA (https://vdataresearch.com/), which focuses on the critical study of surveillance capitalism in Italy, and Research Stream Leader of Algofeed (Feedback culture: assessing the effects of algorithmic recommendations on platformized consumption).

Alessandro Gandini (PhD, University of Milan) is an Associate Professor in Sociology of Culture and Communication at the Department of Social and Political Sciences at the University of Milan. His research focuses on the relationship between technology and society from a cultural perspective, looking at platformisation processes, digital labour, digital cultures and methods. He is the Principal Investigator of the CRAFTWORK project (2021–2025), funded by ERC Starting Grants. He is also the Scientific Coordinator of Algocount (www.algocount.org) and Principal Investigator of Algofeed – two projects that focus on the critical study of algorithms.

Lucia Bainotti (PhD, University of Milan) is Assistant Professor in Digital and Visual Media Analysis and postdoctoral researcher at the Department of Media Studies at the University of Amsterdam. As a postdoctoral researcher, she is working on the Horizon 2020 project SoBigData++, focusing on developing techniques for visual media analysis. Her main research interests revolve around digital consumer cultures, issues of social status and distinction in the influencer economy, and gender-based violence online.

Guido Anselmi (PhD, University of Milano-Bicocca) is a Senior Lecturer in Sociology of Culture and Communication at the Department of Humanities at the University of Catania. His work focuses on digital and computational methods, platform capitalism, and the impact of digital platforms on cities.

Index

Printed in the United States
by Baker & Taylor Publisher Services